Revitalizing Democracy?
Devolution and Civil Society in Wales

POLITICS AND SOCIETY IN WALES SERIES
Series editor: Ralph Fevre

Previous volumes in the series:

Paul Chaney, Tom Hall and Andrew Pithouse (eds), *New Governance – New Democracy? Post-Devolution Wales*

Neil Selwyn and Stephen Gorard, *The Information Age: Technology, Learning and Exclusion in Wales*

Graham Day, *Making Sense of Wales: A Sociological Perspective*

Richard Rawlings, *Delineating Wales: Constitutional, Legal and Administrative Aspects of National Devolution*

Molly Scott Cato, *The Pit and the Pendulum: A Cooperative Future for Work in the Welsh Valleys*

Paul Chambers, *Religion, Secularization and Social Change in Wales: Congregational Studies in a Post-Christian Society*

The Politics and Society in Wales series examines issues of politics and government, and particularly the effects of devolution on policy-making and implementation, and the way in which Wales is governed as the National Assembly gains in maturity. It will also increase our knowledge and understanding of Welsh society and analyse the most important aspects of social and economic change in Wales. Where necessary, studies in the series will incorporate strong comparative elements which will allow a more fully informed appraisal of the conditions of Wales.

Revitalizing Democracy?

DEVOLUTION AND
CIVIL SOCIETY IN WALES

By

ELIN ROYLES

Published on behalf of the Social Science Committee
of the Board of Celtic Studies of the University of Wales

UNIVERSITY OF WALES PRESS
CARDIFF
2007

British Library Cataloguing-in-Publication Data.
A catalogue record for this book is available from the British Library.

ISBN 978–0–7083–2084–6

Printed in Great Britain by Antony Rowe Ltd, Wiltshire

Contents

Figures and Tables

FIGURES

TABLES

BOXES

Series Editor's Foreword

Civil society remains a hot topic in social science but, despite all the attention devoted to it in the last twenty years, it often seems a very hard concept to pin down. Civil society is usually defined as a social space between the state and the market where people take part in more or less formal activities which are meant to achieve something that neither the state nor the market will, or perhaps can, achieve. This attempt at definition shows that the concept of civil society has something in common with the concept of community. Both are generally thought of – in the academic literature as well as public discourse – as fundamentally good things. They are seen as not just necessary adjuncts of, checks on, the state and the market but also as being in some way superior to, or perhaps more authentic than, either. Yet this illustrates the fact that ideas of civil society and community also share something else in common: they seem to encourage rather abstract and sometimes quite vague discussion which is often hard to relate to anything we recognize in practice.

This book sets an example to the academic literature and public discourse because it shows us how much easier it becomes to understand the concept of civil society, and appreciate its potential, if we have thoroughly-researched examples of civil society organisations and initiatives in front of us. Each of the extended case studies presented here confirms how much more we can understand about civil society's potential when we can see what real civil society does, and how it can make progress towards those goals which the state or the market on their own cannot help us with. The case studies also include extended examples and extracts from a number of key sources which help us to make up our own minds about the argument developed here.

Yet Elin Royles, like almost all academics studying civil society, is no neutral observer. By this I do not mean that we cannot trust her to produce balanced, objective and thorough research of the highest quality. After all, this book is based on her PhD which was awarded the Political Studies Association Walter Bagehot Prize for the best dissertation in government and public administration. Elin is one of the very best of the new generation of political scientists and I am not implying that she is not a model researcher, but that she really cares about a more participative and pluralistic democracy. It is because of this commitment that she wants civil society to be more vibrant and prolific. She wants to know, most importantly, how to develop its potential for bringing about positive change.

It is clear from this book that her research findings persuade Elin that one way of developing civil society is to ensure that structures of governance designed to give civil society influence should explicitly be alert to the need to preserve its autonomy. This sounds to be a difficult balancing act as structures of governance that are intended to promote civil society's influence run the risk of turning civil society organisations into the creatures of the political sphere or, worse still, the creatures of government. Both politics and government seem to face chronic problems of failing legitimacy and giving greater influence to civil society seems offer a way out but what about the dangers of contagion? Civil society only offers a way out if it has legitimacy that politics does not and this legitimacy has to come from the people who participate in civil society. Will those participants be put off if they judge that their organisations have grown too dependent on the state so that, in time, the failing legitimacy of politics and government will spread to civil society?

Many books on civil society consider these problems in abstract terms but even those authors who attempt to take their arguments further with the help of empirical evidence generally do not collect the evidence themselves and sometimes rely heavily on contemporary history and journalism. Elin's approach has been much closer to the classic social-science model. She began her work with a thorough grounding in theory and generated some questions which she then sought to answer with her own, extensive and detailed research. Her study is a model of what social science should be but in one respect Elin has also been very fortunate: she has done her research in Wales. As I have noted before in the forewords to other books in this series, social scientists in Wales have been very fortunate to have a sometimes radical experiment in governance taking place on their own doorsteps. Elin has been able to put her ideas about civil society to the test against the experience of the particular kind of governance that has been developing in Wales since the start of the process of devolution in 1999. That governance has been explicitly designed to create structures which will build civil society. Some of these structures were described by the first book in this series (*New Governance, New Democracy?* edited by Chaney, Hall and Pithouse) but Elin Royles has been able to measure their effect on civil society now they have had a reasonable time in which to work.

This book tells us, in considerable detail, how well or badly the difficult balancing act of increasing civil-society influence while not decreasing civil society autonomy has been pulled off. It also tells us much about the struggle to restore and protect legitimacy. From the very beginning of the devolution process. an essential component of the attempt to underpin the legitimacy of the new layer of governance was understood to be that it would reach to the parts of Welsh society that were not reached by politics – and do so in as broad and inclusive a way as possible. There was a recognition that this simply had to be done – otherwise devolution itself would be stalled – but in time this rather desperate conviction became a kind of creed, part of the culture of governance in Wales that most people seemed to share.

All of this might seem wildly ambitious given the general recognition at the start of the process that civil society in Wales before devolution was under-developed (when compared with Scotland for instance). You might think it even more ambitious if you had read what the (empirical as well as theoretical) literature had to say about the impossibility of building civil society in a 'top-down' manner. There seemed to be agreement amongst academics that the 'top-down' approach was, at best, fatally flawed because it would necessarily damage the legitimacy of any civil society organisations it touched. They would be seen as neither autonomous or legitimate, as creatures not partners of their political instigators. The designers of the devolution process in Wales have been aware of this problem but there has been a sort of consensus that, given the weakness of Welsh civil society, there was no practical alternative. Perhaps a more careful and sophisticated top-down approach, with a genuine understanding of the pitfalls, might preserve both the legitimacy of emerging civil society and of the whole new governance project.

Elin's book shows that, as a result of the Assembly's innovative structures, progress has been made, and initiatives like the Welsh Assembly Government's 'Making Connections' (launched in 2004) suggest the work will continue. But the fundamental problem of risking fatal damage to the legitimacy of civil society by appearing to increase its dependency on the state remains. The nature of civil society's engagement with the Assembly falls short of the ideas proposed in the literature on participatory and deliberative democracy. Indeed, the Assembly should investigate the ideas proposed in this rich literature which has already led to theoretically-informed initiatives in other regional governments in Europe. This may be the direction Wales needs to take in order to address the even more fundamental problem which is common to so many Western democracies: the problem of raising levels of participation throughout the public sphere by making sure that both politics and civil society connect with what people really care about.

Preface and Acknowledgements

I grew up under successive Thatcherite and Conserative governments. Devolution had been associated with the failure of the 1979 Welsh Devolution Referendum.[1] The mood expressed by Gwyn A. Williams following the '79 referendum and General Election, that 'Welsh politics had ceased to exist. Wales had finally disappeared into Britain', resonated with my experience (1985: 297).

As I entered university, the political victory of 'New Labour' meant that, in the following two years, Wales embarked on a new political era. The 1997 Welsh Devolution Referendum saw Wales vote narrowly in favour of devolution, the 1998 Government of Wales Act was passed the following year and the first elections to the National Assembly for Wales were held in May 1999.[2] This book originates from the high expectations surrounding political devolution and the discourse on 'new politics'.

Amidst rising expectations, the campaign in the 1990s argued that devolution to Wales would result in open, participative and accountable governance in Wales. As a student, the 'new politics' vocabulary and the aspirations evoked by it filled me with enthusiasm. Academic studies of devolution to Wales and European regionalism and practical experiences with WLGA and the Welsh Office Devolution Unit in 1998 gave me avid interest in investigating whether in post-devolution Wales the language of devolution would be realized in practice. What would be the effects of greater self-governance to Wales on the nature of democracy and political culture in Wales? I expected that the doctoral research on the impact of devolution on civil society in post-devolution Wales – the basis for this book – would produce entirely positive conclusions. It is with some disappointment therefore that the conclusions of the book are less than wholly positive. However, my hope is that the book contributes to enriching our understanding and analysis of Welsh politics and civil society in Wales and points to issues of debate and questions to be addressed in what is still a new and young democracy.

I am extremely grateful to a number of people to who have assisted in developing this research. First, those who were willing to be interviewed for the case studies. They are not named here but I thank them for their time, knowledge and expertise as practitioners and activists in the politics of post-devolution Wales. In particular, I would like to thank the staff and key members of the following organizations: Cymdeithas yr Iaith, Cymuned, Groundwork Wales, Oxfam Cymru and Stonewall Cymru for allowing me to examine their organizations and for being extremely helpful in the research process. Thanks also to a number of colleagues in the Welsh Assembly Government and the Assembly Parliamentary Services for their useful contributions.

I would also like to thank those that make the Department of International Politics, University of Wales Aberystwyth and the Institute of Welsh Politics such a positive environment for work and research. Thanks go to Richard Wyn Jones and Andrew Linklater, my Ph.D. supervisors, for their constructive criticism, their continued support and interest. During the subsequent process of developing the book, I have been grateful for the valuable advice, comments and encouragement to publish the findings by James Mitchell, Andy Thompson and Roger Scully. As editor of the Politics and Society in Wales Series, Ralph Fevre encouraged the further development of the arguments and findings presented here and I owe particular thanks for his openness and wide-ranging advice. I would also like to thank Dafydd Jones and his colleagues at the University of Wales Press for their support and assistance. The usual disclaimer applies.

Finally, I would like to thank my close family and friends for their support and encouragement.

This book is dedicated to my grandparents, Albert and Olwen Royles, Gwyn and Annie Daniel. They each played their part in the civil society of twentieth century Wales.

Notes

[1] 1979 Welsh Devolution Referendum result, 'yes' 243,048 (20.2%) 'no' 956,330 (79.8%) turnout 58.8% (Bogdanor, 1999; 190). Therefore, despite the closeness of 1997 Welsh Devolution Referendum result, it did signify a 30% shift in public opinion in Wales since the 4:1 rejection of devolution in 1979 (Rawlings, 1998: 15).

The day of the 1979 referendum, I became locked in the bathroom. As my father was a Presiding Officer in a polling station, neighbours had to free me and damaged the door in the process. The door has purposely not been replaced with the damage remaining as a reminder of the scars left by the political events in Wales on that day in 1979.

[2] 1997 Welsh Devolution Referendum result, 'yes' 559, 419 (50.3%) 'no' 552, 698 (49.7%) turnout 50.1% (Taylor, Curtice and Thomson, 1999: xxiii). National Assembly for Wales Election 1999 results, out of 60 seats, the Labour Party – 28, Plaid Cymru – the Party of Wales – 17, The Conservative Party – 9, The Liberal Democrats – 6 seats (Trystan, Scully and Wyn Jones, 2003: 639).

Abbreviations

AGW	Auditor General Wales
AMs	Assembly Members
AMS	Additional Members System
ASPBs	assembly sponsored public bodies
BFG	Big Food Group
CAP	Common Agricultural Policy
CBI Wales	Confederation of British Industry Wales
CRE	Commission for Racial Equality
CYLCH	Cymdeithas Y Lesbiaid a Hoywon Cymraeg eu Hiaith
DOE	Department of the Environment
DRC	Disability Rights Commission
EAD	European Affairs Division
EOC	Equal Opportunities Commission
ERDF	European Regional Development Fund
ESRC	Economic and Social Research Council
EU	European Union
FSB Wales	Federation of Small Businesses Wales
FUW	Farmers Union of Wales
GATS	General Agreement on Trade in Services
GDP	Gross Domestic Product
GoWA	Government of Wales Act
Groundwork RCT	Groundwork Rhondda, Cynon Taf
HMSO	Her Majesty's Stationery Office
ILO	International Labour Organization
ISW	Industrial South Wales
LGB	lesbian, gay and bisexual
MPs	Members of Parliament
MTF	Make Trade Fair
NAAG	National Assembly Advisory Group
NAW	National Assembly for Wales
NFU Cymru Wales	National Farmers Union Cymru Wales
NGO	non-governmental organization

OI	Oxfam International
PAGs	project action groups
PDAG	Pwyllgor Datblygu Addysg Gymraeg
PMC	Programme Monitoring Committee
R & D	research and development
SDS	Strategic Development Scheme
SMC	Shadow Monitoring Committee
SPD	Single Programme Document
TJM	Trade Justice Movement
TNCs	transnational corporations
TRIPS	trade-related aspects of intellectual property rights
UK	United Kingdom
WAG	Welsh Assembly Government
WCVA	Wales Council for Voluntary Action
WDA	Welsh Development Agency
WEFO	Welsh European Funding Office
WEPE	Wales European Programme Executive
WLB	Welsh Language Board
WTO	World Trade Organization
WTUC	Wales Trades Union Congress
WWF Cymru	World Wildlife Fund Cymru

1

Introduction: Civil Society in Wales

The effects of regional government are diverse and difficult to predict. These variations arise from the specific context of 'regions', or in some cases 'nations'. There also can be multiple effects arising from a range of economic, political, cultural, historic and external factors. As a result, examining the effects of devolving power to the 'regional' or 'national' level is fascinating. Devolution and the establishment of the National Assembly for Wales in 1999 presented an ideal opportunity for research. It presented a 'real time' experiment and the chance to investigate the effects of regional government on Wales and the UK.

This book investigates questions regarding the influence of regional government on political culture. It does this by focusing on the impact of devolution on civil society in Wales, one of the most under-researched aspects of political culture and contemporary Welsh society. Through empirical case studies, it explores what difference devolution has made to civil society during the first term of devolution to Wales. It concentrates on two areas. It questions whether the high expectations invested by the 'new politics' discourse in civil society are realized in post-devolution Wales. Has civil society contributed to revitalizing democracy and promoted a more civic-based sense of national identity?

This original research complements the existing literature and throws light on the impact of devolution on civil society, specifically civil society's interrelationship with democratic development and national identity. It will, therefore, appeal to those interested in civil society in Wales. It should also be essential reading for those interested in contemporary Welsh politics as well as having considerable appeal to those with a more general interest in devolution in the UK. The study facilitates an assessment of the effects of devolution on political culture and democracy in post-devolution Wales. It also suggests potential policy prescriptions to address some of the problems arising from relations between the National Assembly and civil society. A number of issues raised in this study contribute to a broader literature. The book should appeal to the area of comparative research on regional government. It can inform investigations of the effects of regional government on democracy and in particular the interrelationship between civil society and governmental structures in an existing western liberal democracy (Putnam, 1993). The book should also appeal to scholars working on the theme of civil society: here, it should be of particular interest to those concerned with how theories of civil society can be applied in empirical research. This contemporary research raises wider implications for civil society theory, particularly the need to revisit how civil society's democratic potential is perceived.

This Introduction begins by setting the context and examines the nature of the discussion surrounding civil society in Wales. We also outline the aims of the book, before presenting the methods of inquiry, the case studies and then finally the structure of the book.

CIVIL SOCIETY AND THE 'NEW POLITICS' IN WALES

The political vocabulary associated with the campaign for devolution was forged early in the 1990s and in the short public campaign in the run-up to the Welsh Devolution Referendum in September 1997. Devolution re-emerged on the political agenda in Wales in the late 1980s and early 1990s. One of the key reasons was that devolution was seen as a means to address the 'democratic deficit' and the lack of accountability under the Conservative governments in Wales from 1979 to 1997 (Osmond, 1995). During this period of administrative devolution, there was a vast expansion in the powers and functions of the Welsh Office and the unaccountable quangos (Griffiths, 1996; Bradbury and Mawson, 1999). As a result of the relative weakness of Conservative support in Wales and their method of governance, Wales was characterized as being 'subjected to government without ballot and power without scrutiny' (R. Davies, 1999: 5). Thus, the Wales Labour Party renewed its commitment to devolution in 1990. It argued that 'devolution and democracy went hand in hand and that under an elected Assembly, the governing institutions of Wales would be accountable and responsive' (Chaney and Fevre, 2001a: 22).

In Wales, the discourse of the 'new politics' reflected the aspirations surrounding devolution and raised high expectations. Revitalizing democracy was also a clear aim in the campaign for devolution. It was argued that devolution would result in inclusive, open, participative and accountable governance in Wales. The White Paper on devolution, *A Voice for Wales* published in 1997, stated that an Assembly would address the democratic deficit by developing accountability and partnership in governance. It stated that 'the Government is committed to establishing a more inclusive and participatory democracy in Britain. Its proposals for a Welsh Assembly reflect these aims' (Welsh Office, 1997: 15). Equating devolution with developing a more participative democracy in Wales was also evident in the statements of politicians. Ron Davies, then Secretary of State for Wales, called for devolution to be a participatory democracy as part of 'a new pluralist approach to Welsh politics which was libertarian, decentralist and patriotic' (1999: 6). Similarly, Peter Hain linked devolution with a pluralist conception of democracy and emphasized that devolution to Wales should be a model 'participatory democracy' (1999: 14).

Devolution also drew attention to the analytical and political usefulness of 'civil society', previously an unfamiliar term in the Welsh political lexicon. 'Civil society' gained a currency in the language of devolution following the 1997 referendum. Overall, the usage of 'civil society' by politicians and in political commentary tended to be as a buzzword, and it was treated in idealistic terms. In this respect, 'civil society' was amongst other widely used terms such as 'inclusiveness' and 'participation' that are 'potentially vague and slippery terms' (Chaney et al., 2000: 203). These terms were largely imported into the Welsh discussion of devolution from other parts of the UK in order to make the case for an elected Assembly in Wales. On the one hand, in line with Third Way thinking's stress on deepening and widening democracy that influenced Labour in the UK, it was emphasized that civil society had a central role to play in mobilizing democracy in Wales (Giddens, 1998: 69; 2000: 61). On the other hand, 'civil society' was largely incorporated to Wales from Scotland's discussion of devolution.

On its inclusion in the 'new politics' rhetoric in Wales, an active civil society became associated with the vision of devolution mobilizing a more participative democracy in Wales (Paterson and Wyn Jones, 1999: 183). In the rhetoric of political actors, civil society was a slogan reflecting the aspirations of greater participation in government associated with devolution (Davies, 1999; Michael, 1999; Hain, 1999). By forging greater participation and democracy, civil society was seen as a means of promoting a different kind of politics, thus changing political culture in post-devolution Wales. In one of the first references, Osmond stated: 'the new Welsh politics is about creating a new democracy and a new civil society to make the democracy work' (1998a: 20). Paterson and Wyn Jones raised the potential of civil society in Wales to 'form the locus for the generation of new, more inclusive and participative structures of democratic governance' (1999: 191).

Initially, however, 'civil society' had emerged in political discussion in Wales at the beginning of the 1990s during the Parliament for Wales Campaign attempt to establish a Welsh Constitutional Convention (Wyn Jones and Lewis, 1998). Essentially, incorporating 'civil society' into the devolution discussion in Wales had little to contribute to understanding

Wales better. Rather, it was a politically motivated attempt to influence Labour to broaden discussions of the devolution proposals beyond the confines of the Wales Labour Party (Paterson and Wyn Jones, 1999: 182). In practice, the convention intended to replicate what was understood to have existed in Scotland in the shape of the Scottish Constitutional Convention, a broad-based civil society coalition for Scottish devolution. In reality, the Scottish Constitutional Convention was a meeting of the Scottish elites that involved cross-party working, but was largely distanced from the Scottish public. Nevertheless, this was couched in the terms of 'civil society' in order to gain legitimacy (Mitchell, 1996; Lynch, 1996). In Wales, the attempt to establish a convention failed with little recognition of the potential of civil society and its implications for democracy in promoting participation and legitimization. The devolution debate was internalized in the Labour Party (Paterson and Wyn Jones, 1999).

Following the Welsh Devolution Referendum, 'civil society' re-emerged in Wales as part of the discourse of 'new politics'. As outlined above, the discourse emphasized the importance of an active civil society in promoting greater participation and democracy post-devolution, thus contributing to changing political culture in Wales. The timing of the emergence of 'civil society' into the devolution discussion was significant, as the small minority in favour of devolution in the referendum had forced a rethink. First, it was recognized that confining the devolution debate in the Labour Party until the referendum campaign, as opposed to opening up the discussion to other interests and organizations in Wales, partly explained the poor referendum result. In the 1997 devolution referendum, 559,419 (50.3 per cent) of the population of Wales voted 'yes' and 552,698 (49.7 per cent) voted 'no' on a turnout of 50.1 per cent. Ron Davies, who was genuinely committed to 'inclusive' politics, admitted that 'under pressure from Old Labour we failed to broaden our support amongst the parties and broader Welsh civil society' (1999: 8). Following the referendum, efforts to involve civil society organizations in discussions on the Assembly commenced (Paterson and Wyn Jones, 1999: 181). Secondly, the low turnout in the referendum raised concerns regarding the Assembly's legitimacy and emphasized the imperative of developing a stronger civic sense to Welsh identity. In particular, 23 per cent of Wales's population were born outside Wales (Paterson and Wyn Jones, 1999: 185). The 1997 Welsh Referendum Survey revealed that of those surveyed who were born in England, 2 to 1 were opposed to devolution and were significantly less likely to vote (Wyn Jones and Trystan, 1999: 76). It seemed that elements of the population felt excluded from Welsh society, and to Ron Davies, 'This is a direct challenge to those of us who want to nurture a civic sense of identity' (1999: 8). In this context, the impact of political devolution on national identity was a key concern. Paterson and Wyn Jones asked: 'Will the assembly, and a stronger Welsh civil society, foster a sense of national identity which will be embraced by all those living in Wales whatever their origins?' (1999: 185). Thus, an important role was envisaged for civil society to include citizens, encourage participation, and contribute to a strengthened, civic-based as opposed to ethnic-based, sense of identification with Wales.

While high expectations surrounded civil society's role in promoting a different kind of politics in Wales following devolution, accounts of civil society immediately prior to devolution and in a more historic context pointed to its underdevelopment and weakness. This was the case when Paterson and Wyn Jones compared the relative contribution of civil society in Scotland and Wales to the process of achieving devolution (1999). In Scotland, they argued that 'civil society' (which, as discussed above, was in reality an elite of Scottish society) was central in the campaign for constitutional change. In Wales, the Labour Party dominated the issue. This dominance was underpinned by the weakness and immaturity of civil society seen in its extremely limited contribution to discussions of devolution.

There are limits to our current historical understanding of civil society in Wales and its underdevelopment. Generally, during some periods, civil society has been stronger and subsequently deteriorated. Also in the diversity of civil society, there are exceptions to the image of under-development. One distinction that assists in understanding civil society in Wales is to contrast *civil society in Wales* with *Welsh civil society* (Wyn Jones and Lewis, 1998: 2; Paterson and Wyn Jones, 1999: 175). *Civil society in Wales* is defined as organizations that operate within British terms of reference and are part of England and Wales or UK-wide bodies. *Welsh civil society* can be defined as organizations that have developed and operate within a distinctively Welsh context often with parallel organizations operating on the English or British level (Paterson and Wyn Jones, 1999: 191–3).

It is argued that the weaknesses of *Welsh civil society* are deep-rooted. Wales was integrated into the English state before the age of modernity with which the development of civil society is associated (Paterson and Wyn Jones, 1999: 173). Crucially, therefore, civil society developed in an essentially British context as there were no significant institutional and administrative structures in Wales. Consequently,

> while there obviously are civil society institutions and networks in Wales, it is a moot point to what extent this is a *Welsh* civil society. To what extent do these bodies think in 'Welsh' terms, or do they operate primarily within British terms of reference? (Wyn Jones and Lewis, 1998: 9)

Developments such as national institution-building in the nineteenth century and increasing administrative devolution from the Welsh Office onwards led to decision-making and policy-making structures in Wales. These developments influenced the promotion of a more distinctive civil society in Wales (Paterson and Wyn Jones, 1999: 175). *Welsh civil society* has gradually emerged as organizations became increasingly 'Welsh' in their perspective and context due to the process of national institution-building in Wales. Amongst the examples are for instance, the Farmers Union of Wales (FUW) which was established in 1955 and paralleled the existing UK-wide National Farmers Union. In this case, the impetus was to establish a 'national' organization in Wales that focused specifically on the needs of farmers in Wales. The women's movement, Merched y Wawr, established in 1967, was an alternative to the UK-wide Women's Institute, also established in Wales in 1915.

Administrative devolution also affected some *civil society in Wales* organizations. At a basic level, this was evident as organizations added the suffix 'Wales' or 'Cymru' to their organization's name in Wales. This change, however, suggested broader changes in the identities of organizations and their operation in Wales in response to the gradual increase in decision-making powers and policy-making structures in Wales. Chaney pinpoints that, overall, *civil society in Wales* organizations (referred to as cross-border voluntary organizations) have tended to lack autonomy in their organizations. Devolution has however led some organizations to rethink, restructure and develop more devolved structures in Wales (Chaney, 2002a: 18).

Overall, civil society's direct political role has been limited, and weaknesses remain: 'Welsh civil society remains a fragile plant' (Paterson and Wyn Jones, 1999: 176; Chaney et al., 2000: 212; Chaney and Fevre, 2001a: 42). Yet whatever the case in the past, it was suggested that executive devolution could revitalize civil society in Wales (Paterson and Wyn Jones, 1999: 183). As Chaney et al. state: 'the arrival of the National Assembly for Wales presents an opportunity for a resurgence of civil society in Wales' (2000: 218).

CIVIL SOCIETY IN POST-DEVOLUTION WALES

The specific aim of this book is to investigate the impact of devolution on civil society during the early years of post-devolution Wales. This is approached in four ways. First, the main aim is to develop an empirical understanding of civil society in the post-devolution period. The investigation spans 1997–2003, the Welsh Devolution Referendum (the first time, through the 'Yes' campaign, that civil society was effectively engaged in the devolution project) to the second National Assembly Elections in 2003. It thus focuses on the first term of devolution to Wales. Through case studies, specific organizations and sectors of civil society are examined and a detailed empirical assessment of the initial impact of devolution is developed. Secondly, the study will assess whether the Assembly's 'inclusive' structures achieved the aim of promoting engagement opportunities for civil society organizations. It examines whether the complexities of the devolution settlement and changes during the first term affected the abilities of civil society organizations to engage with the Assembly. Thirdly, the examination of civil society in post-devolution Wales is informed by a theoretical framework. There is nothing new to the expectations expressed in Wales and in western liberal democracies that democracy depends on the health and characteristics of civil society (Putnam and Goss, 2004: 6). A long history of classical theorists point to the role of associations in revitalizing democracy. The theoretical framework developed in this book assists in the task of conceptualizing civil society's contribution to a project of extending democracy and participation in government, and the interrelationship between civil society and national identity. In order to strengthen its findings, a fourth aim of the book is to establish a comparative perspective on civil society and the significance of devolution. The case studies therefore compare organizations pre- and post-devolution.

This book complements the research projects that have developed extensive findings into some sectors of civil society post-devolution, namely 'minority' groups and the voluntary sector and their interaction with the National Assembly.[1] Attempts are made to identify whether these findings are relevant to other sectors and aspects of civil society organizations in Wales. The study also focuses in depth on the interrelationship between civil society and democratic development and national identity.

The limitations in the current literature on civil society in Wales written in the context of devolution are addressed in the volume. The ways in which 'civil society' was utilized in much of the literature in the early stages of devolution tended to reflect the general underdevelopment of civil society in Wales. It underlined the novelty of the concept in Wales and highlighted the lack of adequate research into Welsh politics. The main weaknesses were twofold. First, there were only limited attempts to ensure that 'civil society' was understood in Wales and at times, discussion in the literature was inadequate. A comprehensive theoretical and conceptual underpinning to its discussion in Wales has yet to be developed. The main reason for this is that, as mentioned above, 'civil society' was mostly utilized as a buzzword in the rhetoric of political actors (Davies, 1999; Michael, 1999; Hain, 1999). While it should not be expected that all aspects of the literature developed a comprehensive discussion of civil society, its novelty in the Welsh context and the ambiguities surrounding the concept made deepening understanding of civil society important. A second weakness was that there were certain limits to empirical understanding of the existing situation of civil society in Wales, particularly regarding civil society and the nature of its involvement with the Welsh Office before devolution.

METHODS OF INQUIRY

A case study strategy was adopted as it allowed the development of in-depth and detailed findings through the utilization of a range of sources of evidence across multiple cases. The selection criteria used to determine the civil society organizations investigated in the study are twofold. The first is the requirement that the case studies facilitate the investigation of the five key questions, discussed below. The second is that the cases conform to a four-cell matrix based on the intersection of two axes, devolved and non-devolved and recognition and redistribution. The first axis distinguishes between areas of power devolved to the National Assembly and non-devolved areas that remain under Westminster's control. The second axis is Nancy Fraser's distinction between recognition and redistribution. 'Redistribution' relates to socio-economic issues and inequalities, and 'recognition' relates to what may be termed the politics of identity, including nationality, ethnicity, 'race', gender and sexuality (Fraser, 1995: 68). These were ideal types and were relevant as the key political issues in contemporary politics (Fraser, 1995: 68). Fraser's distinction is particularly useful in conjunction with the devolved and non-devolved axis to develop a matrix for case study selection. The matrix provides a framework to select four case studies that encompass a wide cross-section of civil society organizations engaged in different subject areas post-devolution. The breadth of organizations enables developing indicators of the impact of the Assembly on civil society organizations more generally.

There are strong interrelationships between the five main questions identified for investigation in this study. Overall, the questions can be grouped into two categories. The first category relates to the impact of devolution on the interrelationship between civil society and democratic development. The second category examines the interrelationship between civil society and identity in post-devolution Wales.

The first aspect to be examined in relation to the first category is: To what extent have civil society organizations been involved with the National Assembly? What are the implications of this? The rhetorical emphasis on partnership between the Assembly and different actors including civil society encouraged examining the extent and effects of partnerships. As will be evident from discussing theories of civil society in Chapter 2, there is a concern that some civil society–state relationships can become too close and potentially create an elite in civil society, threaten civil society's autonomy and its ability to scrutinize the state (Gramsci, 1998; Cohen and Arato, 1999; F. L. Wilson, 1983, 1990).

This question seeks to identify whether the supposed 'inclusiveness' of the Assembly was realized in practice. It also assesses the factors that contribute to the variations in the degree to which organizations participate in the Assembly's work. This aids our understanding of whether and how civil society contributes to democratic development or whether power inequalities and practices of exclusion in civil society mean it exacerbates broader inequalities in society. Assessing whether close relationships with the Assembly can affect civil society organizations also provides suggestions regarding the nature of democracy, and serves to identify whether an elitist or pluralist political culture is developing in post-devolution Wales.

Secondly, do civil society organizations have the potential to promote greater participation and thus contribute to enriching the quality of Welsh democracy? This seems a difficult question to investigate as it is very broad. Assessing and measuring the quality of democracy is difficult. As a result, the study focuses on one element highlighted by classical theorists from Tocqueville to contemporary theorists such as Cohen and Arato and Putnam. In their view, civil society's democratic potential to encourage participation and broader civic engagement depends on the extent to which organizations promote participation and high levels of active membership engagement. Consequently, the study investigates the degree to which the internal structures of different organizations promote active membership as opposed to limited participation opportunities. This provides a basis for understanding whether civil society can potentially positively influence the quality of democracy or whether, conversely, patterns of civic participation raise doubts concerning its democratic potential.

Finally, with regard to civil society and democratic development is whether organizations have served to legitimate devolution. Investigation of this focuses on two elements. One is whether the problematic and complex nature of the devolution 'settlement', namely the ambiguity and lack of clarity of the Assembly's corporate body status and the division of powers between the National Assembly and Westminster discussed in Chapter 3, influenced the degree to which different organizations interact with the Assembly. The second element is whether organizations contributed to legitimizing the devolution process and advocated greater powers for the National Assembly. Considering that civil society played a limited role in the campaign for devolution, identifying that civil society legitimized the

Assembly and sought to increase its powers would be a strong indicator of devolution's contribution to revitalizing and empowering civil society.

The second grouping of questions relate to the impact of devolution on the relationship between civil society and identity in post-devolution Wales. Firstly, what impact does devolution have on the identity of organizations? The distinction discussed above, *civil society in Wales* and *Welsh civil society*, has been widely accepted (Chaney, Hall and Dicks, 2000; Chaney and Fevre, 2001a; Chaney, 2002a; Day et al., 2000; Thompson and Day, 2001; C. Williams, 2001). Previous research highlighted the utility of the distinction and the potential impact of devolution on the identity of sectors of civil society. Nevertheless, there was little detailed investigation of the distinction – such as what are the nature and characteristics of *civil society in Wales* and *Welsh civil society* – or questioning of its usefulness. Therefore, the distinction will be examined in greater depth through the case studies. The book assesses the relative impact of devolution on the identity of civil society in Wales. It investigates the characteristics of *civil society in Wales* and *Welsh civil society*. It examines how devolution affects *civil society in Wales* and *Welsh civil society* organizations. If devolution spurs *civil society in Wales* to develop an increasingly Welsh outlook, this may indicate that devolution has had a significant impact on the identity of civil society organizations.

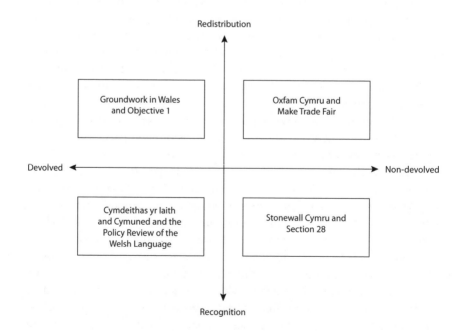

Figure 1.1: The case study selection matrix

A final issue to investigate is whether devolution leads civil society organizations to promote the civic elements of national identity. As mentioned earlier, there were high expectations that civil society would have an important role in this respect post-devolution. Investigating the impact of devolution on the relationship between civil society and national identity is challenging. By examining the impact of devolution on the interrelationship between civil society and national identity, the study will seek to provide an initial assessment grounded in an empirical investigation on a potentially very important aspect of the devolution project.

The case study criteria call for selecting organizations with different experiences of interaction with the National Assembly. These include organizations that receive Assembly funding; organizations with different types of internal structures and civil society organizations that can be characterized as *civil society in Wales* and *Welsh civil society* on their inception. The four-cell matrix (Figure 1.1) based on the devolved and non-devolved and the recognition and redistribution axes along with the research questions discussed above provided the basis to select the specific cases. These cases are now briefly outlined.

1. Devolution and Redistribution: Groundwork Wales and Objective 1

Groundwork Wales was selected for investigation in relation to the devolved/redistribution intersect. Groundwork is a sustainable development organization and an all-Wales level, Groundwork Wales, was established in 1998 by the Groundwork Trusts in Wales. The case study focuses on Groundwork's involvement in the Objective 1 programme as a means of highlighting broader issues regarding the impact of devolution on Groundwork Wales. This case provides valuable insights as the Groundwork Trusts form part of *civil society in Wales*, receive Assembly funding and work in areas of community development and sustainable development, the latter being an area where the Assembly has a statutory duty to promote sustainable development.

2. Devolution and recognition: Cymdeithas yr Iaith and Cymuned and the Policy Review of the Welsh Language

It is almost inevitable that the subject to be located in the devolved/recognition intersect is a case study on the Welsh language. This is due to the language's central role in Welsh national identity. The Welsh-language movement has been the sector of civil society most proactively involved in identity politics. Two organizations are selected in this case, Cymdeithas yr Iaith and Cymuned, with the National Assembly's Culture Committee's Policy Review of the Welsh Language providing the focus to the case study. Examining Cymdeithas and Cymuned's attempts to influence the Review allows for broader reflections on the interaction of the pressure groups with the National Assembly. This case provides important contrasts with our other case studies. Cymdeithas was established prior to devolution and Cymuned was founded post-devolution. While the organizations in the other case studies are more 'constitutional' in their methods of engagement with political processes, these two organizations can be characterized as 'social movements'. Both organizations have financial autonomy in the sense that they do not receive government funding and depend on voluntary financial contributions.

3. Non-devolved redistribution: Oxfam Cymru and Make Trade Fair

Oxfam is one of the best-known international development agencies. In 1998, its organization in Wales changed from Oxfam in Wales/yng Nghymru to Oxfam Cymru. Although Oxfam's work includes some areas devolved to the National Assembly, the main areas of its work are international development issues, a policy area that is definitively non-devolved. This case study focuses on campaigns to reform the international economic system: Oxfam Cymru's contribution to the Oxfam International Make Trade Fair campaign to reform international trade rules. This focus illustrates the degree to which devolution has influenced Oxfam Cymru's work on international issues and serves to highlight ways in which devolution has affected *civil society in Wales* organizations, primarily involved in non-devolved areas.

4. Non-devolved recognition: Stonewall Cymru and Section 28

Stonewall Cymru (initially Lesbian, Gay and Bisexual Forum Cymru/ Stonewall Cymru) was established in 2001 as one of the first all-Wales organizations focusing on lesbian, gay and bisexual (LGB) issues. This case study was selected on the basis that recognition of sexual orientation issues is an area where the main functions and responsibilities remain non-devolved. The focus of the case study is on Section 28 of the 1988 Local Government Act that prohibits local authorities from intentionally promoting homosexuality and Stonewall Cymru's contribution to the Stonewall campaign regarding issues surrounding Section 28. The merits of selecting this case study are numerous. The contrast between the largely absent campaigning for recognition of sexual orientation before devolution and the post-devolution establishment of an all-Wales body to represent LGB interests is significant and deserves investigation. Stonewall Cymru was established in the post-devolution period with part-funding by the National Assembly for Wales and Stonewall; this receipt of financial support raises interesting questions. On its establishment, the organization could be characterized as *Welsh civil society* but it provides an interesting example of tensions in the identity of organizations.

STRUCTURE OF THE BOOK

This volume is divided into two parts. Part I is titled 'Studying Civil Society in Post-devolution Wales'. The two chapters focus on key aspects that provide a foundation for the detailed case studies in Part II of the book titled 'Civil Society in Wales: The Case Studies'. Chapter 2 reviews the relevant theoretical literature to develop a conceptual framework for understanding civil society that places the study on a sound theoretical footing. One of the key points to emerge from the discussion is the vital necessity of studying organizations individually rather than relying on generalizations made on the basis of abstractions. Civil society is a complex phenomenon – in theory as well as in practice. Chapter 3 analyses the political context of the study. It develops a comprehensive assessment of the impact of the Government of Wales Act 1998 and political developments on civil society's engagement with the National Assembly during devolution's first term. It highlights that, despite a number of 'inclusive' structures, the shift to a more parliamentary system of government meant that in order to gain influence in the Assembly, organizations needed to be professionalized and well resourced, and to have close connections with the Welsh Assembly Government.

Part II focuses on the four individual case studies. Chapter 4 examines Groundwork in the Objective 1 programme post-devolution. Chapter 5, discusses the role of Cymdeithas yr Iaith and Cymuned in the National Assembly's Policy Review of the Welsh Language. Chapter 6 analyses Oxfam Cymru's contribution to the Make Trade Fair campaign. Chapter 7 investigates Stonewall Cymru's involvement in issues surrounding the non-devolved Section 28 of the Local Government Act 1988. Based on the four case studies, the Conclusion draws out the main findings of the study that point to the profound impact of devolution on civil society organizations during the Assembly's first term. It also highlights concerns regarding the impact of devolution on civil society's ability to enhance democracy post-devolution and the potentially negative democratic effects of civil society–Assembly relations. On the basis of these findings, the Conclusion also highlights some of the broader implications of the study for our understanding of devolution to Wales, and of civil society theory more generally. It also suggests potential policy prescriptions to address problematic issues surrounding civil society–Assembly relations.

Part I

Studying Civil Society in Post-Devolution Wales

The 'Toolkit': Concepts and Theories

This chapter discusses key aspects of the conceptual and theoretical literature on civil society in order to provide a sound basis for the study and
to enrich understanding of 'civil society' in Wales. Although there is an
extensive literature on civil society in Wales from 1997 to the end of the
first term of devolution in 2003, there has been little by way of reflection
on the concept of civil society. As Chaney et al. comment regarding
terms such as 'civil society', 'participation' and 'inclusiveness': 'In public
pronouncements, as can be expected, these terms and phrases have generally
been employed as slogans and hardly developed at all as analytical concepts'
(2000: 219). Consequently, civil society was utilized with a lack of precision
and became a 'catch-all' term. For instance, in the interviews for this study,
some individuals included aspects such as local government and the private
sector when asked to define civil society. Overall, there is inadequate
definition of what constitutes civil society, reflecting broader problems
arising from a lack of adequate political debate and the novelty of civil
society in political discussion and academic research in Wales.

A more extensive conceptualization of civil society that highlighted its
complex and problematic nature was necessary. Some sources in the early
literature on 'civil society' made an important contribution in this respect
(Hain, 1999; Wyn Jones and Lewis, 1998; Paterson and Wyn Jones, 1999).
The greater academic content of the literature produced following the
Assembly's establishment also enriched the discussion. It provided greater
conceptual and theoretical discussion of civil society and referred to an
extensive academic literature (Day et al., 2000; Thompson and Day, 2001;
Chaney et al., 2000; Dicks et al., 2001; Chaney and Fevre, 2001c; K. Morgan
and Rees, 2001; Chaney, 2002a, 2002b; Chaney and Williams, 2003). Projects
also produced a volume of literature on social capital, 'minority' groups,
the voluntary sector's interaction with the Assembly, some of the aspects
of civil society in post-devolution Wales. However, civil society was not
their focus. As a result, many of the theoretical issues surrounding civil
society are yet to be fully addressed.

Therefore, a theoretical discussion of 'civil society' is important to provide firm footings for this study. As the extant literature on civil society in Wales emphasized, a two-way relationship between theory and empirical practice of civil society is important to academic research (Chaney et al., 2000: 220). Overall, the literature on civil society theory and democratic theory is very extensive and wide-ranging and this chapter focuses on the main issues that are essential to informing this book: the relationship between civil society and democracy, and civil society and national identity. As we saw in the Introduction, these are areas where there were high expectations of civil society with the onset of devolution. In contrast, while economic democracy is an important issue, it does not feature in this chapter as it is not covered in this book. Overall, we chiefly draw on the literature associated with civil society in western liberal democracies and attempt to counterbalance the tendency within a large amount of the literature to be overtly normative and see civil society as inherently 'good' or 'democratic' (McLaverty, 2002: 303).

This chapter is divided into four sections. The first discusses theoretical definitions of civil society. The second and third sections discuss the relationship between civil society and democracy. Finally, the literature that assists our understanding of how civil society, in conjunction with government, can contribute to the development of a greater civic sense of national identity is examined.

DEFINING CIVIL SOCIETY

During the 1980s and into the 1990s, civil society became the subject of intense global interest. Some have questioned the value of resurrecting the concept of civil society (Kumar, 1993: 390). However, the rich tradition of theorizing civil society has provided the foundations to contemporary conceptualizations of civil society (Bryant, 1993). Here we examine key developments in civil society theory, characterized as the 'classical theory' of civil society (Fine, 1997: 9). It highlights the background to the contemporary diversity and conflicting definitions of 'civil society', that partly explains the 'catch-all' usage of the term in Wales. Then, Cohen and Arato's contemporary framework of civil society that provides a basis to this study is introduced.

The 'classical theory' of civil society

Though the long tradition of theorizing 'civil society' can be associated with medieval and classical thought, it was the Scottish Enlightenment philosophers in the eighteenth century that first articulated the modern conception of 'civil society' (Baker, 2002: 4). Prior to this, civil society was equated with the state or political society and emphasized the development of 'civilized' society (Kumar, 1993: 376–7). However, with modernity came centralized states, markets and political movements. These developments influenced Adam Ferguson's understanding of civil society in *An Essay on the History of Civil Society* (1767). Ferguson initiated the distinction between civil society and the state by recognizing civil society as a distinct sphere with its own principles. From this standpoint 'the refashioned concept of civil society was tied to the emergence of a distinct sphere of private property whose principal feature was an unprecedented degree of autonomy and independence from other social spheres' (Kumar, 1993: 377). Ferguson also elaborated on civil society and its moral foundations, signifying the first normative usage of civil society. To Ferguson, civil society was not a sphere for individual interests but rather promoted shared ethical relations that were crucial for moral and intellectual development (Ehrenberg, 1999: 91). However, Ferguson contended that capitalism and complex political institutions in modernity threatened the autonomy of civil society and made inequality and individualism increasingly prevalent within civil society. Ferguson therefore contributed to distinguishing civil society from the state and provided a greater understanding of the underpinnings of civil society and the threat it faces from other spheres.

Ferguson's work was translated into German and influenced the development of Hegel's modern idea of civil society (Baker, 2002: 5). In his *Philosophy of Right* (1821), Hegel conceived of civil society as an autonomous sphere that mediated between the state and the family. In addition to the market, Hegel emphasized professional associations as a key feature within civil society, reflected in the usage of *Bürgerliche Gesellschaft* (bourgeois or civil society). This was influenced by his identification of the role of property and the modern economy in spurring civil society. Hegel also elaborated on civil society's internal values and stressed its potential to develop individual interests and social solidarity. However, he echoed Ferguson in his awareness of how inequalities were increasingly embedded within civil society which undermined ethical unity and called for state regulation (Baker, 2002: 5). Therefore, this reading posits that a degree of interdependence exists between the state and civil society and that the state is essential for the rational organization of society and for addressing inequalities in civil society.

A further influential contribution was made by the Sardinian Marxist, Antonio Gramsci in the twentieth century. Gramsci was influenced by Hegel's thinking, but in contrast, Gramsci located civil society at an equal distance from the state/political sphere of society and from the market

(Honneth, 1993: 20). He states: 'Between the economic structure and the state with its legislation and its coercion stands civil society, and the latter must be radically transformed' (Gramsci, 1998: 208). Gramsci emphasized the non-economic dimensions of civil society, which include the social sphere and the associational sphere where public opinion is formed and ideas and values develop as the status quo (Bobbio, 1988: 83). The struggle for hegemony in Gramsci's view takes place in civil society: 'It is where values and meanings are established, where they are debated, contested and changed' (Kumar, 1993: 383). Gramsci's conception has been extremely influential, as it developed a three-part framework of civil society, state and market, illustrating the interrelationships between different spheres. It highlighted the centrality of civil society in the power struggle in society as a whole and emphasized the emancipatory potential of civil society.

The three theorists examined here made significant contributions to theorizing civil society. There are fundamental differences between their conceptions of civil society, in both descriptive and normative terms. This diversity is reflected in the ambiguities and contrasting notions of civil society in contemporary theory and in the practical usage of the term. To some degree, it could be argued that the concept has reverted to its earliest roots: 'Increasingly, "civil society" is used as the shorthand for the kind of society in which we want to live' (Edwards, 2004: 38). How we define civil society has clear implications for whether or not civil society can be viewed as a force for democracy. Honneth points to the more negative implications of this diversity: 'The use of the notion *civil* society ... in the course of over two hundred years of the history of political theory, has acquired so many strands and strata of meaning that today it appears to lack any definite contours' (1993: 19). As a result, in order to make a valid contemporary contribution, Ehrenberg contends that the theory of civil society needs to be reconstructed (1999: xvi).

Cohen and Arato and civil society

A key contemporary theoretical model that posits that the category of civil society must be reconstructed is that developed by Cohen and Arato in *Civil Society and Political Theory* (1999: 422). This approach has been selected as the most relevant framework to inform investigating civil society in this book. Cohen and Arato aim to demonstrate the relevance of civil society to all contemporary societies, and its potential to promote greater democratization in existing western liberal democracies (1999: vii). They contend that existing models and theories of liberal democracy are not adequately democratic and that civil society is central in promoting greater democratization in existing liberal democracies (Cohen and Arato, 1999: 564).

The background to Cohen and Arato's theory will be provided here as well as outlining their three-part framework of civil society, before discussing some of the drawbacks of their work.

Cohen and Arato develop their framework based on a Habermasian and post-Marxist understanding of civil society (1999: xvii, 2). Cohen and Arato attempt to fill a void as discussion of civil society broadened but no systematic theory has been developed (1999: 3). However, the Habermasian influence and the aims of the authors make explicit the high normative value attached to the concept of civil society in their model and their idealistic treatment of the term. Therefore, the framework developed by Cohen and Arato has a tendency to reflect that 'Civil society theory is not just a theory of civil society but a theory which privileges civil society over all other moments or spheres of social life' (Fine, 1997: 9).

Cohen and Arato develop a three-part model, whereby civil society is differentiated from the state and the economy, and also from political society and economic society. The latter is composed of organizations of production and distribution such as firms, partnerships and cooperatives. Due to the focus of the book, economic society and economic democracy will be excluded from the following discussion. Cohen and Arato argue that only a three-part model can serve to identify the critical potential of civil society in liberal democracies (1999: ix). In essence, civil society is conceptualized as the sphere of social interaction. There are several components: the family, which is the intimate sphere; also forms of public communication such as the media; and the associational sphere including voluntary associations and social movements (Cohen and Arato, 1999: ix). The definition is narrowed, as other features that characterize civil society are conscious association, self-organization and organized communication (1999: x). Cohen and Arato stipulate that a basis of laws and subjective rights are fundamental to civil society's ability to self-mobilize. Its continuation and reproduction depend on its capability for independent action and its institutionalization (1999: ix). This reflects the two-way relationship between civil society and a representative democracy. They presuppose one another as they share similar characteristics and are founded on a common basis of rights. This basis is crucial for civil society's existence and defence against the state and the economy.

Political society is an innovative inclusion into Cohen and Arato's model. They contend that many commonalities exist between political society and civil society, being rooted in civil society, sharing its forms of organization, communication with both depending on the same basis of rights in a representative democracy (Cohen and Arato, 1999: 413). Political society refers to political parties, political organizations and publics, including parliaments. In a representative democracy, the public sphere and voluntary associations are common to both civil and political society and mediate between them (Cohen and Arato, 1999: 412). Moreover, political society is presupposed to be open to the influence of civil society (1999: 413). The main difference between political society and civil society is that the former is directly involved with state power and does not operate as civil society that is characterized by normative integration and open-ended communication (Cohen and Arato, 1999: ix).

Following from this, we can examine Cohen and Arato's conception of civil society's potential to promote greater democracy in a representative democracy. Civil society should be self-limiting in relation to democratizing the state to avoid damaging the self-regulation of the subsystem (Cohen and Arato, 1999: 487). Civil society can potentially promote the democratization of a representative democracy by defending existing forms of democracy, by extending rights and demanding further democratization (Cohen and Arato, 1999: 414–15). Due to its mediating role, political society is central to civil society's potential to influence the nature of a representative democracy and contribute to its democratization (1999: ix, 415). However, there are limits to civil society's ability to democratize a representative democracy, as 'Civil society can directly transform only itself, and it can have at most an indirect effect on the self transformation of the political system' (Habermas, 1996: 372; Cohen and Arato, 1999: 415).

Cohen and Arato emphasize the importance of social movements as 'a key feature of a vital, modern, civil society and an important form of citizen participation in public life' and civil society's main method to indirectly influence the democratization of other spheres (1999: 19). These 'constitute the dynamic element in processes that might realize the positive potentials of modern civil societies' (1999: 492). They defensively target political society that mediates between civil society and the state and exert the 'politics of influence' on this sphere (1999: 531–2). According to Cohen and Arato, social movements can influence policy and political culture without endangering liberal democratic institutions through civil disobedience (1999: xviii). It is defined as a form of collective action that takes place in the public spaces of civil society. Civil disobedience is justified in that it aims to democratize decision-making processes further and is viewed as legitimate if there are insufficient channels for civil society to influence political society (Cohen and Arato, 1999: 600). However, civil disobedience as a form of collective action must be self-limiting and conduct should be appropriate to the situation (Cohen and Arato, 1999: 602).

Cohen and Arato's three-part framework of civil society is very revealing. Their work has been acclaimed as the 'most comprehensive study of civil society', but it has also received criticism (Habermas, 1996: 367).[1] Within their framework, political and economic society are seen as 'probably Cohen and Arato's single most innovative contribution' (Alexander, 1993: 799). In addition, they provide greater clarity on the interrelationships and differences between the spheres, and organizations that can be categorized in each sphere. These are also central to understanding civil society's abilities to promote the democratization of representative democracies.

However, the main criticism directed at Cohen and Arato's model is that their work leads to an overly idealized vision of civil society (Alexander, 1993: 801). Cohen and Arato point to differences within civil society: 'there can be very different types of civil society: more or less institutionalized, more or less democratic, more or less active', but their work has been criticized on this count (1999: 17). Competing normative values within civil society are not adequately recognized and Cohen and Arato do not sufficiently consider the issue of difference within civil society (Calhoun, 1995: xii–xv). A related critique of their normative approach is that Cohen and Arato take the democratizing potential of civil society for granted. Overall, the difficulties with the theoretical framework can be overcome by accepting that Cohen and Arato's model is an ideal model and by discussing other literature that tempers their approach.

To conclude, this section has outlined the 'classical theory' of civil society and elaborated on Cohen and Arato's definition of civil society that is:

- defined as a sphere of social interaction including the intimate sphere, forms of public communication and the associational sphere;
- characterized by conscious association, self-organization and organized communication;
- differentiated from the state and the economy, and from political society and economic society.

The main drawback of the model is the idealism surrounding the discussion of civil society. Nevertheless, the three-part framework is extremely revealing in highlighting the interrelationships between civil society and other spheres in a liberal democracy, and its potential to promote greater democratization. On this basis, we move on to consider the main approaches to issues of civil society and democracy, and civil society and national identity.

CIVIL SOCIETY AND THE PROMOTION OF DEMOCRACY

The relationship between civil society and democracy has been a crucial issue in civil society theory and democratic theory. In the past few decades, it has become increasingly clear that the 'orthodox' representative democracy is in crisis (Hirst, 2002; McLaverty, 2002). Trends such as declining voter turnout, trust and the alienation of citizens from political systems compounded with the weakening of the state and increased privatization have emphasized the limited political participation of citizens. Voting in periodic elections to elect representatives has been seen as providing a minimal role for citizens to influence decision-making and hold governments accountable (Pateman, 1970; Barber, 1984; Hirst, 1994). In response, different models of democracy have proposed alternatives means to democratize representative governments, particularly through more continuous opportunities for participation in the political system, more akin to the original conception of 'democracy' as rule by the people. Consequently, 'civil society' is now central to the majority of accounts of democracy and democratization (Baker, 2002: 81).

This book concerns the interaction between civil society and devolution. Both the project of devolution itself and Cohen and Arato's framework of civil society emphasize efforts to democratize an existing representative democracy. We therefore briefly examine the role envisaged for civil society in developing a healthy democracy in key contemporary models of democracy. Then we focus in greater depth on two interrelated issues associated with civil society's potential contribution to enrich democracy. We examine whether it has the ability to enhance democracy by promoting civic engagement and active participation. Then, considering the various functions of civil society in its interaction with the state, in the next section we examine different approaches to civil society–state relations and the implications for civil society's democratic role.

Most contemporary theories of democracy emphasize the contribution of civil society, or its constituent parts, to developing a healthy democracy. In response to elitist theories of democracy, Pateman's classic text *Democracy and Participation* (1970) was central to the revival of participatory politics. Pateman highlights that in a participatory democracy, citizens should participate in decision-making on all levels and in different spheres of life: 'for a democratic polity to exist it is necessary for a participatory society to exist' (Pateman, 1970: 43). Pateman emphasizes the importance of learning democracy through participation. Civil society would promote openness and participation, thus contributing to realizing 'democracy', the collective participation of citizens in decisions (Pateman, 1970: 42). Similarly, Barber points to representative democracy as a 'thin democracy' and advocates a 'strong democracy' to, 'associate democracy with a civic culture nearer to the themes of participation, citizenship and political activity that are democracy's central virtues' (1984: 25). He emphasizes the importance of institutional reforms to provide citizens with a variety of forms of participation to promote active deliberation and decision-making at both the local, regional and state levels (1984: 266).

In associative democracy, Hirst focuses on the role of organizations in a democracy: 'political theorists from Alexis de Tocqueville to Robert Dahl have stressed the central role of secondary associations in providing the institutional foundations of political pluralism and thus viable multiparty political contestation' (2002: 413). He argues for improving representative government and for democratizing civil society and promoting habits of association and participation (see also Cohen and Rogers, 1995). As a result, he advocates reducing the burden on representative institutions through decentralization, devolving social activities and public functions to voluntary associations.

Finally, as part of the shift 'from "vote-centric" to "talk-centric" democratic theory' (Kymlicka and Norman, 2000: 9), deliberative democracy advocates political equality and, 'collective decision making with the participation of all who will be affected by the decision or their representatives' (Elster, 1998: 8). Amongst the diversity of approaches in deliberative democracy, some emphasize the importance of creating spaces for deliberation within state institutions, thus tending to stress the role of representatives (see Gutmann and Thompson, 1996). As is the case with Cohen and Arato's work, following Habermas's discursive democracy, others give greater attention to civil society's role in developing deliberative politics (see Habermas, 1996; Young, 2000: 167). In the context of diversity and in order to protect minorities in modern societies, Gargarella emphasizes the problems of elected representatives and the importance of representing all groups in civil society: 'If we want to fulfil the criteria of both deliberation and full representation, we need to introduce substantive changes into the present representative system' (Gargarella, 1998: 260).

After establishing that civil society is central to contemporary theories of democracy, we can now examine one of the main ways that civil society can promote a healthy democracy and examine contending debates surrounding its potential to promote participatory norms and civic engagement thus increasing citizen participation in the political system. This discussion suggests that generalizations are unhelpful and that, in order to understand civil society's democratic potential, organizations need to be considered individually within the broader political context in which they are located.

Alexis de Tocqueville was a classical theorist writing in the 1830s who highlighted the central role of civil society in ensuring a stable and healthy democracy (Whitehead, 1997: 98). He asserted that associational life and local participation promoted habits of association and cooperation on political issues (Foley and Edwards, 1996: 39). Cohen and Arato emphasize civil society's democratic potential and build on Tocqueville's work (1999: 19). They argue that civil society can become more democratic and that its norms call for further democratization (Cohen and Arato, 1999: 411). Democratizing and modernizing the internal structures of modern civil society organizations would lessen domination, exclusion, inequality and discrimination and encourage universal inclusion, so increasing the chances of direct participation (Cohen and Arato, 1999: 516, 19). Cohen and Arato argue that norms of interaction, equality and solidarity are promoted within civil society. They view civil society as essential to developing participatory norms and argue that:

> Without *active* participation on the part of citizens in *egalitarian* institutions and civil associations, as well as in politically relevant organizations, there will be no way to maintain the democratic character of the political culture or of social and political institutions. (Cohen and Arato, 1999: 19)

To Cohen and Arato, social movements have a central role in promoting civil society's democratization by making structures and associations within civil society more democratic and egalitarian (Cohen and Arato, 1999: 505, 531).

Also influenced by Tocqueville is Putnam's work, which elaborates on civil society's democratic potential (1993: 15). 'Civil society' does not feature extensively in Putnam's work, but civil society is fundamental to 'social capital', his main conceptual focus. He explains the connection: 'voluntary associations and the social networks of civil society that we have been calling "social capital" contribute to democracy in two different ways: they have "external" effects on the larger polity, and they have "internal" effects on participants themselves' (Putnam, 2000: 338). *Making Democracy Work* (1993) highlights the impact of social capital on the quality of democracy and governance in Italian regions.[2] Putnam argues that 'civic community', produced from high levels of social capital, can strengthen democratic institutions and culture. High levels of social capital result from extensive active participation in networks of civil associations that embed virtues of solidarity, trust, cooperation, and reciprocity (Putnam, 1993: 177). Elements of citizenship in a civic community are revealing. Putnam distinguishes between horizontal and vertical networks. A community with social capital, 'is bound together by horizontal relations of reciprocity and cooperation, not by vertical relations of authority and dependency' (1993: 88). Horizontal networks within civil society create norms of reciprocity, can develop social trust, promote collective action and democracy (1993: 173). In contrast, vertical networks do not promote social trust and cooperation and are less helpful in addressing dilemmas of collective action (1993: 174–5). On this reading, civil society can embed democratic values through horizontal networks that can promote active participation in public affairs (1993: 88). In addition to the practical skills that can be developed from participation in organizations, the emphasis on reciprocity encourages members to seek a consensus in a democratic debate when they do not agree. Associations are also 'forums for thoughtful deliberation over vital public issues' (Putnam, 2000: 339–40).

Other aspects of the literature question civil society's democratic credentials. In *Bowling Alone* (2000) Putnam identifies the impact of declining social capital on American society and pinpoints contemporary trends in associations and diversity within civil society that weaken the claims of its ability to promote participatory norms. Change in the nature of membership casts doubt on civil society organizations' propensity to enhance democracy. There has been a steep decline in the membership of voluntary associations from the 1960s to the 1990s, and a growth in smaller-sized groups (Putnam, 2000: 49). Similar evidence of limited associational membership is evident in the UK context and it is suggested that active and involved membership in organizations is even lower (McLaverty, 2002: 309). However, McLaverty argues, echoing Cohen and Arato, that from a democratic standpoint, limited membership of organizations is potentially counterbalanced by the 'quality' of involvement, particularly in social movements and locally organized associations (2002: 309; Cohen and Arato, 1999: 492–563).

Crucially, the nature of membership has changed in voluntary associations and social movements with shifts to more contemporary rather than traditional affiliations leading to a mass membership boom and direct mail becoming the main method to gain membership and support. Internal changes within organizations has led to a greater emphasis on staff-led development and more hierarchical structures: 'new organizations are professionally staffed advocacy organizations, not member-centered, locally based associations' (Putnam, 2000: 51). Often organizations are powerful, but their practices are similar to mail-order commercial organizations (Putnam, 2000: 51–2). Active and involved membership is weak and in many respects organizations are less democratic and participatory (Putnam, 2000: 58; McLaverty, 2002: 309; Skocpol, 2003: 13). Edwards explains the effects,

> since the skills of democracy are best learned through practice rather than in the classroom or by reading fund-raising leaflets sent by mail, the increasing dominance of lobby groups and service-providing NGOs may threaten the norm-generating effects of associations by reducing citizen involvement to cheque or letter writing and attendance at the occasional rally – the 'junk food' of participation as Sidney Verba calls it. (2004: 79)

Compared with the emphasis on a participatory civil society in Toqueville's era, Skocpol states: 'early-twenty-first-century Americans live in a diminished democracy, in a much less participatory and more oligarchically managed civic world' (2003: 11).

Secondly, the assertion that norms such as equality and solidarity are embedded within civil society is contested. Exclusionary aspects surround civil society and, according to Edwards, 'norms vary between different associations in the same society or culture and between different cultures and societies' (2004: 43). Putnam states that 'urban gangs, NIMBY ("not in my back yard") movements, and power elites often exploit social capital to achieve ends that are antisocial from a wider perspective' (2000: 21). Civil society can therefore perpetuate limitations to democracy: 'voluntary associations . . . can reinforce antiliberal tendencies; and they can be abused by antidemocratic forces' (Putnam, 2000: 341). In this regard, civil society reflects the context in which it is located: 'civil society can support authoritarianism as easily as it can advance freedom' (Ehrenberg, 1999: 244).

Thirdly, civil society can exacerbate inequalities of power that mean that it can create exclusion and negatively influence the democratic process. Edwards argues: 'The persistence of serious inequalities and insecurities endangers civil society as a democratic enterprise and places too much influence in the hands of elites' (2004: 97). Exclusionary aspects within civil society reflect that external factors such as distributions of power are perpetuated within civil society (Whitehead, 1997; Ehrenberg, 1999). Indeed, Whitehead suggests that these inequalities cannot be overcome: 'however we specify the precise components of civil society, some sections of the citizenry will be over-supplied with "dense associative life", while others will be under-provided' (1997:101).

Fourthly, these three factors underline the diversity within civil society. Issues of difference within civil society cannot be ignored as difference can promote exclusion and competition. Civil society does not equal democracy and its democratic credentials depend on how we define civil society and call for examining organizations on an individual basis. As McLaverty argues, 'There is nothing inherently democratic about "civil society" or about the voluntary organizations which are found within it' (2002: 310). Kopecky and Mudde's comments regarding civil society in eastern Europe are also relevant to the West:

> civil society is itself hugely diverse and heterogeneous, including a plethora of different and sometimes opposed agents. Hence, it is not useful as a unitary concept in empirical research; i.e. statements like 'an active civil society is good for democracy' are invalid, as this depends on which groups *within* civil society dominate. (2003: 11)

To conclude, civil society has the potential to be both positive and negative to democracy. Changes in the nature of some organizations suggest that they are less democratic and less conducive to developing active participation. Diversity and the inequalities of power and influence within civil society question its democratic potential. Civil society can however have potentially positive effects on democracy. In particular, organizations that promote high levels of active participation in non-hierarchical horizontal networks can generate norms that are conducive to a participatory democracy. On balance, civil society's democratic potential cannot be generalized. Attention needs to be directed to organizations individually, in particular to their internal structures, their actions and the setting in which civil society is located.

CIVIL SOCIETY–STATE RELATIONS AND DEMOCRACY

An interrelated aspect of the relationship between civil society and democracy is different types of civil society and state relations and the implications for civil society's democratic role. While there is a spectrum to relations between civil society and the state, there are two potentially conflicting aspects of civil society–state relations that could affect civil society's democratic role. Through interaction with the state, civil society can promote and protect different interests within civil society and society, and hold government to account and check state power. For instance, civil society has a role in protecting minorities: 'If minorities are to have any real influence in a majoritarian system, it will be through participating in the formation of public opinion, rather than through winning a majority vote' (Kymlica and Norman, 2000: 9). Overall, 'independent associations provide the channels or mediating structures through which political participation is mobilized and states are held accountable by their citizens' (Edwards, 2004: 74). From this standpoint, civil society's autonomy needs to be safeguarded in order to fulfil these democratic functions. Another aspect is that civil society can have strong relations with the state by engaging in partnerships with the state for the purposes of policy-making and implementation and receiving state funding. Partnership could have positive effects in improving the quality or relevance of policies but could also be viewed as threatening civil society's autonomy.

Here we firstly elaborate on Cohen and Arato's approach to civil society and state relations. Then two literatures are investigated, the Third Way and neo-corporatism, discussed in the existing literature on civil society in Wales (Hain, 1999; Day et al., 2000; Thompson and Day, 2001; Chaney and Fevre, 2001a). In this literature, it was argued that the former influenced the adopted model of civil society–Assembly relations, and the latter was highlighted as relevant to understanding the nature of relations between civil society and the Assembly post-devolution.

Cohen and Arato contend that civil society faces threats from state expansion, particularly the welfare state, and the growth of the capitalist economy (1999: 426). They explain the threats to modern civil society as the colonization of the lifeworld, following Habermas's dualistic model of the lifeworld and the system. The concept of the lifeworld is translated into the institutional expression of civil society which is differentiated from the economic and political/administrative subsystems (Cohen and Arato, 1999: 531). As a result of these threats, the task is to guarantee the autonomy of the modern state and economy while simultaneously protecting civil society from destructive penetration and functionalization by the imperatives of these two spheres (Cohen and Arato, 1999: 25).

Cohen and Arato nevertheless emphasize the state's importance to civil society's existence. They accept the interrelationship between civil society and the state and reject positioning civil society against the state (1999: 471). As explained, a representative democracy establishes a foundation of basic rights that underpin the institutional existence of modern civil society (Cohen and Arato, 1999: 346). While representative democracy is at times seen as limiting the participation opportunities available to citizens, it has an important role. Cohen and Arato state that:

> a plural, dynamic civil society finds in a parliamentary structure the most plausible general framework in which the conflicts of member groups and individuals can be politically mediated, rival interests can be aggregated, and the possibility of reaching consensus can be explored. (1999: 413)

Thus, Cohen and Arato simultaneously point out that the distinction between civil society and the state is essential to democracy, while recognizing the interdependencies that exist between the state and civil society. This explains why they emphasize the need for civil society to be self-limiting when attempting to democratize other spheres.

Other aspects of the literature express similar viewpoints. On the one hand, civil society advocates argue that retaining the distinction between civil society and the state is essential to democratic society in order for civil society to protect the autonomous development of public opinion, counterbalance state power and promote accountable government (Baker, 2002: 7; McLaverty, 2002: 306). According to Ehrenberg: 'civil society *does* often serve democracy by checking state power' (1999: 239). On the other hand, some theorists stress the role of the state in providing a basis of rights for civil society and addressing conflicts within civil society (Kumar, 1993: 391). Others take this argument further and emphasize the deeper interdependencies and greater complexities. Many civil society organizations receive state funding, and thus 'Financial independence is another key, yet highly problematic, criterion on which the distinction between civil society and the state is based' (Kopecky and Mudde, 2003: 6).

The Third Way and neo-corporatism point to two opposed types of relations between the state and civil society, and highlight the different implications to democracy. The Third Way philosophy became popular internationally during the 1990s. The focus here is on the Third Way strand that influenced New Labour's agenda in the UK as discussed by one of its most influential proponents, Anthony Giddens (1998; 2000). Third Way politics calls for a transformation of government and state and argues that there is a need to attempt to address the crisis facing liberal democracies due to being insufficiently democratic (Giddens, 1998: 71). To facilitate this, Third Way politics advocates deepening and widening democracy, or 'democratising democracy' (Giddens, 1998: 69; 2000: 61).

Civil society is an essential element of Third Way politics (Giddens, 2000: 64). Giddens argues that 'The fostering of an active civil society is a basic part of the politics of the third way' (1998: 78). A flourishing civil society is essential to a democratic order (Giddens, 2000: 51). The process of democratizing democracy should include 'downward democracy' that 'presumes the renewal of civil society' from its present, weakened situation (Giddens, 1998: 77). Giddens argues that civil society and the state should act in partnership 'to facilitate, but also to act as a control upon, the other' (1998: 79). In this partnership between state and civil society, civil society protects individuals from state power, but the state also protects individuals from the conflicts of interests within civil society (Giddens, 1998: 85–6). This partnership, with particular reference to the third sector, can promote community renewal in deprived local communities to develop a new mixed economy (Giddens, 1998: 69). In order to achieve this renewal, the state has a direct role to play in developing an active civil society and in supporting local groups. Therefore, in Third Way politics, the state is central in promoting the revitalization of civil society. A partnership with civil society is important for the purposes of democratic renewal, enhancing civil society's participation in government, delivering public services and potentially generating economic development (Giddens, 2000: 81).

The neo-corporatism literature, however, points to the potentially negative effect of close state/civil society relations on civil society's democratic role.[3] While it must be recognized that the nature of relationships between the state and interest groups is more complex in practice than propounded by the literature, it provides interesting insights (Moore and Booth, 1989: 2). To explain neo-corporatism, the literature differentiates between pluralism and neo-corporatism. Schmitter explains pluralism as:

> a system of interest intermediation in which the constituent units are organized into an unspecified number of multiple, voluntary, competitive, non

hierarchically ordered and self-determined (as to type or scope of interest) categories which are not specially licensed, recognized, subsidized, created or otherwise controlled in leadership selection or interest articulation by the state and which do not exercise a monopoly of representational activity within their respective categories. (1979: 15)

Neo-corporatism presents an alternative framework to understanding interest group politics that contrasts with the open political process of pluralism (Wilson, 1990: 67). According to Wilson:

The neo-corporatist model stresses the exclusive relationships between a handful of privileged groups and the state. Instead of the multiplicity of relevant interest groups predicted by pluralism, the neo-corporatist model posits the presence of a single group for each interest sector ... That one group is viewed as the only legitimate vehicle for that sector. There is thus little competition from rival groups within the various sectors. (1990: 69)

Through formal engagement with governmental structures, groups directly engage in developing and in some cases implementing government policies (Wilson, 1990: 69). The greatest benefit for government is that it leads to greater expertise that positively affects the decisions taken (Wilson, 1990: 69). Limiting the number of groups that directly engage addresses the difficulties facing government (Wilson, 1990: 70).

The literature on neo-corporatism suggests that such arrangements do not necessarily advance democracy. First, the state's selection of a single group as representative of each sector raises a number of issues. It is unclear to what extent the group is representative of the wider interests of their sector. Moreover, the privileging of one group over others creates inequalities, particularly as Wilson argues that groups and the state guard these arrangements. This constrains other organizations from engaging in the political system. Wilson argues that:

The government may limit the organization of new groups by requiring the licensing of interest associations and restricting entry of groups deemed by the government to be 'unrepresentative'. It may refuse to consult with all but the officially recognized groups or accord privileged access only to them. (1990: 69)

This in turn reinforces exclusion and marginalization both within civil society and in relations between civil society and the state. One effect of this can be that groups take alternative action:

Frustrated by their inability to gain a hearing for their concerns by the policy-makers, outside groups resort to unconventional methods such as demonstrations, boycotts, political strikes, sit-ins, and even violence to draw the attention of the public or the policy-makers to their concerns. (Wilson, 1990: 71)

A second element that suggests that neo-corporate relations between the state and civil society hinder democracy is that they tend to promote consensus and assimilation. Close relationships are established with the state, and organizations do not want to threaten this. As a result, a consensus develops between the state and organizations that makes the latter unwilling to go against the state. Wilson explains:

> The effectiveness of the groups' participation in these corporatist bodies renders other forms of action unnecessary ... Other forms of pressure – such as demonstrations or political strikes – are not only unneeded, but are avoided out of fear that they might damage the harmony and spirit of accommodation that is the essence of the corporatist process. (1990: 69)

Furthermore, neo-corporatist arrangements can affect the democratic role of 'inside' groups. The state's extensive influence over organizations means that they are less likely to act as a check on the state and to hold it accountable. It is unclear whether the state's influence is more intense when groups receive state funding, as little research appears to have been undertaken into this matter, but it would hardly be surprising if this were the case (Wilson, 1983: 119).

Finally, neo-corporate structures can affect the internal cohesion of organizations in strong relations with the state as consensus-building develops between the state and organizations' leaders. As a result, elite leaders of groups are potentially torn between retaining the privileged relations with the state and being responsive to their membership who could have competing agendas or demands. According to Wilson, 'The elitist character of corporatism inevitably produces tensions both within existing associations and among latent outside groups that feel that their concerns are neglected' (1990: 70). This can damage accountability within representative organizations, limit the opportunities for membership engagement and create tensions within organizations.

To sum up, the discussion of different types of civil society–state relations provided by the Third Way and neo-corporatism literature has highlighted potential benefits and threats of strong relations with the state to civil society's democratic potential. Third Way politics emphasizes the state's ability to promote the renewal of civil society and generate partnerships that can contribute to democratizing democracy and increasing civil society participation in government. From a neo-corporatist perspective, however, strong partnerships between the state and civil society can hinder democracy. Selecting specific organizations to represent a whole sector can create an elite of interest groups to the exclusion of other organizations. In addition, such arrangements can promote consensus in state–civil society relations, thus making organizations less able to hold the state accountable and therefore further hinder democracy. In practice, the situation is more complex: 'It is not enough to say that civil society serves democracy only if it sustains political opposition, for there are too many examples of state-sponsored associations that have served plurality, facilitated voluntary activity and encouraged equality' (Ehrenberg, 1999: 238–9). As was evident when considering civil society's potential to promote active participation, attention needs to be given to organizations on an individual basis: 'as always, theory needs to be informed by solid analysis. Much depends on the nature of the state and the character of the associations, groups and movements that populate civil society' (Ehrenberg, 1999: 239).

CIVIL SOCIETY AND NATIONAL IDENTITY

The final section of this chapter briefly discusses literature that can assist in identifying the relationship between civil society and a civic sense of national identity. This question is particularly pertinent due to the pre-devolution expectations that, in parallel with the National Assembly, a stronger civil society would promote a more civic sense to Welsh identity (Paterson and Wyn Jones, 1999: 185). In Scotland, Wyn Jones and Lewis stated 'The institutions of civil society . . . have therefore been the medium through which Scottish national identity was both expressed and trans-mitted' (1998: 7). In contrast, in Wales, while Welsh national identity is diverse and multifarious, it has essentially been characterized as more 'ethnic' (Fevre and Thompson, 1999: 22). The relative paucity of institutional structures partially accounted for the weak sense of civic identity. From the establishment of the Welsh Office onwards, administrative devolution to Wales promoted institution-building which fostered a greater civic sense to Welsh identity. Based on research conducted in 1998, Hasely argues that:

> Scotland and Wales are simultaneously civic and ethnic because many Scottish and Welsh citizens accept aspects of an ethnic conception of what it means to be Scottish or Welsh, whereas others embrace civic notions of what it means to be Scottish or Welsh. (2005: 254)

It was envisaged that the National Assembly could act as a springboard for the expansion of civic aspects within Welsh identity post-devolution. In order to inform an examination of the impact of devolution on civil society's contribution to the development of a civic sense of Welsh identity, attention is paid to the interrelationship between national identity and civil society. As a result, we draw on the distinctly different literature on civic nationalism and identify the links with the idea civil society. We examine two aspects: conceptualizing a civic sense of national identity; and civil society's contribution to the promotion of a civic sense of national identity.

How does the literature characterize a civic sense of national identity? The literature differentiates between civic and ethnic types of national identity. Initially, a note of caution must be sounded as the analytical value of the civic/ethnic distinction has been questioned. They are fundamentally ideal types of identity that are 'normative and value-laden' and must be essentially considered as a theoretical distinction (Keating, 2001: 8; Hasely, 2005: 252). However, the distinction assists in identifying the characteristics associated with a civic identity. A civic identity is based on the premise of:

> shared allegiance to civic institutions, understood in broad terms to include for example legal norms and institutions, political representative organs, branches of public and local administration, the organization of education, churches and religious communities in their secular aspect and other like institutions having an understood territorial location with which they are connected. (MacCormick, 1996: 562)

In contrast, ethnic identity involves:

> A distinctive culture, including perhaps a language thought of as the special possession of those and only those belonging to the original ethnic community, grounded ultimately in some kind of shared ancestry or genetic bond. You are either a member of this nation or not. (MacCormick, 1996: 563)

On this basis, civic identity is less exclusive than ethnic identity. Civic identity is based on common values, allegiance to institutions is voluntary and can be aquired, thus incorporating all resident within the territory of a nation. MacCormick states: 'the community defined by allegiance to institutions is open to anyone who chooses to dwell in the territory and give allegiance to the institutions' (1996: 563).

If these are the characteristics associated with a civic sense of national identity, how can civil society be an expression of national identity, particularly a civic sense of national identity? In *Nations Against the State* (2001), Keating examines Quebec, Catalonia and Scotland as examples of minority nationalisms. He explains that civil society can be an expression of national identity: 'where the nation does not have its own state, national identity may be borne by institutions and practices in the civil society and shared values to which all can adhere' (Keating, 2001: 7). Indeed, Keating contends that, in the cases under discussion:

National identity has become plural rather than singular and exclusive, though with a steady increase in identification with the minority nation. In all three, there is a consciousness that the national project, in the contemporary world, cannot be carried by governmental institutions alone but must be rooted in civil society. (2001: 265)

This suggests that civil society can play a role in projects of civic nationalism if it promotes a plural rather than exclusive expression of national identity.

Bryant discusses civic and ethnic nationalism, but his discussion provides some pointers to understanding the values associated with a civil society that promotes a civic sense of national identity. He argues that:

Civic nations may attribute a leading role in their formation to one or more particular ethnies but they also extend citizenship to all who permanently and lawfully reside within their territory and who join in the national imaging or at least refrain from contesting it. By definition they are pluralist and/or assimilationist. (Bryant, 1995: 145)

On the other hand, he argues that ethnic nations:

Relate citizenship and full participation in society to ethnicity and descent. They can and do develop civil societies but these are exclusive; residents of other ethnic origins, even of long standing are denied citizenship. There is a suspicion of difference and a rejection of pluralism. (Bryant, 1995: 145)

This discussion suggests that a plurality of interests and identities and voluntary membership would be expressed in a civil society that promotes a civic sense of national identity. An exclusive and elitist civil society would, in contrast, be related to a more ethnic sense of national identity.

Overall, civil society can play a role in developing a more civic sense of national identity in two ways. The idea of civic identity and a civic nation emphasized that national identity is voluntary, open to all and based on allegiance to political institutions. In this sense, civil society organizations can promote a civic sense of national identity by encouraging allegiance to these institutions. Civil society can also contribute to developing a more civic sense of national identity. If one accepts that a civic sense of national identity is multifaceted and plural, then a civil society within which a plurality of interests and organizations are represented can potentially promote the development of a more civic sense of identity.

CONCLUSION

This chapter has attempted to provide strong theoretical foundations to inform the examination of the impact of devolution on civil society in post-devolution Wales. The sophisticated theoretical understanding of civil society developed by Cohen and Arato was identified as a sound conceptual basis for this empirical study. Subsequent discussion of civil society's potential contribution to a healthy democracy has gone some way to counter-balancing Cohen and Arato's highly idealistic approach to civil society. Civil society does not necessarily promote active engagement and can indeed exacerbate inequalities. This highlights the need to pay attention to individual organizations, focusing in particular on their internal structures and degree of membership engagement.

The chapter also discussed different types of civil society–state relations and the implications for democracy. This has underlined that a study of civil society needs to give attention to the nature of relations between the state and individual organizations in order to identify whether these have positive or negative democratic effects.

Overall, the chapter has emphasized that 'civil society' is ambiguous and problematic. How we define civil society is crucial to assessing its democratic credentials. Civil society can be a force that promotes and hinders democracy. Furthermore, it could be argued that the two characteristics of how civil society can contribute to promoting a healthy democracy discussed here, through participatory engagement structures and its relations with the state, do not necessarily go hand in hand. For instance, on the one hand, an organization that promotes active participatory engagement may not also hold the state accountable. On the other hand, an organization that directs extensive energy into scrutinizing the state may have hierarchical internal structures, thus promoting limited membership involvement. This leads us to the conclusion that accepting only those groups with both characteristics as 'civil society' would be extremely narrow: 'there is nothing *intrinsically* democratic about "civil society organizations" – unless that is, you so define "civil society" as to exclude, by definitional fiat, any organizations which are not completely democratic' (McLaverty, 2002: 310). A crucial point is that groups can change over time and may operate in different ways in relation to different activities more or less 'democratic'. Therefore, in practice, the means by which civil society organizations can potentially promote democracy differ both within and between organizations.

Finally, the chapter has provided a basis for examining the impact of devolution on the interrelationship between civil society and national identity in post-devolution Wales. Civil society can contribute to the development of a greater 'civic' sense of national identity. It can promote allegiance to civic institutions. Secondly, civil society can contribute to developing a civic sense of identity if a plurality of interests are represented within civil society.

3

New Institutions, New Opportunities?

This chapter provides the political and constitutional context to this study and explains how institutional change created new opportunities for civil society in Wales. It examines the implications of the constitutional settlement established by the Government of Wales Act 1998 for civil society's engagement with the Assembly. It also assesses the direct effects of the 'unsettled' nature of the devolution settlement and political developments during the first term of devolution on the terms of engagement, so to speak, of civil society organizations. Therefore, the chapter attempts a comprehensive assessment of the impact of the changing devolution 'settlement' and associated political developments on civil society's engagement with the Assembly.

This chapter is divided into three sections. The first section sets the scene by providing a broad outline of the National Assembly for Wales' powers and structures as prescribed by the Government of Wales Act 1998. The second section examines the opportunities arising from the 'settlement' to promote civil society engagement in the Assembly's work. The third section considers the converse, the difficulties that discourage civil society involvement arising from the devolution settlement and the political context of the Assembly's first term. Overall, the chapter concludes that, in theory, a number of the Assembly's features suggest extensive opportunities for civil society organizations to engage in its work. However, changes to a more cabinet style of government had multiple and contradictory effects. This meant that the degree to which organizations are well resourced, professionalized, have expertise and connections with the Assembly and Welsh Assembly Government became more important in order to secure meaningful engagement with the Assembly.

THE DEVOLUTION 'SETTLEMENT'

This section briefly outlines the main steps in the process of establishing the National Assembly particularly in order to familiarize those not aware of the nature of Welsh devolution. It then outlines the key relevant elements of the Assembly and its political composition during the first term. The Government of Wales Act that established new constitutional arrangements for Wales received Royal Assent in July 1998. Preceding this, soon after Labour's victory in the May 1997 General Election, a pre-legislative referendum on devolution to Wales took place on 18 September 1997. Its basis was Labour's proposals for the Assembly as outlined in the *A Voice for Wales* White Paper issued in July 1997 (Welsh Office, 1997). With a narrow majority, a 'yes' vote was returned in the referendum; this represented a 30 per cent shift in favour of devolution since the Welsh Devolution Referendum in 1979 (Rawlings, 1998: 15). Labour's proposals bore the strong influence of the internal Labour Party policy commission's recommendations outlined in the 1995 *Shaping the Vision* document. The devolution proposals were developed almost exclusively within the Labour Party following the Labour Party Executive's refusal to participate in a proposed cross-party Constitutional Convention for Wales (Wyn Jones and Lewis, 1998).

Though the broad principles of the White Paper were reflected in the Government of Wales Act 1998, a number of changes were made to the legislation during the passage of the Act (Lambert, 1999: 60). These changes significantly altered the structures of the National Assembly. In addition to the Act itself, two other components formed the 'constitutions' of the National Assembly. The first was the National Assembly Advisory Group (NAAG) recommendations. NAAG was established in December 1997 with cross-party representation as well as representatives from the voluntary and business sectors. It produced recommendations to ensure that the internal processes of the National Assembly would make it a 'democratic, effective, efficient and inclusive' institution (Rawlings, 2003: 43). This group therefore undertook preparatory work that informed the work of the Standing Orders Commission that drafted the standing orders for the Assembly (McAllister, 2000a: 640–1). Much of the Commission's work was already determined by the requirements of the Government of Wales Act, but the Assembly's Standing Orders, completed in April 1999, provided detail on the internal architecture of the Assembly, particularly its operating procedures and structures (Sherlock, 2000: 64). The Standing Orders formed the third element of the 'constitutions' of the National Assembly for Wales (Laffin and Thomas, 2000: 557).

The foundations of the National Assembly were established in the Government of Wales Act 1998. The powers and functions of the Assembly were broadly those previously under the remit of the Welsh Office and the Secretary of State for Wales as set out in a raft of previous primary and secondary legislation. The Assembly therefore inherited powers in education, health, agriculture, forestry, fisheries and food, transport and roads, industry and training, local government and housing, the environment, planning, economic development, the arts and culture, the Welsh language, sports and recreation. Section 22 (1) of the Act established the procedures for the transfer of Welsh Office functions and activities in a Transfer of Functions Order and provides for further transfers (Rawlings, 2003: 61). Matters of foreign affairs, defence, taxation, macro-economic policy, financial markets policy and common markets, social security and broadcasting remained in central government control. Furthermore, primary legislative and tax-raising powers were not transferred by Westminster. However, as during the Welsh Office period, the Assembly had the ability to utilize secondary legislation to adapt legislation for the needs of Wales.

Regarding the Assembly's composition, sixty directly elected Assembly Members (AMs) were elected for four years. These were responsible for the functions and powers previously exercised by the Secretary of State for Wales. More proportional election procedures were introduced with forty Assembly Members elected via first past the post and another twenty elected from five electoral regions, in a version of an Additional Members System (AMS). With regards to the Assembly's structures, the White Paper had proposed that the Assembly would replicate the committee or local government model of committee structures (Welsh Office, 1997: 25). However, during the passage of the Act, a cabinet government model was superimposed on the local government model of the Assembly. Therefore, the Assembly as a whole elected the First Secretary who then appointed an executive committee (subsequently a Cabinet) made up of Assembly Secretaries (subsequently Assembly Ministers). The Assembly's subject committees reflected the portfolios of a maximum of eight Assembly Ministers. Committee membership reflected party balance in the Assembly, and the ministers were members of the committees, but did not act as chairs (Laffin and Thomas, 2000: 557, Rawlings, 2003: 99). Other Assembly committees included: the Business Committee, responsible for the Assembly's work programme; scrutiny committees; Audit and Legislation Committees; advisory committees in the form of four Regional Committees; and two cross-cutting committees in areas of Equality of Opportunity and European and External Affairs (Rawlings, 2003: 106). In addition, the Assembly's 'corporate body' status arising from the local government model was retained despite the decision that the Assembly should operate with a cabinet system (Sherlock, 2000: 61). Osmond explains: 'The Assembly was established as a corporate body, combining its legislative and executive functions rather than separating them as is normal in parliamentary institutions' (2000: 37).

The first election to the National Assembly for Wales in May 1999 determined the political composition of the Assembly for the first term and was significant in affecting the direction of the National Assembly during the infancy of devolution to Wales. As with UK General Elections in Wales since 1945, Labour gained the greatest number of the Assembly seats reflecting its status as the largest party in Wales (McAllister, 1980: 79). However, the elections were characterized as a 'quiet earthquake' as Labour won only 28 of the 60 seats, thus failing to win an overall majority. Plaid Cymru won 17 seats; the Conservatives won 9 seats and the Liberal Democrats 6 seats. Therefore, from the beginning of the Assembly's operation in July 1999, Labour operated as a minority administration that was led by Alun Michael, as First Secretary, until his resignation in February 2000. At this point, Rhodri Morgan became First Secretary (subsequently, First Minister) and a period of cohabitation with the other parties ensued. However, in October 2000, a Partnership Agreement was instituted between the Labour Party and Liberal Democrats and they formed a coalition government that governed until the end of the Assembly's first term in May 2003.

OPPORTUNITIES FOR CIVIL SOCIETY ENGAGEMENT WITH THE ASSEMBLY

Now we examine the opportunities for civil society during the Assembly's first term. The discussion examines the Assembly's powers, its composition, then its structures, and finally examines other factors arising from the constitutional settlement and features of the Assembly that promote civil society engagement. It will be argued that elements of the Assembly's structures and working practices and its emphasis on freedom of information reflect the aspiration to realize the 'new politics'.

The powers and functions of the Assembly reflected a continuation of arrangements from the Welsh Office era. While primary legislative duties were not transferred to the Assembly, 'there is substantial executive power to elaborate upon primary legislation and, depending on the framing of the laws, there can be wide-ranging discretion of real consequence for the people of Wales' (Chaney, Hall and Pithouse, 2001b: 226). Therefore, there was a sense that while the National Assembly's powers were no more extensive than during the Welsh Office era, it had the potential to make a difference. One key element was its power to allocate the spending of a financial budget of around £8 billion annually (Rawlings, 2003: 7). The emphasis placed on the Assembly's potential to 'make a difference' could be viewed as an encouragement for organizations to engage with the

Assembly. This seemed the case for those sectors of civil society organizations involved in devolved areas of powers that were affected by the Welsh Office before devolution. Furthermore, there was a stark difference from the Welsh Office era. Rather than being under the authority of one Secretary of State for Wales, now, due to the 'corporate body' principle, sixty directly elected Assembly Members were responsible for these powers and functions. This 'democratization' of a tier of government in Wales greatly expanded the political opportunities for civil society organizations to influence AMs and engage in the National Assembly's work. Indeed, most AMs promoted participation and in practice encouraged actors such as civil society groups with which they had contact to foster strong relations with the Assembly. Therefore, this involvement was in part due to the previous contact of organizations with politicians and due to the broader commitment to openness in the Assembly that encompassed civil society (Chaney, 2002a: 14).

One obvious opportunity for organizations to engage with the Assembly's work upon which there were high expectations at the onset of devolution was through the subject committees. Prior to the Assembly's establishment, Ron Davies claimed that the committees would be 'all-round policy workhouses of the Assembly. They would make day-to-day decisions, but would be more powerful than the House of Commons select committees' (in Laffin and Thomas, 2000: 568). In a similar vein John Osmond envisaged that subject committees would be 'the engine room of the Assembly's activities' (1998b: 9). The cross-party composition of the committees was seen as a means of ensuring that all parties could influence policy-making and thus 'give ordinary Assembly Members more input into policy-making than is enjoyed by backbench MPs' (Wyn Jones and Trystan, 2001: 24). It was widely expected that the link between the subject committees and decision-making would be strengthened through Assembly Ministers' membership of the committees (Rawlings, 2003: 108). For civil society organizations, the intention for committees to be proactive in policy-making suggested extended opportunities for gaining influence through interaction with the committees and their members. Indeed, the subject committees were viewed as a facet of the 'new politics' with their working practices, not only a matter of cross-party collaboration but also of partnership working and inclusiveness toward external actors. In this respect, committees would consult and receive representations from external actors in both policy reviews and policy development to a greater extent than at the Westminster level. Wyn Jones and Trystan confirm the potentially greater opportunities to civil society organizations:

> the committee structure is important in this context, as its openness and transparency is also intended to allow civil society groupings to be far more

intimately involved in the policy-making process than is usually the case at the UK level. (2001: 25)

With regard to the other committees, the Assembly's four regional committees were viewed as having the potential to facilitate the interaction of civil society organizations from different areas of Wales with the National Assembly. The regional committee's ability to receive representations was seen by Osmond as part and parcel of creating 'an interactive network of policy communication that will be a building block of a new civil society' (1998a: 6). As committees met in various locations across Wales, they also provided opportunities for organizations to express their views to the Assembly without travelling to Cardiff. This was most advantageous to organizations not directly represented in Cardiff, or organizations with fewer resources, or those that operate only on a local level. Therefore various aspects of the Assembly's committee structure, their working practices and political composition suggested multiple, meaningful channels through which organizations could input into the Assembly's work.

Another potentially crucial route through which civil society organizations might be involved in the Assembly's work was the result of the legal requirements of the Government of Wales Act. First, Clause 114 of the Act placed a statutory duty upon the National Assembly to develop a Voluntary Sector Scheme (Box 3.1) outlining how the Assembly aimed to assist and promote the interests of voluntary organizations, and consult with organizations on matters that affected them (NAW, 2000a: 1). A Compact existed between the government and the voluntary sector in Wales before devolution (NAW, 2001a: 2). According to the Assembly, no similar scheme existed in the UK and this was the first of its kind in Europe (NAW, 2001a; NAW, 2000a: i). The scheme, developed in consultation with the voluntary sector, was approved in July 2000. In accordance with the scheme, a Voluntary Sector Partnership Council was established. The council was composed of 11 AMs (chosen to reflect party balance), 3 representatives of the Wales Council for Voluntary Action, and 21 sectoral representatives from the voluntary sector, and met four times a year (NAW, 2000a: 9–10). WCVA and National Assembly officials supported the council's work, the former acting as a secretariat by coordinating voluntary sector members and selecting representatives, so ensuring the voices of a cross-section of the voluntary sector on the Council (NAW, 2000a: 9). In 2001–2, the WCVA received a grant of £70,000 to undertake this work (NAW, 2001m). In addition, in accordance with the scheme, each Assembly Minister held twice-yearly meetings with 'representatives of the relevant networks of voluntary organisations' (NAW, 2000a: 8). Again, WCVA was responsible for the coordinating work for these meetings.

Box 3.1: Voluntary Sector Scheme

Chapter 2: The General Principles of Assembly–Voluntary Sector Relations

2.1 In this Scheme, the term 'voluntary sector' includes voluntary organisations, community groups, volunteers, self-help groups, community cooperatives and enterprises, religious organisations and other not-for-profit organisations of benefit to communities and people in Wales.

2.2 The National Assembly is committed to recognising, valuing and promoting the voluntary sector as it builds a genuine partnership with the sector.

2.3 This Scheme sets out the broad principles and shared values, which will govern the relationship between the National Assembly and the voluntary sector in Wales.

2.4 In consultation with the sector, the Assembly Government will develop and maintain a separate Action Plan by which performance against the Scheme can be monitored effectively.

2.5 A review of the implementation and impact of the Scheme and Action Plan will be conducted annually and a report submitted to the National Assembly.

2.6 In working in partnership with the voluntary sector the National Assembly seeks to:

- encourage good practice and cooperative methods of decision making; review performance, particularly where organizations receive Assembly Government finance directly as service providers;
- encourage the voluntary sector through cooperation and training as well as through financial support;
- encourage volunteering initiatives and the idea that voluntary activity is an essential part of active citizenship;
- encourage the work of umbrella organisations and cooperation between such organisations;
- recognise the specific needs and special contributions of particular groups within the sector;
- encourage a growth in the contribution of different age groups to ensure that voluntary activity is seen as a part of active citizenship irrespective of age or other circumstances;
- measure and recognise what matters to the voluntary sector; and,
- assess carefully, in consultation with relevant voluntary organisations, the potential impact of policy changes upon the sector.

Shared values

2.7 The National Assembly and the voluntary sector share a number of common values about the role of individuals and communities in a modern democracy, which will underpin all aspects of this Scheme. The goal is the creation of a civil society which:

- has a duty to promote equality of opportunity to all its members regardless of race, colour, sex, sexual orientation, age, marital status, disability, language preference, religion or family/domestic responsibilities;
- is inclusive and enables people to participate in all its economic, social and cultural activities;
- empowers people to participate in the development of their communities and recognises the value of such a contribution;

- relies on people's voluntary action to foster community leadership and enhance local democracy;
- comprises public, private and voluntary sectors which complement each other and seek to tackle social issues in a spirit of partnership between them;
- enjoys the benefits of a healthy environment and a thriving competitive economy, alongside vibrant community life, as a result of its commitment to sustainable development.

2.8 The relationship between the National Assembly and the voluntary sector must be built on integrity, trust and mutual respect.

2.9 The National Assembly recognises that partnership means working together towards a common set of goals and appreciation of each party's distinctive contribution.

2.10 The National Assembly recognises:

- the wide scope and diversity of voluntary activity across the whole spectrum of society; the contribution voluntary and community organizations and volunteers make to the economic, social, environmental, cultural and linguistic life of Wales; and the role they play in formulating and delivering public policy;
- that voluntary and community organisations are independent organisations which determine their own priorities and manage their own affairs;
- that volunteering is an important expression of citizenship and is an essential component of democracy. It is the commitment of time and energy for the benefit of society and the community and can take many forms. It is undertaken freely and by choice, without concern for financial gain;
- that the voluntary-sector has an obligation to represent the interests of its constituents;
- that voluntary-sector organisations operate within the principles upon which they are founded, and are accountable to their members and the individuals and communities with whom they work.

2.11 The Assembly:

- designates the First Minister to have overall responsibility for the Voluntary Sector Scheme.
- designates an Assembly Minister to have specific responsibility for the interests of the voluntary sector;
- expects every part of the National Assembly – Cabinet, committees and officials – to promote the interests of the voluntary sector in its work and decision-making;
- will maintain:
  - a policy on working in partnership with the voluntary sector and measures to support this (Chapter 3);
  - arrangements for consulting the voluntary sector (Chapter 4);
  - a policy on volunteering and measures to promote volunteering (Chapter 5);
  - a policy on community development and measures to promote it (Chapter 6); and,
  - a Code of Practice for funding the voluntary sector which is published as a separate document.

(NAW, 2000a)

The Voluntary Sector Scheme brought civil society organizations into close and high-level relations with the Assembly's work, to a far greater degree than achieved previously. From the onset, the Partnership Council reflected sincere efforts on the Assembly's part to develop dialogue with civil society organizations in the voluntary sector, and it seemed that there was strong cooperation. The strongest expression of the high-level relations was the interface between Council members and Assembly Ministers that provided unprecedented regular access to ministerial channels and was a way of gaining influence. The meetings with ministers were valued by the voluntary sector as 'an opportunity for dialogue with Ministers; an opportunity to share information and contact; to contribute to policy development' (NAW, 2002n: 2). Also, the Assembly's responsiveness to the voluntary sector led to improved relations with the sector and increased transparency. For instance, the Code of Practice for Funding the Voluntary Sector took the sector's needs on board including emphasizing its role in delivering policy objectives and established more stable funding relations, not only with the WAG but also with assembly sponsored public bodies (ASPBs) (NAW, 2003j). Other examples are efforts to promote greater transparency and developing tools for involving the voluntary sector in policy-making and providing details on public-sector funding to the voluntary sector (NAW, 2002n: 12; NAW, 2003j). The work of the Partnership Council also influenced relations with other public bodies, local government and the ASPBs, for instance, guidance to relationships between local government and the voluntary sector was produced in 2003.

Furthermore, Clauses 48 and 120 of the Government of Wales Act placed a duty on the Assembly to conform to the principle of equality of opportunity.[1] These clauses were viewed as 'the second principal area where Members of the National Assembly have targeted the voluntary sector in order to achieve inclusive governance' (Chaney and Fevre, 2001c: 140). Research projects identified that the Equality Policy Unit and the Equality of Opportunity Committee have been central in engaging sectors of civil society related to 'minority' groups, particularly by establishing and funding Assembly-sponsored structures (Chaney, 2002d: 26). Networks and Assembly consultative bodies intended to act as umbrella organizations that received Assembly funding included the Wales Women's National Coalition (WWNC), Disability Wales, the Black Voluntary Sector Network Wales (BVSNW), Minority Ethnic Women's Network (MEWN Cymru), All Wales Ethnic Minority Association (AWEMA), Lesbian, Gay and Bisexual Forum Cymru/Stonewall Cymru and Transgender Wales (Chaney and Fevre, 2002b: 56). These structures were pioneering in facilitating engagement and consultation with under-represented groups related to race, gender, disability and sexuality.

While the above has identified the main channels for civil society engagement with the Assembly's work, other avenues have also promoted accessibility. The White Paper proposed that the Assembly would be 'a modern, progressive and inclusive democratic institution' and specific steps have been taken to realize this (Welsh Office, 1997: 24). In accordance with Freedom of Information legislation, the Assembly has provided public access to Assembly proceedings and its documentation (Rawlings, 1998: 23). Under Rhodri Morgan, the commitment to freedom of information was extended with Assembly Cabinet and Business Committee minutes published six weeks in arrears. While freedom of information and improving accessibility is a broader UK phenomenon, Rawlings notes that the 'Assembly has gone further and faster than is strictly necessary' (2003: 115). In addition, the Assembly has established information, research and education services that further suggest efforts at openness. An emphasis was also placed on utilizing information and communication technology in government and access to Assembly documentation and consultations was available through the relatively user-friendly website. Processes that promoted accessibility and openness can be viewed as extremely important in encouraging civil society involvement in the Assembly's work. They can assist in addressing the difficulties of acquiring information that particularly affect smaller and more poorly resourced organizations. This openness seemed important in familiarizing organizations with the Assembly's structures and the opportunities for engagement. In addition, it has the potential to be an ongoing tool so that organizations have regular and in-depth opportunities to monitor and interact in the Assembly's work.

A final feature that has potentially expanded opportunities for civil society involvement in the Assembly's work relates to the civil service in Wales. Under the previous Welsh Office, civil servants were solely accountable to the Secretary of State for Wales. The Assembly's corporate body status meant that they were responsible to all Assembly Members. In practice, however, while all staff remained part of the Home Civil Service, there was some difference between which part of the corporate body staff were responsible. The majority worked for the Assembly Administration (officially the Welsh Assembly Government since March 2002) while a smaller number worked for the Office of the Presiding Officer and thus supported Assembly Members and the committees. Sherlock explains:

> Unlike the position in Northern Ireland and Scotland where the legislative bodies have their own staff separate from the general civil service (in the same way as the Houses of Parliament do), in Wales no separate administration was established. (2000: 71)

Devolution was a steep learning curve for the 'Welsh Office' civil service. Two interrelated issues arising from the pre-devolution context suggested opportunities for civil society organizations to engage with the Assembly. Considering the fundamental changes taking place with the inception of devolution and the dramatically increased workload, the number of civil servants that worked in the Welsh Office in the run-up to devolution was limited and only minimal increases took place in the early stages of devolution (Chaney et al., 2001a: 12).[2] Rawlings describes the situation as ' "Devolution on a shoestring": the Assembly was starting from an exceptionally low base, such were the minimalist staffing and resources of the Welsh Office' (2003: 159). More significantly, the policy-making capacities of the Welsh Office civil service were particularly weak. Before devolution, the Welsh Office had an administrative role in implementing policies determined in Whitehall and in adapting these to the needs of Wales where necessary. Indeed, Rawlings even characterizes pre-devolution Wales as a 'policy-free zone' (2003: 168). He elaborates:

> Such was the historical legacy of the administrative character of the Welsh Office – notwithstanding pockets of creativity in certain fields like education – or what the then Permanent Secretary memorably referred to as its 'colonial' role: transmitting London policy to Wales. Indicative of the internal constraints on the Assembly being able to make the most of its autonomy, the local cadre of senior civil servants with substantial hands-on experience in policy formulation and development has been stretched very thinly. (2003: 168)

Against this backdrop, attempts by the Assembly to make use of its current powers by being more proactive in policy-making highlighted weaknesses within the administrative structures (Osmond, 2000: 44; Sherlock, 2000: 73).

The need to compensate for deficiencies in staffing levels and policy-making capacity within the Assembly civil service suggested a willingness to capitalize on external expertise and engage actors such as civil society. The limited number of staff that supported the Assembly committees potentially meant that opposition Assembly Members would be more eager than might otherwise have been the case to engage with civil society organizations, informing their committee work and serving as a counterbalance to the support provided to the executive by the civil service. Devolution also expanded the functions and policy role of the civil service working for the Administration, and this suggested greater opportunities for civil society to directly engage with civil servants. In the policy process, the Administration arranged consultations, developed strategy and policy documents, and decided on policy implementation. Furthermore, it selected others to contribute expertise to policy-making through task forces and groups of outside 'specialists' and advisers that directly interacted with civil servants. Therefore valuable opportunities seem to have been provided for civil society to engage directly in the Assembly's work through contacts with the civil service. The smaller number of civil servants working for the Office of the Presiding Officer (subsequently Presiding Office) suggested that opportunities to influence the Assembly's work through this channel could arise.

To sum up, the 'democratization' of governance in Wales opened up opportunities to influence a new tier of politicians. The main channels by which organizations could have influenced and directly participated in the Assembly's work were the Assembly's committee structure and the Voluntary Sector Partnership Council. The openness of the Assembly illustrated its efforts to engage different actors, including civil society, in its work. Morgan and Rees confirm this new openness: 'the new governance structures – the Assembly itself, the office of First Secretary, the Cabinet, the subject committees and the regional committees – have created *multiple* points of entry to the policy-making system' (2001: 145). They also emphasize the new opportunities to engage in policy-making:

> Whatever the limits of the National Assembly, and the constraints of the model of executive devolution on which it is based, the Assembly's policy-making process is more open, more transparent and more inclusive than the semi-secret world of administrative devolution which preceded it. (Morgan and Rees, 2001: 164)

COMPLEXITIES AND AMBIGUITIES: CIVIL SOCIETY'S ENGAGEMENT AND THE EVOLUTION OF DEVOLUTION

Here we examine the shifts in the devolution settlement. These shifts potentially hindered civil society involvement with the Assembly during its first term, the converse of that examined above. Many of the challenges and difficulties facing the Assembly were embedded in its constitution and had been forecast before its establishment, particularly by Richard Rawlings (1998). The implications of these challenges for civil society engagement are investigated here. This section discusses the Assembly's powers, its composition, its structures including the committees, the situation of the Assembly civil service and other key aspects that are relevant to understanding civil society engagement with the Assembly.

With regard to the Assembly's powers, the previous section noted the similarities with the pre-devolution period. However, the nature of the powers and functions inherited by the National Assembly under executive devolution had potentially negative effects on the engagement of all civil society organizations with the Assembly. Dependent on secondary legislation, the Assembly's ability to act on its own initiative was limited.

Rawlings argues that 'The impact of no primary legislative power in terms of a restricted policy-making framework is a political and administrative issue' (2003: 500). The Assembly depended on its ability to influence the primary legislative process at Westminster through the Secretary of State for Wales. This proved problematic. Formally: 'as machinery for preserving Welsh input into primary law making, these provisions [i.e. using the good offices of the Secretary of State] are typically skeletal', with the greatest danger being 'the uncomfortable prospect of the Assembly as supplicant or lobbyist in the Westminster process' (Rawlings, 1998: 490). During the first term, the Assembly was not able to secure more than one or two Wales-only bills every year (Rawlings, 2003: 500). Overall, the Assembly was weak in its interaction with Whitehall/Westminster and over-dependent on concordats as non-statutory agreements to ensure good relations with Whitehall departments. Instead of a sound constitutional base, there was 'high dependency of the Welsh scheme of devolution on administrative and political good will' (Rawlings, 1998: 509).

A number of other problems arose from the nature of the Assembly's powers. On the one hand, the Transfer of Functions Order, the statutory functions delegated to the Assembly previously exercised by the Secretary of State and other ministers on matters that affect Wales, were criticized for being limited. Rawlings states:

> it is a cardinal principle of government policy to retain overarching functions which operate on a common basis in the different territories: not only foreign affairs, defence and macroeconomics, but also social security, taxation, and policy on fiscal and common markets. (1998: 487)

On the other hand, it was argued that the structure of the Transfer of Functions Order was problematic. In the Scotland Act 1998, the Scottish Parliament was given general legislative powers and the Act listed matters reserved to the UK Parliament rather than specifying devolved matters. For the National Assembly for Wales, a detailed procedure was undertaken of compiling all specific functions held by the Secretary of State in every section of statutes and these were transferred to the Assembly (Sherlock, 2000: 66). Reflecting previous practice whereby powers were gradually passed to the Secretary of State for Wales in a piecemeal fashion, the powers transferred to the Assembly were consequently an uneven and incoherent package. As Rawlings noted, 'the division between primary and secondary powers has tended to be ad hoc', and 'the Assembly will find that its powers are of uneven width and depth' (1998: 487–8). Furthermore, the ongoing transfer of powers in this mode since devolution exacerbated the inconsistencies surrounding the Assembly's powers. Many problems arose. The Assembly's powers were unclear and there were complexities in the process of identifying whether power lay with the Assembly or central government. Rawlings argues that:

> the principle of intelligibility, which is considered so important in constitutional documents, is offended. Who other than a lawyer or official could give any meaningful guidance on the legislative competence of the Assembly? This feature is the more striking because of the great stress that has been placed in the devolutionary design on transparency and bringing government closer to the people. (2003: 70)

Wyn Jones and Trystan concur with this: 'the chronic lack of clarity in the division of powers between the Assembly and Westminster/Whitehall must make it extremely difficult for citizens to know which body is responsible for what, and whom, therefore, to hold accountable' (2001: 25).

This lack of clarity and the limitations of the Assembly's powers had direct consequences for civil society organizations. Generally, it raised questions regarding the utility of engaging with the Assembly, as its powers were limited and difficult to comprehend. Overall, there was general complexity and confusion for all organizations. Moreover, it required organizations to be able to influence both the Assembly and Westminster in order to ensure that they could influence all their areas of interest. As limited resources affected many, if not most civil society organizations, it is possible that they had to decide where to channel their resources. As Chaney states:

> Such confusion is expensive in that it requires civil groups to simultaneously lobby and monitor two centres of political decision-making in two countries, and it further disinclines citizens towards participation owing to the opaqueness of the political process. (2002d: 31)

These complexities and ambiguities surrounding the Assembly could also have deterred new civil society organizations from engaging with the Assembly.

The democratizing impact of having sixty Assembly Members replace a Secretary of State was also not as straightforward as expected. The number of Assembly Members was still inadequate. Rawlings forecast that the sixty members specified in the Government of Wales Act would be inadequate to undertake the Assembly's workload effectively. In particular he suggested that the limited number of Assembly Members would face multiple roles including contributing to the work of various committees. This could potentially result in overdependence on the civil service (Rawlings, 1998: 478). His worries were more than borne out. Indeed, the introduction of a Partnership Agreement in October 2000 exacerbated the problem by expanding the number of ministerial portfolios from fourteen to sixteen. Taken with the Presiding Officer and the deputy Presiding Officer, this meant that only 42 Assembly Members were available to undertake the Assembly's non-executive work (Osmond, 2001: 17).

With regard to civil society engagement, limitations on the number of Assembly Members had, amongst other factors, an effect on the efficacy of the Assembly's committees and decreased their potential role in civil society's engagement with the Assembly. Regional committees were less effective and played a more limited role than was envisaged at the onset of devolution. They had little success in providing a channel for civil society organizations to influence the Assembly's work. Indeed, organizations that interacted with the committees tended to be organizations with good relations with the Assembly. As Rawlings explains, ' "Insider" groups and organizations have also featured prominently amongst the participants; that is to say, the same bodies which exercise substantial voice in the structures and processes of Welsh governance' (2003: 222).

Furthermore, as there were limited mechanisms for the committees to feed back into the Assembly's work, they were not viewed as an effective means of engaging with the Assembly. The subject committees did not play the role that was initially anticipated, even if, as Rawlings reminds us, 'by reason of their extended remit, and of the immediate problem of the Members' lack of experience, one should beware of rushing to hasty conclusions about the effectiveness or otherwise of the subject committees' (2003: 110). Their most positive contribution was as a forum for collecting evidence and information on key policy areas through engagement with organizations, such as universities and interest groups, and undertaking extensive inquiries in which evidence was heard from a number of organizations (Rawlings, 2003: 207–12). However, resource constraints were clear from the onset. In addition to limited numbers, Assembly Members were overloaded due to the demands arising from membership of several subject committees, and this particularly affected less experienced AMs (Chaney, Hall and Pithouse, 2001b: 226). There were also problems arising from the limited staff resources available to support the work of committees in the Presiding Office (Rawlings, 2003: 111). Overall, the expectations that surrounded subject committees were unrealistic and overambitious. The subject committees were not able to fulfil the dual role envisaged for them: scrutiny of the minister and legislation, and policy development. Problems were compounded by the ambiguities arising from the minister's membership of subject committees.

It could be argued however that political developments during the Assembly's first term made the ability of civil society organizations to influence the subject committees less crucial, as these tended to reduce the role of these committees in the Assembly's work. Rawlings explains that

'The Assembly's subject committees are a unique feature, a talisman of concerns about the undue concentration of power. They have in turn been caught up in the stresses and strains associated with the ongoing constitutional development inside the Assembly' (2003: 117). The key explanatory factor was that during the Assembly's first term the corporate body principle was rejected, *de facto* if not (yet) *de jure*, and there was a gradual shift to a more parliamentary style of government, particularly following the establishment of Partnership Government. In this respect:

> the arrangements have veered sharply in the direction of a parliamentary system, premised first on the operational independence of the Presiding Chair and Clerks and second on the practice and conventions of Cabinet government. A strong 'executive branch', aka the Welsh Assembly Government, thus reflects and reinforces basic constitutional ideas of separation of powers. (Rawlings, 2003: 7)

With regard to the committees, the end result of the emergence of an executive distinct from the legislature was that the ability (or otherwise) of civil society organizations to influence the subject committees decreased in importance. Rather, it was the ability (or otherwise) to influence the executive that became increasingly important. The process by which this occurred may be briefly summarized as follows. Initially, under the leadership of Alun Michael, there was a tight control on policy-making, the committees were overburdened and under-resourced and, along with the plenary, tended to play an advisory role (Morgan and Rees, 2001: 144; Rawlings, 2002: 4). When Rhodri Morgan became First Minister in February 2000, he governed through making deals and agreements with Plaid Cymru (Osmond, 2000: 43). In this period, the position of the Labour Party and party balance suggested that there was a greater emphasis on the policy-development role of subject committees (Rawlings, 2003: 122). Therefore, at this point there seemed some opportunities for subject committees to gain influence, thus making it worthwhile for organizations to make use of these channels to engage with the Assembly. However, the Partnership Agreement between Labour and the Liberal Democrats in October 2000 instigated extensive change. It brought about a government majority with a Partnership Agreement as a programme of action across the Assembly's powers. Though this programme, *Putting Wales First,* emphasized collaborative and inclusive ways of working and called for a strong Assembly to hold the executive to account, the Partnership Agreement had profound effects and reduced the role of subject committees (Rawlings, 2003: 9). This is evident in the 'erosion of the (much-vaunted) role of the subject committees, as indicated by the claim by one Minister of no greater status for their conclusions than that of public consultees' (Rawlings, 2003: 124).

Osmond notes that the committees have not only been weak in holding the executive to account but 'did not engage in policy *making*. Rather they were involved in generating a great deal more information about their policy areas and contributing in a general way to policy *development*' (2000: 47). In an executive-dominated process, the role of subject committees in policy development led to 'legitimate concern about the potential for co-option into an administrative process or elongated decision-making chain over which they can hope to exercise only limited influence' (Rawlings, 2003: 213). The shift to executive decision-making and a more advisory or informative role for subject committees as devolution progressed reflected the limited influence of opposition political parties in the Assembly's structures. This emphasized that, in order to gain any influence, civil society's interaction with the governing parties, especially Assembly Cabinet Ministers and the civil service in Wales, developed as the most important channels to influence the Assembly's work.

In short, political developments decreased the potential of subject committees as a channel for civil society organizations to be involved in the Assembly's work. This in turn increased the importance of the Voluntary Sector Partnership Council. However, questions surrounded the Partnership Council. A key issue is the degree to which the Council and its membership represented the diverse interests within the voluntary sector and civil society. Kopecky and Mudde's comments in the previous chapter emphasized the extensive diversity and heterogeneity within civil society that includes conflicting interests (2003: 11). Could twenty-one members represent this diversity? As the neo-corporatism literature identified, does the practice of selecting representatives privilege some groups over others (Wilson, 1990: 69)? In addition, the Code of Practice for Funding the Voluntary Sector, developed in conjunction with the Partnership Council, stated that the Assembly did not intend to directly fund local groups but to 'provide support to partnerships or representative intermediary voluntary organisations to deliver specific funding support at a local level' (NAW, 2005: 6). This suggests that there was little awareness that such actions could perpetuate hierarchy by promoting the status of national and larger organizations. Furthermore, the 'representativeness' of members was under question on the Partnership Council (Wilson, 1990).

From the early meetings, the Partnership Council identified the importance of ensuring that the representatives were accountable and had the capacity to engage their networks properly and proposals to promote capacity-building were implemented. The Partnership Council attempted to monitor the development and effectiveness of networks and the Assembly provided partnership capacity-building funding to support this work, £85,000 for 2001–2, and £126,000 for 2002–3 (NAW, 2004: 16). However, problems persisted and there were inconsistencies between sectors. Well-established networks with umbrella bodies had structures at the local and regional level in Wales. Other sectors had no previous networks to rely on, making disseminating information more difficult. There were disparities in the number of organizations that formed part of different networks in specific sectors. In addition, the number of organizations that were active within the networks, that interacted with and responded to the representatives, was narrower. The challenge of developing effective networks therefore raises issues regarding the 'representativeness' of the council itself.

Another key issue is how the views of the voluntary sector can influence the Assembly. It seemed that the members of the council were aware that they had to act with one voice in order to have their views taken on board. The WCVA arranged pre-meetings for both the Partnership Council and the ministerial meetings to decide on their strategy and approach. The need for a 'line', and the selection of a representative for each sector suggests that these structures were of limited use as a dependable channel for individual organizations to exert influence on the Assembly.

The Assembly's approach to funding the voluntary sector as outlined in its Code of Practice for Funding the Voluntary Sector questioned whether there was adequate awareness of the importance of the autonomy of the sector and the potential effects of funding. The Voluntary Sector Scheme itself states: 'voluntary and community organisations are independent organisations which determine their own priorities and manage their own affairs' (NAW, 2000a: 5). 'Respect for the sector's independence' was detailed as one of the principles of the funding code, but under this heading it stated: 'recognition that the sector can often reach groups that the Assembly cannot and provides innovation' (NAW, 2005: 2). This suggests a lack of awareness of the potential effects of funding on the voluntary sector's autonomy in the Assembly's interaction with the Partnership Council. Finally, the position of the WCVA on the council highlighted its powerful role and again reflected neo-corporate arrangements (Wilson, 1990). WCVA administered the Partnership, selected organizations to be representatives on the council and played a central role in setting the agenda for council and ministerial meetings. Its credentials of being representative were somewhat overshadowed despite its central role in representing the diversity of the voluntary sector in the Assembly (Chaney and Fevre, 2001c: 148; Chaney, 2002a: 6).

Despite these issues, during the first term of devolution, the Partnership Council represented the main formal channel by which civil society organizations may have hoped to be involved in the Assembly's work. Similar problems regarding the ability of umbrella groups to represent specific needs within diverse communities were raised in relation to the

Assembly-sponsored networks. These structures however had the potential to gain influence within the Assembly and were another channel for those 'minority' groups within civil society.

Some positive advances affected civil society arising from the shift towards a greater formalization of a cabinet structure. The greater separation and enhanced division between the executive and the Assembly can be viewed as a step that clarified the differences in the potential of various channels to gain influence within the Assembly. Previously, the complexity of the internal structures was seen as detrimental to promoting the engagement of external actors, particularly organizations with limited resources (Chaney et al., 2000: 213). Wyn Jones and Trystan stated that 'the Assembly's status as a body corporate serves to further muddy the waters. It is difficult to conceive how participation can be maximised in a context in which responsibility, and hence lines of accountability, are so opaque' (2001: 25). Changes in role were clarified by changes in the nomenclature of government introduced in March 2002 due to the Assembly Review of Procedure report produced in February 2002. This established Assembly Ministers rather than Assembly Secretaries, a Cabinet replaced the Executive Committee, a Presiding Officer instead of the Office of the Presiding Officer, the Executive Board of senior civil servants instead of the Management Board, and a Welsh Assembly Government and National Assembly instead of a 'corporate body' (Osmond, 2003: 13). These changes provided greater clarity and were welcomed by the Administration and opposition parties.

In addition to changes in nomenclature, other practical shifts clarified the separation between the Assembly and Assembly Government. These directly affected civil society's interaction with the civil service. With regard to the Presiding Office element of the Assembly, a significant extension of parliamentary services took place (Rawlings, 2003: 133). Due to the Assembly Review of Procedure Group, additional resources were provided to the Presiding Office, including an expert member of staff for each of the seven subject committees (Osmond, 2003: 24). Such steps contributed to improving the capacity and support for the committees. This made them less dependent on policy officials serving the Cabinet (Rawlings, 2003: 141). Yet, by comparison with the staff and finance provided to support the legislature in the Scottish Parliament, there were continuing limitations on the resources of the Presiding Office (Osmond, 2003: 14, 23, 24). One of the implications of this was, of course, that while staff were willing to engage with civil society organizations, this channel may not have provided organizations with as strong a degree of influence as some may have envisaged.

Arguably, more significant for civil society organizations were two developments. For as Rawlings notes, 'the political quest for ways of "making a difference" has been working to promote a substantial thickening of the administrative core of the Welsh Assembly Government' (2003: 158). The transformation of the civil service Management Board into an Executive Board in 2001 was part of a process that strengthened internal coordination within the civil service. In particular, it bolstered the policy-making and implementation structures within the Assembly Government (Osmond, 2003: 20). Secondly, in the aim to improve policy development capacities, the role of the Strategic Policy Unit was expanded with the Special Advisers relocated to the unit. The unit promoted policy development and joint working across departments and had a role in promoting increased participation and consultation with external partners including representatives of the three Partnership Councils (Rawlings, 2003: 177). These developments highlighted concerted efforts within the civil service to increase policy-making capacities in order to complement the Assembly Government's aspiration to be proactive in policy development and develop policy divergence for Wales post-devolution. It also emphasized the benefits for those civil society organizations that were members of the Partnership Council.

The changes to the structures charged with developing Assembly Government policies highlighted the increasing centrality of the civil service to policy-making during the first term and the greater policy autonomy for Wales compared with the Welsh Office period. The openness of the Assembly's structures implied broader opportunities for civil society to contribute to the civil service's work compared with the pre-devolution period, particularly in the initial stages of Assembly Government policy-making. There was a danger that excessive public consultation would result in little attention paid to the diversity of viewpoints received. As a result, more direct engagement with Assembly civil servants was more valuable.

However, requirements point to which organizations benefited from the Assembly's policy autonomy and were able to effectively input and influence its policy processes. Organizations needed to be aware of the potential opportunities to engage with the civil service. As part of this, informal contacts within the civil service were increasingly important and organizations needed to be aware of which channels to target to gain influence. Issues of expertise, specialization and adequate resources were essential in gaining access to civil servants and in carving out opportunities to input into their work. These were fundamental in determining the degree to which organizations could have a direct role in policy deliberation as opposed to a more limited role of submitting responses to consultations during the policy-making process. Two previous requirements tend to suggest continuity in Welsh governance. In order to gain influence, previous contact with civil servants and the Welsh Assembly Government were increasingly beneficial during the first term. Involvement with the Welsh

Office before devolution would have led to familiarization with civil servants and their working practices. Building on good working relations would facilitate civil society attempts to influence different stages of the Assembly Government policy process. Good contacts with the dominant political parties in the Partnership Government and with Cabinet Ministers also expanded opportunities to gain substantial participation.

CONCLUSION

This chapter has examined in broad terms the opportunities for civil society engagement with the National Assembly during the first term of devolution. It assessed how political and constitutional developments during the first term changed the locus of power in the Assembly and in turn altered and constrained opportunities for most organizations to engage with the Assembly. Many of the Assembly's internal structures, which were designed to promote 'inclusiveness', were downgraded. As Rawlings sardonically points out, 'the capacity of the Westminster-style parliament tradition to reinvent itself in other settings was grossly underestimated' (2003: 89). Perhaps the shift towards a greater cabinet system of government particularly after the establishment of Partnership Government in October 2000 was of no great surprise to many. As a result, however, the key channels for civil society organizations to attempt to influence the Assembly's work were the Voluntary Sector Partnership Council and access to the Welsh Assembly Government and its civil service. Consequently, the ability of organizations to gain substantial influence on the Welsh Assembly Government's work came to depend on their awareness of the potential and limitations of different Assembly structures. This in turn depended on the expertise and connections with governmental actors. The degree to which organizations became professionalized and well-resourced enough to articulate themselves coherently and cogently became decisive. In the early days of devolution, the willingness of organizations to work with all political parties had been important. It increasingly seemed that formal and informal contacts with the dominant political parties and the Assembly Government civil service were decisive. The case studies which follow will give attention to these changes and in particular to the structures and methods used by organizations to engage with the National Assembly.

Part II

Civil Society in Wales:
The Case Studies

4

Devolution and Redistribution:
Groundwork in Wales and Objective 1

The accession of the UK, Ireland and Denmark to the European Community in 1973 signalled the commencement of two processes; the expansion of the Community, and the establishment of the Structural Funds as part of the European Community's regional policy. Since then, Wales has benefited from a number of Structural Fund programmes. These funds were devolved to the Welsh Office whose European Affairs Division (EAD) was set up in 1973 with responsibility for administering these funds.

In March 1999, only months before the National Assembly for Wales was established, West Wales and the Valleys was designated as an Objective 1 area for the 2000–6 Structural Funding period. Objective 1 for West Wales and the Valleys was the largest Structural Funds programme in the UK, and one of the biggest in the EU as a whole.[1] As a result, Objective 1 was a major first-term priority for the National Assembly. The coincidence of developing Objective 1 and the Assembly's establishment provides a unique opportunity to consider the dynamic between civil society and the Assembly in relation to its devolved functions in economic redistribution. Furthermore, the timing allows for a comparative perspective between civil society's involvement in Objective 1 and its participation in the pre-devolution Structural Funds programmes in Wales from 1994 to 1999. This chapter focuses on the role of Groundwork, a sustainable development organization, and examines its involvement in Objective 1 during the Assembly's first term compared with Groundwork's involvement in pre-devolution Structural Funds programmes. Focusing on Objective 1 illustrates how devolution has affected Groundwork's involvement in Structural Funds programmes. It also highlights the impact of devolution on the organization's broader development post-devolution.

The chapter is divided into four sections. Firstly it outlines Groundwork during the pre-devolution period. The second section details the main processes and structures entailed in Objective 1. The next section then examines Groundwork's role in different stages of Objective 1. Finally, the fourth section highlights the main points of Groundwork's involvement in Objective 1 and reveals devolution's impact on Groundwork. It concludes that devolution was a catalyst for the establishment of Groundwork Wales, which has expanded the organization's capacities post-devolution. It has extensively engaged with the National Assembly and Welsh Assembly Government, and the post-devolution shifts within the organization suggest greater convergence with *Welsh civil society*.

GROUNDWORK

Groundwork is a network of trusts established in some of the most disadvantaged parts of the UK. Groundwork Trusts were first established in the early 1980s and expanded in the UK to claim the status of 'the leading independent agency in the UK promoting sustainable regeneration and development' (Groundwork Wales, 2000a). It is an example of state agency in the establishment of a civil society organization. The first Groundwork trust was established following Countryside Commission proposals to improve the physical environment of the urban fringe (Groundwork UK, 2002b). By 2000, however, a UK-wide federation of forty-seven charitable Groundwork Trusts was established, the Groundwork approach had been adopted internationally, with projects in central and eastern Europe and the European Union (Groundwork UK, 2002c).

This section outlines the background of the first of the four existing Groundwork Trusts in Wales, currently known as Groundwork Merthyr & Rhondda Cynon Taff. The organization's involvement with the public sector and its role in the Objective 2 Industrial South Wales 1994–9 programme is examined.

Groundwork Merthyr and Rhondda Cynon Taff

From the first Groundwork Trust established in Merseyside in 1981, partnership working has been important. The trust's role was to bring together 'a partnership of public, private and voluntary sector interests in a coordinated effort to upgrade the environment, to realise the full potential of under-used land, to convert waste ground to productive use and to improve access to the countryside' (Groundwork UK, 2002b). During the 1980s and 1990s, Groundwork Trusts expanded and a Groundwork Foundation (now Groundwork UK) was established by the Countryside Commission 'to coordinate expansion and to support the network by building national partnerships and raising new resources' (Groundwork UK, 2002b). As an environmental regeneration charity, the trusts work in partnership with local people, local authorities and businesses. They therefore have close relations with different levels of government and the

---

Box 4.1: Groundwork Wales

Welcome to Groundwork Wales

Groundwork is a federation of 47 charitable trusts working in many of the most disadvantaged areas in the country to bring together people, places and resources from all parts of the community in effective long-term partnerships. The purpose is to achieve sustainable communities through joint environmental action.

Groundwork Wales is a part of the Groundwork network, working with local communities in areas of need.

We have been active in Wales for more than ten years, weaving together environmental, social and economic programmes in a holistic approach to regeneration.

There are four *Trusts in Wales,* in *Merthyr and Rhondda Cynon Taff, Bridgend, Caerphilly* and *Wrexham.* All have been in operation for over twelve years and have a substantial track record of excellent projects on the ground. Between them they employ over 100 staff and last year turned over some 8.4 million. Last year Groundwork Wales assisted the Wrexham and Bridgend Trusts to complete their extensions into Flintshire and Neath Port Talbot respectively and the overall turnover is now budgeted to be approximately 9 million.

(Groundwork Wales, 2000d)

---

private sector, thus highlighting the interrelationships between the spheres of civil society, the state and the economy. This is inevitably the case in areas such as community development. Apart from being a civil society organization, Groundwork could be viewed as a 'third sector' body or an organization that forms part of the 'social economy'.

Merthyr Groundwork Trust was established in 1987, the first in Wales (Groundwork UK, 2002b). Its approach reflected the Groundwork ethos of partnership and community involvement; local authorities have been key partners. At the end of the 1980s, this led to increased involvement in local strategies and accessing Welsh Office funds such as Urban Aid and Strategic Development Scheme (SDS) grants through local authorities. Subsequently, the trust's work expanded from small-scale practical projects to medium and major landscape improvement works, and rolling programmes of community strategies. Building relations with local government also led to expanding its activities into the Cynon Valley Borough Council area in 1990 with the consequent renaming of the Trust as Merthyr and Cynon Groundwork Trust. Again, local government reorganization in 1996 and establishing Rhondda Cynon Taff County Borough Council extended

Groundwork's activities. Thus, it currently operates in two local authority areas and is known as Groundwork Merthyr and Rhondda Cynon Taff (RCT). In terms of funding, Groundwork Trusts in England were funded directly from central government. In Wales, funding for the Groundwork Trusts in Wales was administered by the Welsh Office and channelled via local authorities, who topped up the funds.[2] As a result, the trusts in Wales have had a stronger bond with local government than trusts in England.

Groundwork Trusts interacted with the broader public sector before devolution. Individually, trusts held periodic meetings with Welsh Office civil servants to negotiate issues such as the work programme for their baseline funding and SDS funding. Ministers were also engaged in their work, making presentations and being invited to launch projects or new Trusts. Groundwork projects also led to joint working with statutory bodies such as the Countryside Council for Wales and the Welsh Development Agency (WDA). Despite the direct contacts with the civil service and ministers, Groundwork Merthyr and RCT felt that it had little potential to affect policy. One member of staff stated:

> I don't think Groundwork was seeing itself as a major lobbying organisation. Most of what we were doing in terms of talking to the Welsh Office was with the division or the department that was responsible for the money for Groundwork and so we would have periodic meetings with them ... So I guess we didn't really have serious channels to affect policy previously.[3]

During the second half of the 1990s, although local authorities remained an important source of match funding, Groundwork Merthyr and RCT also developed a more strategic approach to raising funds. One key source became European funding, particularly the Objective 2 Industrial South Wales (ISW) Programme for the 1994–9 programming period. This funding aimed at the economic conversion of declining industrial areas (European Commission, 2000: 12). The Objective 2 ISW Single Programming Document (SPD) for this period was divided into two phases, 1994–6 and 1997–9. During the 1994–6 programme, Groundwork Merthyr and RCT sponsored projects relating to tourism and community development, specifically the Taff Trail and Gurnos regeneration work (Ecotec, 1999).

During the 1997–9 programme, Groundwork Merthyr and RCT became more prominent as a sponsor of numerous bids, including large-scale projects.[4] Again these included regeneration projects in areas such as the Gurnos, Gelli Deg and Fernhill, related tourism and environmental projects, and also expanded to include business and the environment projects.

This illustrates the increasing focus on community work and partnerships established with a range of organizations from community groups to strategic partners. Groundwork often played the role of project lead that implied 'getting the partnerships together, building the trust between them as well as then working up the bids, undertaking some of the roles and the financial monitoring and audit'.[5] Furthermore, it expanded its sources of match funding to include other grants from the private sector and other sources of European Funding.

During Objective 2 ISW programme, Groundwork Merthyr and RCT was a project applicant and one of the main organizations bringing projects forward. Other key civil society organizations were WCVA, Scope, ARENA Network, Groundwork Caerphilly, Groundwork Bridgend, Valley Kids, Chwarae Teg and Antur Teifi.[6] Groundwork Merthyr and RCT was not involved in strategic discussions surrounding the programme, and this was characteristic of the role that civil society organizations played in Objective 2 ISW (WEPE, 1997). European Commission regulations promoted a partnership approach in 1994–9 programmes from the preparatory to the implementation stages. It called for

> 'close cooperation' between the European Commission, and the authorities competent in each State at national, regional, local or other level, including the economic and social partners designated by the Member State. This principle is applied as of the preparatory stage up until implementation of the measures. (European Commission, 2000: 26)

However, in the Objective 2 ISW programme, drafting and decision-making structures such as the Programme Monitoring Committee (PMC) were public-sector dominated (see Table 4.1). There was some gradual increased civil society representation evident in the 1997–9 phase of the Objective 2 ISW programme. The main actor was the Wales Council for Voluntary Action (WCVA), which had made concerted attempts to be involved in Structural Funds from 1994. WCVA and the Community Development Foundation sat on the working group assisting in preparing the Single Programming Document (WEPE, 1997: 227). Other organizations partook in project action groups (PAGs) which ranked and selected projects. A greater number of civil society organizations sat on the Programme Monitoring Committee (Ecotec, 1999: 71). This demonstrated some broadening of partnership in accordance with the European regulations. Moreover, it also perhaps reflected shifting the main administration of the Structural Funds in 1997 from EAD of the Welsh Office to an independent secretariat, the Wales European Programme Executive (WEPE).[7]

While Groundwork's role in Objective 2 was as project applicant, it developed its profile. A member of staff stated that despite its relative inexperience, 'we worked about the whole process but the whole process was newer and we were much newer in terms of what we were doing on European projects'.[8] Furthermore, it fulfilled the criteria to receive funding and successfully completed all subsequent audits. This suggests that Groundwork developed a greater capacity than other organizations. Overall, the Objective 2 ISW Programme had found difficulty in fully involving community and voluntary organizations, particularly in community development projects. The main reasons were the complexities of the process, match funding and cash-flow difficulties (Ecotec, 1999: 37, vi).

Groundwork Wales

Before devolution, the four Groundwork Trusts established in Wales in Merthyr and Rhondda Cynon Taff, Bridgend, Caerphilly and Wrexham identified the need for greater coordination.[9] The executive director of Groundwork Merthyr and RCT had a contract to undertake all-Wales work for the trusts. This meant that an all-Wales organization would be beneficial. According to a member of staff, 'It was a combination of the different finance, the need for a more coordinated approach to some of the programmes and probably above all almost the need to be able to speak with our own voice on policy issues'.[10] Proposals for a Groundwork Wales organization were put forward by the trusts in Wales, but 'it was seen to be a bit before its time and Groundwork UK, I don't think, was ready to consider regionalization'.[11] The Trusts, however succeeded, and 'finally when the

Table 4.1: **Structural Fund Programme Monitoring Committee Membership of the 1994–1999 programmes**

	Rural Wales Objective 5b 1994–9	*ISW Objective 2 1997–9*
Commission	4	2
Government actors	3[a]	3
Government agencies	6	10 (6 + 4 WEPE)
Local authorities	6	5
Private sector		1
Third sector	1 (TGWU)	1 (Wales Cooperative Development and Training)
Higher education	2	3
Voluntary sector	3 (WCVA, Disability Wales, Cymad)	2 (WCVA + Disability Wales)
Total	26	28

[a] Two of these are central state actors: Department for Education and Employment and Department of Trade and Industry.

Source: WEFO. These numbers are based on membership lists of 1998–9.

report went to the Board just before devolution, they took a view that the world was changing, Wales was a separate country and therefore we needed a structure that could relate to that'.[12] Consequently Groundwork Wales was established in 1998 with a role in raising the profile, assisting in increasing the capacity of the trusts and in developing networks between them (Groundwork Wales, 2000b) (see Box 4.1).

Therefore, Groundwork was essentially a *civil society in Wales* organization as its presence in Wales was developed from a UK-wide organization. During the pre-devolution period, its interaction with the Welsh Office was based on funding and it felt it had little ability to influence policy. However, with the onset of devolution, an all-Wales level was established with Groundwork Wales. This suggests a shift towards *Welsh civil society*.

OBJECTIVE 1

The 2000–6 programming period was the first time that West Wales and the Valleys had been eligible for Objective 1 funding.[13] Gaining Objective 1 designation had involved concerted political efforts under the leadership of Ron Davies, then Secretary of State for Wales after Labour's victory in the 1997 General Election. Objective 1 was the EU's strongest regional policy instrument to address regions lagging behind in the competitive Single European Market. European Regulations continued to require a partnership approach. In comparison to the 1994–99 programming period:

> The general definition of partnership is unchanged, but its composition is extended including now: the Commission; the Member State; the regional and local authorities (including environmental authorities); the economic and social partners; other relevant organisations (including those working to protect the environment and to promote equality between men and women). (European Commission, 2000: 26)

This section outlines the key decision-making stages and implementation structures of Objective 1 West Wales and the Valleys. This enables a greater understanding of the potential opportunities for Groundwork's involvement in Objective 1, examined in the third section.[14]

Following the confirmation of West Wales and the Valleys' eligibility for Objective 1 designation in October 1998, a European Task Force was established. Its role was to advise the Secretary of State on the new Structural Fund Regulations and to develop strategies and programmes to implement the funds in Wales post-2000. The Task Force's work continued after the Assembly's establishment in May 1999 and in the preliminary stages, it was the main body charged with preparing the Objective 1 Single Programming Document (SPD), the development strategy for the region. The Task

Force comprised public, voluntary and private-sector representatives, but it largely reflected the make-up of the 1994–9 Structural Funds programmes (see Table 4.2). Civil society representation was restricted to the WCVA and Disability Wales. Two regional partnerships were established; one in West Wales and the other in the Valleys. In reality, these, together with lead bodies, compiled the SPD and developed the Programme Complement from March to October 1999. Although most of the lead bodies were statutory bodies, WCVA led on drafting Priority 3 (Community Development), and Chwarae Teg was key in drafting the cross-cutting theme of equal opportunities.[15]

Between July and September 1999, a public consultation was held on a draft of the SPD and this offered opportunities for a broad input into Objective 1. Alun Michael, then Secretary of State, delayed the consultation until the National Assembly was up and running in July 1999. This avoided the programme becoming politicized during the first Assembly elections. Following the Assembly's establishment, the Economic Development Committee became engaged in Objective 1. In the final month of the consultation, the Assembly's Director of Economic Affairs announced the termination of the European Task Force. Then, from October 1999 to April 2000 the Programme Document was taken in hand and revised by the civil service.

Table 4.2: European Taskforce membership[16]

	October 1998	May 1999
Politicians	1 (MEP)	2 (AM/MP/ MEP)
Government actors	5	8
Government agencies	6	13
Regional agencies	1[a]	4[b]
Local authorities	2	5
Private and third sector	5 (FSB, CBI, NFU, UW, FWTUC)	5 (FSB, CBI, NFU, FUW, WTUC)
Higher education	2	2
Voluntary sector	1 (WCVA)	2 (WCVA, Disability Wales)
Other	1[c]	1[c]
Total	24	42

[a] North Wales Economic Forum represented all regional economic fora.
[b] These are the four Economic Regional Fora.
[c] Hywel Ceri Jones was European adviser to Ron Davies, the Secretary of State for Wales.

They took on board the detailed critique of the SPD produced by the European Commission.

A Shadow Monitoring Committee (SMC) with a role in establishing the structures for Objective 1 was initially convened in March 2000. In May 2000, the Assembly established a Structural Funds Working Group that advised the SMC. The Shadow Monitoring Committee made crucial decisions on the direction of Objective 1, and a key decision was on Programme Monitoring Committee membership. It was decided to constitute this on the basis of equal representation for each of the three sectors of the partnership. That is, one-third public or statutory sector, one-third private sector and social partners, and one-third community and voluntary sector, the so-called 'one-third principle'. Moreover, the Shadow Monitoring Committee decided that the 'one-third' principle should be adhered to in all partnership groups at all levels (WEFO, 2000c). In addition, the Committee called for the equal representation of men and women on all partnership levels.

The Single Programming Document was submitted to the Commission in April 2000 and eventually approved in July 2000. Commission approval allowed for the Programme Monitoring Committee (PMC), the main decision-making body in the programme, to be established. Its chair was an Assembly Member and another AM was a committee member as a public-sector representative.[17] During 2000, a fundamental overhaul in the main administration and management of Structural Funds took place. Following devolution, aspects of WEPE and EAD were combined in the Welsh European Funding Office (WEFO). This was an executive agency of the Welsh Assembly Government that was established in April 2000 and became the Managing Authority for the programme.

The Commission's approval of the SPD set the implementation structure of Objective 1 into action (see Figure 4.1). Implementation centred on Local and Regional Action Plans. The former were to be delivered by fifteen local partnerships, one for each local authority in the Objective 1 area, and the latter were to be implemented by ten regional partnerships based upon specific sectors of the economy. The main role of the partnerships was to identify, support and assist in developing projects that complied with the priorities of the SPD. A review of the implementation of Objective 1 was undertaken by the Task and Finish Group, and this was completed in December 2000 (Benfield et al., 2000). Amongst its proposals was refining the partnership structure by including four strategy partnerships, established in April 2001, as final arbiters on project applications. The composition of these partnerships was drawn equally from local and regional partnerships. The Task and Finish Group also called for establishing a Voluntary Sector Unit in WCVA to mirror the Private Sector Unit established in WEFO to encourage the engagement of these actors in Objective 1 implementation.

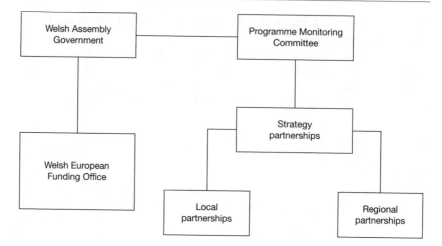

Figure 4.1: The Objective 1 decision-making and implementation structures in Wales (AGW, 2002: 16)

This section has outlined the range of participation opportunities opened to civil society organizations in Objective 1 at all levels, from the Programme Monitoring Committee at the apex to local partnerships. The key aspects that created such extensive opportunities were the emphasis on partnership and the decision that all partnership levels should replicate the 'one-third' principle. The very significant enhancement of opportunities for civil society engagement illustrated here cannot be adequately explained simply by reference to the impact of Commission regulations. Rather, devolution was the main driver for more intense involvement by civil society in Objective 1.

GROUNDWORK AND OBJECTIVE 1

After outlining the Objective 1 structures and processes, we can now examine Groundwork Wales and Groundwork Merthyr and RCT's involvement in the structures. Groundwork's engagement in Structural Funds was dramatically transformed as it engaged in all stages of Objective 1 and was one of the leading civil society organizations in the decision-making structures.

As previously outlined, the number of civil society organizations directly engaged in the first stages of developing Objective 1 was limited. During the drafting of the SPD, Groundwork fed in its viewpoints through the WCVA. There was some feeling that due to administrative changes, there was a lack of learning process between the two programming periods, mainly in terms of the activities that would be supported. A voluntary sector worker stated that during Objective 2:

> We did learn, we did speak to the Welsh Office direct and said, 'look this is an issue,' and they said, 'put it in writing and we'll deal with it,' sometimes speaking to Brussels. And then when we got to Objective 1 we went right back to square one.[18]

However, overall, another worker felt that civil society representation in the early drafting stage was satisfactory:

> I'm not sure whether you could have done it much better at the time. I mean the time-scale, the amount of literature that was coming out on documentation. It was quite a fairly open process; there was a lot of access for individuals who'd got comments to make and the representatives that were there were definitely representative. I used to e-mail papers through so if there were any comments coming through some of the other organisations then I would always pass them on.[19]

Inputting through the main voluntary sector organizations and the public consultation aided Groundwork Wales's efforts to change drafts of the programme document. As a member of staff stated:

> We were particularly keen on the communities side to ensure that environmental projects and programmes were seen as part of community regeneration and capacity-building. We got more recognition for the whole notion of sustainable development and aspects with business through some of the programmes on innovation and R&D. So we did see some changes in wording as a result of comments that were put forward.[20]

The number of organizations involved in Objective 1 expanded with the establishment of the Shadow Monitoring Committee (SMC) in March 2000 and Groundwork Wales formally participated on this (see Table 4.3). Furthermore, Groundwork Wales was a member of the Structural Funds Working Group with WCVA, Chwarae Teg, LEADER Network, Valleys Partnership and Wales Wildlife Trust (see Table 4.4). This advised the Shadow Monitoring Committee on issues regarding Objective 1 implementation, and undertook work such as preparing guidance for partnerships. The decisions of the Shadow Monitoring Committee, namely that the 'one-third' principle should be reflected on all partnership levels, profoundly affected Groundwork and other civil society organizations' role in Objective 1.

Following the approval of the SPD, the SMC became the Programme Monitoring Committee proper. Groundwork was amongst the civil society

Table 4.3: Objective 1 Shadow Monitoring Committee membership[21]

Politicians	2 AMs
Government actors	4
Government agencies	7[a]
Local authorities	2
Social partners	6 (British Telecom, FSB, North Wales Chamber, TGWU, NFU Cymru Wales, Wales Cooperative Centre)
Higher education	1
Voluntary sector	6 (WCVA x 2, Chwarae Teg, Wales Wildlife Trust, Groundwork Wales, Cymad)
Total	28

[a] One was from the Wales European Programme Executive. Some of these were included as specialist statutory bodies.

Table 4.4: Objective 1 Structural Funds Working Group membership[22]

Government actors	1 (NAW)
Public sector	6 (3 local authorities, 2 government agencies, 1 higher education)
Social partners	6 (FSB, CBI, Chamber Wales, Wales TUC, NFU Cymru Wales, FUW)
Voluntary/community	6 (WCVA x 2, Chwarae Teg, Wales Wildlife Trust, LEADER, Groundwork)
Specialist statutory bodies	8
Total	27

organizations that now constituted the one-third voluntary sector membership on the PMC, and it represented the social economy group (WEFO,
2000c) (see Table 4.5). It was emphasized that these organizations reflected
a cross-section of the voluntary sector, represented their members and
liaised with a variety of other groups (WEFO, 2000c). Groundwork Wales'
membership of the PMC was a catalyst. It created opportunities to participate
on other levels, the regional and the strategy partnerships. A voluntary
sector official stated:

> I guess there'd be a request for Groundwork to sit on certain things. I mean
> I've had requests, some have come from the Assembly, or WEFO, and then
> others who get to know you; it's more like a process of osmosis. People know
> who you are, they know what your track record is and then you tend to have
> an invitation to sit on whatever people think are relevant for you.[23]

Table 4.5: Objective 1 Programme Monitoring Committee membership[24]

Government actors	8 (2 AMs, 6 WEFO officials)
Public sector	5 (2 local authorities, 2 government agencies, 1 higher education)
Social partners	4 (FSB, CBI Wales, Chamber Wales, NFU Cymru)
Voluntary/community	6 (WCVA x 2, Chwarae Teg, Wales Wildlife Trust, LEADER, Groundwork)
Specialist statutory bodies	7[a]
Total	30

[a] These include three European Commission officials.

As a result, Groundwork Wales was engaged in four regional partnerships and was a member of the Community Assets strategy partnership. Groundwork Wales viewed its role as ensuring that the Objective 1 process worked effectively:

> It's very much been part of trying to make sure that the process runs smoothly if there are any changes on policy, and obviously seeing the applications that come through and commenting on them. So that has been quite a significant role.[25]

The Groundwork Trusts were central on other partnership levels. Groundwork Merthyr and RCT played a key part on Local Partnerships Boards in Merthyr Tydfil and RCT. A Groundwork officer was a member of the four subgroups of the RCT Objective 1 partnership and they led on the Rural Assets and Community Assets subgroups. In addition, the Trust's executive director was a member of the tourism regional partnership, and the Community and Rural Assets strategy partnerships. Groundwork Merthyr and RCT and Groundwork Wales also played a role in implementing Objective 1 through project sponsorship, and several project applications were successful.[26]

Overall, Groundwork Wales and Groundwork Merthyr and RCT played an extensive role in Objective 1. All levels felt stretched by their engagement. One issue is that no financial recompense was provided for engaging in the Objective 1 decision-making structures. In addition, submitting projects cost both time and money. A member of staff explained:

> It has cost us in terms of time; it's also cost us in terms of having to put in place people at a senior level who can run these programmes. So in other words, the financial expertise, the monitoring, the evaluation, the actual bid-writing. I do think that's an issue for the voluntary sector. We're all in there doing our bit, but it's quite a significant resource.[27]

Furthermore, in contrast to previous programmes, responsibilities for management, implementation and monitoring were delegated to partnerships, and therefore the work was more extensive. As was evident, the density of partnerships in Objective 1 meant that Groundwork Trusts sat on a number of partnerships and subgroups while also involved in other Assembly programmes. As a member of staff stated,

> We have in Rhondda Cynon Taff 25 Communities First areas and 9 in Merthyr. The current experience is a stretchy one. Add to that Objective 1 where Rhondda Cynon Taff has its hardships and assets groups and Merthyr have their assets groups, and you're stretched, but not too bad. Because it's a small area within which the expert team is limited and we're all trying to serve these areas as well as Communities First and actually do your job and good running of the organisation.[28]

This suggests that it had simply been assumed that all partners could participate effectively in Objective 1, and disparities in experience and resources were not adequately recognized. The contrasts in resources available to the public sector is quite clear in one voluntary sector official's response:

> I do think there is an issue for the voluntary sector. Because when you see the statutory sector, whether it's WDA or the local authorities, those officers are being paid, that is part of their mainstream job. And they set up European officers – we don't have the capacity for that, we're doing that on top of a day job.[29]

To sum up, in stark contrast with Objective 2 1994–9, Groundwork was significantly involved in all stages of Objective 1 from the Shadow Monitoring Committee onwards. As one member of staff stated, 'now in Objective 1 we're part of the whole deliberation process, the whole consultation as well as delivering and putting bids in, so that has changed'.[30] Groundwork's participation was greater than ever before and it changed from being an organization implementing projects in Objective 2 ISW programme to being one of the most prominent voices for civil society in Objective 1.

GROUNDWORK IN POST-DEVOLUTION WALES

This section examines how Groundwork's participation in Objective 1 reflects the impact of devolution on the organization's development post-devolution.

Groundwork was heavily involved in all stages of Objective 1. Its involvement in the programme highlights the greater opportunities afforded to organizations such as Groundwork due to the National Assembly's openness. EU regulations, which require partnership, do not fully account for the difference between 'partnership' on the European Task Force and the Shadow Monitoring Committee. Rather it reflected the Assembly's efforts to be more inclusive. For example, the Economic Development Committee was pivotal in ensuring that the one-third principle became enshrined in Objective 1. Groundwork staff concurred with this: 'if we hadn't had the Welsh Assembly, I don't believe we would have had this whole partnership approach to the level that we got it'.[31] Groundwork staff also referred to the Assembly's open government working practices:

> I don't think that there's another government that has as much stuff for example on the Internet. You know all their committee papers, all these things. There's never any difficulty in getting hold of information of what's going through the Assembly.[32]

However, Groundwork was fully aware of how to take advantage of the opportunities for participating in Objective 1 and in other Assembly policies and programmes. This was crucial in ensuring its in-depth involvement.

A second factor that explained Groundwork's deep engagement with the Assembly, evident in Objective 1, was Groundwork's area of work. Before devolution, Groundwork implemented community development and environmental projects on a trust level. The setting up of Groundwork Wales allowed for programmes to be developed across the trusts. Its involvement in Objective 1 was mostly in implementing Priority 3, Community Economic Development, and in its work on business and the environment. Groundwork's expertise in community development and sustainable development were not only important in Objective 1 but to the Assembly itself. Sustainable development was an area where the Assembly had a statutory duty, and along with community development was a key area where the Assembly attempted to make its mark. However, developing Objective 1 occurred simultaneously to the Assembly's establishment. At the time, its civil service had limited capacities to deal with the transition pressures. It also lacked capacity in areas of community and sustainable development. Groundwork's expertise compensated for this lack of expertise and also explained its role in projects such as Communities First. Overall, it was a valuable partner to the Assembly and Assembly Government. To some degree, this represented symmetry between Groundwork's work and the Assembly's agenda. One member of staff explained: 'you've got the Assembly giving you funding but a lot of the key objectives and targets of the Assembly in their main policies are what we want to do anyway'.[33] However, it also illustrates the partnership and participation opportunities provided to some resourced organizations with expertise and the ability to fulfil the Assembly and Assembly Government's aims.

Thirdly, Groundwork's increased internal capacity through the estab-lishment of Groundwork Wales in 1998 complemented the trusts and facilitated its involvement in the Assembly's work. In Objective 1, Ground-work Wales's role on the PMC opened up extensive opportunities to influence the programme's direction. Though at times stretched by the degree of engagement, Groundwork Wales and the trusts could contribute effectively to national, regional and local decision-making and implementa-tion structures. More generally, in addition to receipt of funding that almost by definition provided greater access, Groundwork's high profile and greater capacity resulted in strong direct engagement in the National Assembly and Welsh Assembly Government's policy-making processes since devolution.

Groundwork was engaged in the Assembly's work through a number of different channels. The first and most indirect channel was responding to policy consultations. This allowed inputting into policy-making and ensured that Groundwork was subsequently involved in further develop-ments. Groundwork Wales staff emphasized the opportunities available to contribute: 'the Assembly . . . because it wished to create its own policies and not simply accept policies from central government in England, it has been considerably more open about reviewing subject areas and the ways in which it works'.[34]

A second channel was Groundwork Wales's engagement in networks of organizations relating to its subject area and working through groups representing a range of organizations. Networks included the WCVA, the social economy network, its role on the LINK organization's Council and steering group and the Sustainable Development Forum. These were seen as an alternative channel for influencing Assembly Government policy:

> If there are organizational things being set up where it is appropriate for us to be represented on them, then Groundwork will be, or will attempt to be there. You don't get on all of them by any stretch, but we try to pick things that we are most interested in. That means you actually do engage in the decision-making.[35]

A third channel was that Groundwork Trusts continued to receive funding from the National Assembly, and since devolution Groundwork received greater financial acknowledgement for its work:

> We're the same as a number of organizations in that we get funding from the Assembly. I have to say the Assembly was the first body; certainly the Welsh Office didn't give us any extra funding. The Assembly's given us extra money.[36]

This funding relationship led to regular sessions with key civil servants and involvement with Assembly Members, particularly on the Local

Government and Housing Committee responsible for its funding. Groundwork also interacted with the Assembly on other issues. Groundwork Trusts liaised with their AMs to build a rapport and draw attention to their work. Groundwork Wales engaged with key individuals in the Assembly Government: 'when it's appropriate, we've spoken to some of the Assembly Members but more often if it's a subject area that's ongoing and developing, it's a question of building a relationship with the civil servants'.[37]

The changes within Groundwork's structures strengthened its ability to engage with governmental structures. Groundwork Wales provided a coordinated and targeted response at an all-Wales level drawing on the expertise of the organization as a whole. This signalled a transformation. Its representative explained: 'the way I relate to the Assembly would have been impossible under the old structure'.[38] Building on its pre-devolution contacts and its funding relations, its main links continued to be key civil servants that formulated and drafted policy, and it gained direct representation on working groups. In addition, it could take advantage of more closed mechanisms and formally and informally liaise with the Welsh Assembly Government. Interestingly, Groundwork Wales did not regard its activities as lobbying. Considering the numerous channels available to Groundwork and its executive-level access through strong relationships developed with the Assembly and Assembly Government, lobbying was perhaps not as necessary as was the case with other organizations.

Groundwork's ethos also made it a key organization both in Objective 1 and amongst the civil society of post-devolution Wales. Partnership principles were embedded in its working practices. In Objective 1, it engaged the grassroots and community level in its project work. It also used its position within the decision-making structures to facilitate the involvement of organizations and to improve the accessibility of Objective 1. For example, referring to Groundwork Wales's effective role on the PMC, another voluntary-sector member on the committee stated that it had 'taken a very strong line on defending the process and making sure that it is more accessible'.[39] This was also evident in Groundwork Merthyr and RCT's approach to Objective 1:

> Considerable effort is being focused into the whole Objective 1 planning process to both secure the role for the Trust to deliver locally as well as disseminate information and facilitate local organizations in the Community and Enterprise Sector to be active and empowered participants in the Local Plan delivery. (2000c)

More generally, Groundwork's approach was one of its fundamental strengths and suggested its ability to promote participatory norms. This was most clear as, in its working practices, Groundwork promoted a strong 'bottom-up' approach to working with those that participated in grassroots and community projects being involved in the decision-making. This approach was conducive to social inclusion. The partnership principle incorporated into Structural Fund programmes in Wales and into other Assembly programmes has always been a guiding principle of Groundwork's approach. One Groundwork member of staff explained: 'the example of our work has now become mainstream way of working'.[40] Emphasis on encouraging participation and incorporating groups that can be challenging to involve underlined Groundwork's potential to contribute to developing participatory norms that can generate civic engagement, thus improving the quality of democracy.

Finally, establishing Groundwork Wales at an all-Wales level in response to devolution unleashed its potential in Wales and signified a shift in Groundwork's identity in Wales towards a greater sense of *Welsh civil society*. Groundwork Wales characterized itself as 'a Welsh based organization because Groundwork Wales is an independent company in its own rights so are the Welsh Trusts, so we're part of a federation but we're all independent companies'.[41] Traces of *civil society in Wales* remained as respondents referred to Wales as a country and the UK as the national level. Groundwork Wales was referred to as a 'regional' office and Groundwork UK as the 'national' office and it remained part of a UK-wide federation (Groundwork Wales, 2000a). However, devolution was a catalyst for the development of its greater Welsh outlook. This was evident in the restructuring and the greater autonomy afforded to the organization. Establishing the post of an executive director along with a team of staff working on an all-Wales basis represented a heightened internal capacity. In the past, though autonomy was afforded to Groundwork Trusts as independent companies, Groundwork UK determined the main policy direction. This resonates with the idea raised in the Introduction that *civil society in Wales* organizations tended to lack autonomy. Establishing Groundwork Wales led to greater autonomy for the trusts in Wales and a growth of activity on an all-Wales basis. One member of staff explained:

> Previously we were a national organization, we didn't have Groundwork Wales and basically, the way that Groundwork developed was because a lot of the push came through the DOE [Department of the Environment]. Well now our response and the way we choose to develop our organization is about responding to Welsh issues.[42]

Decisions on Groundwork Wales's work programme and coordination between the trusts were now developed through regular meetings of individual officers and the board comprising the chairs of the four trusts. This trend of responding to objectives set in Wales suggested that establishing

Groundwork Wales has shifted towards a more 'Welsh' approach and a greater convergence with the *Welsh civil society* spectrum, as opposed to *civil society in Wales*. As noted in the Introduction, the characteristics of *Welsh civil society* are organizations that are more 'Welsh' in their perspective, and Groundwork highlights that this relates to organizational structures, the autonomy of organizations and their decision-making and policy-development capacities to respond to 'Welsh' issues. One public sector official noted concerning the contribution of different organizations to Objective 1:

> Most of these organizations operate on a UK basis which means that their Welsh basis is very weak. Those organisations which are Wales-focused, and there are more of those in the voluntary sector, tend to be stronger . . . Examples are the WCVA is a good one, Wales Cooperative Centre, Groundwork Wales I think is quite a good example – they focus on a particular area.[43]

This case has highlighted a number of interesting points regarding the *civil society in Wales/Welsh civil society* distinction. The tendency of a shift in the identity of *civil society in Wales* organizations towards *Welsh civil society* in the context of devolution was clear. While there were continuing *civil society in Wales* tendencies, Groundwork Wales viewed itself as a Welsh organization; it was geared to the Welsh context and had a greater propensity to collectively develop policies relevant to Wales.

CONCLUSION

This chapter has demonstrated that Groundwork in Wales greatly expanded its capacities since the pre-devolution period. Groundwork was deeply involved in Objective 1 decision-making and implementation through the trusts and also on an all-Wales level. Its contribution reflected the Assembly's emphasis on partnership working with organizations that had expertise. This compensated for the Assembly's limited policy capacities in areas of sustainable and community development. However, the unique step of establishing Groundwork Wales cannot be overestimated. It trans-formed Groundwork's ability to bring its expertise to the fore. As a result, through a number of formal and informal channels, Groundwork Wales was directly involved on a high level in influencing and engaging in the National Assembly and Welsh Assembly Government's work. This reflected broader enthusiasm on the part of civil society organizations that engaged in partnerships with the Assembly and contributed to demonstrating that devolution 'makes a difference'.

Groundwork in Wales developed a high profile amongst the civil society of post-devolution Wales. At the same time, its partnership and bottom-up approach meant that it could potentially contribute to generating participatory norms. Its high profile was in contrast to the lack of capacity and resources that impeded other organizations from the sector from fully engaging in the opportunities that have arisen due to devolution. The establishment of Groundwork Wales in 1998 before setting up the Assembly demonstrated the organization's foresight in recognizing the need for restructuring and developing a unified voice. One member of staff explained: 'Groundwork Wales was set up in 1998 by the Welsh trusts largely as a response to devolution'.[44] Devolution was therefore a catalyst to the expansion of Groundwork in Wales and it shifted the identity of the organization towards a greater Welsh outlook in the direction of *Welsh civil society*. This was evident in that it identified itself as a Welsh organization, and its structures and policy-development capacities were geared to interacting with the National Assembly and responding to the needs of Wales. The organization subsequently was a key player in realizing the aims of the National Assembly and Welsh Assembly Government during the first term of devolution.

5

Devolution and Recognition:
Cymdeithas yr Iaith and Cymuned

Nancy Fraser states that 'The "struggle for recognition" is fast becoming the paradigmatic form of political conflict in the late twentieth century' (1995: 69). The struggle for recognition for the Welsh language made the language movement a prominent and robust facet of civil society in twentieth-century Wales.[1] Language campaigning enhanced Welsh political nationalism and the need for self-governance by creating an awareness, 'that there were areas of Welsh life in which the British State actively opposed manifestations of a separate Welsh identity' (C. A. Davies, 1989: 50).

As a result of devolution, the National Assembly for Wales under Section 32 of the Government of Wales Act 1998 'may do anything it considers appropriate to support the Welsh language' (HMSO, 1998a). This clause made the Assembly the first democratically elected institution in Wales with responsibility for the language. Indeed, the wording of the Wales Act suggested that the language is where 'the Assembly's powers are most generously drawn' (Rawlings, 2003: 218). The National Assembly's first significant initiative in relation to Welsh was the Culture Committee's Policy Review of the Welsh Language. In May 2001, amidst renewed controversy surrounding the Welsh language, the committee's year-long review commenced.[2] It provided extensive opportunities for public, private and civil society organizations to present evidence. It was regarded as groundbreaking and 2001 was compared to 1588 and 1962 in terms of its importance to the Welsh language (Lewis, 2001: 42).[3]

Devolution therefore presented a new context for campaigns to recognize the Welsh language and this chapter examines Cymdeithas yr Iaith (the Welsh Language Society) and Cymuned's role in the policy review. As *Welsh civil society* organizations from within the language movement, one was established before devolution and the other post-devolution. Examining their involvement, as the more political rather than cultural strand of the Welsh language movement located outside the 'consensus' of the new Welsh politics, provided an opportunity to investigate the extent to which the Assembly's rhetoric of 'inclusiveness' became reality. Moreover, a paradox surrounded the topic of the Welsh language in post-devolution

Wales. While the Assembly had greatest statutory power in this area, it raised the greatest problems due to the contentiousness of the topic and the negative attitudes of some politicians towards the Welsh language during the Assembly's first term.

The chapter is divided into four sections. First, it provides the background to the two movements. The next section outlines the background to the review, the Policy Review of the Welsh Language's process and subsequent Welsh Assembly Government policy. The third section then examines Cymdeithas and Cymuned's engagement with the Welsh language review. The final section assesses what the review illustrates of Cymdeithas and Cymuned's broader relationship with the Assembly. It highlights the effects of limited resources; the negative attitude of some AMs to the groups; the impact of the Welsh language policy network and the effect of civil disobedience on engagement with the Assembly. Furthermore, it discusses the groups' propensity to promote active engagement, their efforts to promote further devolution and the indications of the effects of devolution on *Welsh civil society*.

CYMDEITHAS AND CYMUNED

Cymdeithas

During the twentieth century, the decline of the Welsh language and the transformation of the linguistic fabric of Wales became visible. This led to the establishment of Plaid Cymru as a Welsh nationalist party in 1925. During the second half of that century, concerns about the future of the Welsh language intensified. In 1962 Saunders Lewis expressed this concern in the radio lecture *Tynged yr Iaith* (the fate of the language).[4] Lewis presented an apocalyptic vision of the decline of the Welsh language by the twenty-first century. His aim of shifting Plaid Cymru from its emphasis on achieving self-government through parliamentary channels to being devoted to safeguarding the Welsh language through civil disobedience was unsuccessful (Adamson, 1991: 196). However, the lecture intensified political protest from the nationalist movement and Cymdeithas yr Iaith Gymraeg was founded in 1962.

As a Welsh language pressure group, Cymdeithas reflected the nationalist upsurge in Wales in the early 1960s. As its founders were mainly young professionals and students, it also paralleled the era's international youth movement campaigning for civil and minority rights (C. H. Williams, 1977: 429). The prime concern was the status of the Welsh language, and Cymdeithas attempted to secure its official and equal recognition in

Wales. In terms of its methods, Cymdeithas adopted civil disobedience and non-violence, thus rejecting parliamentary constitutional methods. This was influenced by pacifist practices of conscientious objection. Limited acts of symbolic damage against property were deemed legitimate as they had previously been effective and were an expression of frustration due to the 'target group's unwillingness to enter into reasonable negotiations' (Williams, 1977: 448). Acts of non-violent direct action varied from sit-ins and mass demonstrations and withholding of payments to the state, to more direct action of occupying or damaging property. This led to 'confrontation with the state and the use of court appearances to publicize and draw attention to the specific claims of the defendants' (Adamson, 1991: 128). Cymdeithas members were charged with conspiracy, faced heavy fines and imprisonments. From 1962 to 1992, 1,105 individuals made court appearances in Cymdeithas's name and 171 received prison sentences (Phillips, 1998a: 68).

Cymdeithas's decision-making structures provided opportunities for membership involvement. The Senate, its main decision-making body composed of the society's officers elected by members, reflected Cymdeithas's traditional base amongst students and the younger generation. Membership opportunities also existed through working groups and cells. Furthermore, the organization's cell structure (similar to branches) encouraged member engagement on a local/regional basis. The degree of cell activity largely depended on individual members in different areas.[5] It could also be argued that Cymdeithas's campaigning methods, including letter-writing, petitions and non-violent direct action, encouraged membership input.

Cymdeithas campaigning stimulated a number of policy and legislative changes that enhanced the Welsh language's status and provided legal protection. C. A. Davies argues: 'prior to this form of language activism, decades of conventional post-nationalism had had no impact on the pervasive official disregard for the Welsh language' (1989: 46). Cymdeithas language campaigning covered diverse policy areas from housing, education, broadcasting to the economy. Of most relevance to this chapter, in the 1980s it campaigned to address the effects of outward migration and inward immigration both in terms of pricing out local young people in the housing market and the subsequent erosion of Welsh-speaking communities. In 1989, it began a campaign for a Property Act to regulate the sale of all properties, according to plans developed by local government in local communities where in-migration threatened the way of life (see Griffiths, 1992). In the 1980s and 1990s, Cymdeithas campaigned for a language Act that resulted in the 1993 Welsh Language Act and the creation of a statutory Welsh Language Board. Thomas emphasizes Cymdeithas's effectiveness as a pressure group:

Cymdeithas yr Iaith can, with some justice, point out that perpetual protest has served them well in the past. It played a significant role in setting the policy agenda which led to the introduction of two Welsh language Bills, PDAG and a Welsh Language Television Channel. (1997: 341)

A number of campaign successes were associated with coalition-building with other groups and eminent politicians. For example, the decision to establish the Welsh language channel was taken following protests by Cymdeithas, pressure by parliamentarians and a hunger strike by Gwynfor Evans. A Language Act Committee that led to the Welsh Language Act 1993 was set up following pressure from Cymdeithas and key politicians such as Dafydd Wigley and Gwilym Prys Davies (Thomas, 1997: 335–6).

Although Cymdeithas attracted cross-party affiliation and employed members of several political parties as full-time officers, the public closely associated Plaid Cymru and Cymdeithas. Overlapping membership and family links explain this. Indeed, Cymdeithas has experienced a complex and ambiguous relationship with Plaid. As Plaid headed for electoral respectability, it sought to distance itself from Cymdeithas's radical campaigns. In the long term, Cymdeithas's existence released Plaid from being responsible for safeguarding the language and allowed it to develop broader public appeal. McAllister states: 'a separate language pressure group presented Plaid with the opportunity to scale down its own campaigns for the language and develop more fully other policies related to the goal of self-government' (2001: 104). More broadly, Cymdeithas influenced all political parties. C. A. Davies refers to 'the clarification, even polarization, of attitudes about the Welsh language that was forced upon all political parties in Wales as a consequence of public reaction to Cymdeithas campaigns' (1989: 47).

Before devolution, various UK governments were largely reactive to Cymdeithas demands. During Conservative governments, Cymdeithas's interaction with the Welsh Office was in flux. A number of Conservative Secretaries of State refused to meet Cymdeithas members while it adhered to civil disobedience. Deacon characterizes Cymdeithas on the outer edge of the policy periphery during the Welsh Office era in comparison with other actors in the 'Cathays Park Village' (2002: 165). According to Deacon, they 'were regarded as illegitimate to the Welsh Office's policy goal/strategy mix' (2002: 166).

Labour's accession to power in 1997 saw Ron Davies as Secretary of State for Wales. Reflecting the new 'inclusiveness', Davies stated: 'we threw the doors open to groups that wanted to come in, groups like Cymdeithas yr Iaith [Gymraeg]' (cited in Chaney and Fevre, 2001a: 30). Cymdeithas engaged in the National Assembly Advisory Group consultation and produced documents arguing that Welsh should be an issue cutting across subject areas, and for bilingualism to permeate the Assembly's work (Cymdeithas yr Iaith Gymraeg, 1998). By the end of the 1990s, Cymdeithas commenced a campaign for a new Welsh Language Act to counter the perceived inadequacies of the 1993 Act which had been passed by a Conservative government without the support of Welsh MPs, many of whom favoured stronger legislation.

Cymuned

In January 2001, a tense public dispute commenced, sparked by the remarks of Seimon Glyn, a Gwynedd Plaid Cymru councillor. He stated that inward migration of non-Welsh speakers contributed to the decline of Welsh-speaking communities in north-west and west Wales, the 'heartlands'. The remarks broke the political truce on the language that had developed following the 1993 Welsh Language Act and continued in the run-up to devolution. Glyn's comments roused tension in Plaid Cymru and between the political parties during the 2001 General Election. Some Labour figures made charges of 'racism' against Plaid Cymru (Osmond, 2002: 3). In the wake of renewed language debate, the attitudes of the press and Plaid Cymru, Cymuned was founded as a pressure group in June 2001.

Cymuned was formed by a group of nationalists in Ceredigion that met from March 2001. Cymuned's public launch was delayed until after the June General Election and its first public meeting was held in July 2001, attended by 600 people. Rather than founding a second nationalist party, Cymuned was established as a pressure group. It aimed to fill the political vacuum by providing intellectual support to discussing in-migration to Welsh-speaking areas and exerting pressure on all parties. Its constitution described the group as anti-racist and anti-colonialist that sought to ensure the survival of Welsh as a community language in those areas where it existed as a community language (Cymuned, 2002d). At the onset, Cymuned attempted to undertake constitutional lobbying rather than being a direct action protest group in the tradition of the language movement.

Cymuned's main decision-making body, the Executive Committee, had no formal roles extended to its membership of 12 (9 directly elected and 3 co-opted) except for a treasurer. This intentionally avoided hierarchy within its structures and prevented the possibility of one person being identified as the movement's leader. The Executive Committee was directly elected by Cymuned's membership. The Annual General Meeting provided a forum for policy formulation and decisions on amendments to the constitution. Membership involvement was promoted through other structures, its standing committees and *ad hoc* subcommittees. However, initially, the greatest strength of Cymuned's structure was the local branches, with over twenty branches established across Wales but concentrated in Gwynedd. At a community-based level, activities included campaigns against local estate agents, protests, fundraising and cultural events. This illustrated the community nature of the movement with some branches more active than others. By 2004, local activity had reduced significantly with only one extremely active branch. While there were overlaps between the membership of Cymdeithas and Cymuned, the latter tended to attract local membership, from a wider age group in Welsh-speaking areas.

Cymuned policies included controlling migration into Welsh-speaking areas, halting outward migration, linguistically assimilating newcomers, and establishing the Welsh language as the primary language in the Welsh-speaking areas. In this regard, Cymuned viewed itself as part of the struggle for minority rights: a worldwide struggle for the survival of indigenous minority communities (Cymuned, 2001a). The group focused on developing its community base, but also engaged in constitutional lobbying, with the greatest emphasis in its early existence on the Welsh language review.

Therefore, there were distinct differences between Cymdeithas and Cymuned. Cymdeithas had a long history as a protest movement committed to civil disobedience whereas Cymuned was established post-devolution as a community-based movement with a greater emphasis on constitutional lobbying. Cymdeithas campaigns influenced policy and legislative changes relating to the Welsh language despite its unstable relationship with the Welsh Office before devolution. Focusing on the organizations' involvement in the policy review will assist in identifying trends within both organizations post-devolution.

THE POLICY REVIEW OF THE WELSH LANGUAGE

The Culture Committee's Policy Review of the Welsh Language resulted in an extensive investigation. This had not happened since the Consultative Welsh Language Board developed recommendations for a Welsh Language Act published in 1991 (Welsh Language Board, 1991).[6] This section briefly explains the origins of the review, outlines the participation opportunities for organizations before identifying the degree to which the review fed into the Welsh Assembly Government's policy.

The review originated in an Assembly plenary debate on the Welsh language held on 4 July 2000. The Post-16 Education Committee resolved on 16 February 2000 to treat the creation of a bilingual Wales as 'an achievable national aim' (NAW, 2000d). In plenary, Christine Humphreys proposed an unsuccessful amendment that 'the Post-16 Education and Training Committee should make time in its timetable to discuss the need for a new Welsh Language Act for Wales' (NAW, 2000c). However, a motion tabled by Elin Jones was passed: 'The National Assembly calls upon the Post-16 Education and Training Committee to allocate time in its forward work programme ... to conduct a comprehensive policy review into the Welsh language in order to form a strategy for the future' (NAW, 2000d).

The Partnership Agreement in October 2000, led to a restructuring and a new portfolio of Minister for Culture, Language and Sport was created with Jenny Randerson appointed as minister. The Culture Committee, chaired by Rhodri Glyn Thomas, was given responsibility for the main review of the Welsh Language. The Education and Lifelong Learning Committee gained responsibility for reviewing the Welsh language in formal education.

The review's terms of reference were 'to seek to define more closely the National Assembly's established objective of "creating a bilingual Wales"' (NAW, 2001b). In undertaking the review, the committee exercised two of its functions outlined in the Standing Orders. It considered a matter referred to it by the Assembly, and contributed to policy development. However, it must be emphasized that the committee's recommendations were to inform Welsh Assembly Government policy rather than to be an integral part of policy-making.

The Culture Committee chair and secretariat determined the format of the review along with the review's appointed expert adviser, Euryn Ogwen Williams. Consultees were informed that the review was inviting written submissions, and information-gathering sessions through 'open microphone' sessions were also held in four roadshows across Wales (NAW, 2001d). During the review, 178 written responses were received and evidence was submitted by a cross-section of ninety-three public, private, civil society actors and Assembly committees (see NAW, 2002h).

The formal consultation took place from May 2001 to March 2002. The committee then drafted the report, and the final content was decided in the last meetings. The report *Our Language: Its Future* was published on 9 July 2002, unanimously agreed by all committee members (NAW, 2002h). It included forty-five recommendations in seven subject areas and illustrated a shift in ideas concerning the Welsh language. According to Rawlings the review reflected:

> a heightened sense of political cooperation on a most sensitive subject in the novel conditions of small-country governance: the fact that leading actors from both Labour and Plaid Cymru could hail the process as an example of the Assembly working at its best also speaks volumes. (2003: 217)

Subsequently, the Welsh Assembly Government's Policy Statement *Dyfodol Dwyieithog: A Bilingual Future* was published on 29 July 2002, and the document reflected the spirit of the Culture Committee's recommendations (WAG, 2002a). Following the budget round, the Assembly Government launched *Iaith Pawb* (Everyone's Language) as a draft National Action Plan in November 2002 (WAG, 2002b), and this was published in its final form in February 2003 (see C. H. Williams, 2004). The definition of a 'bilingual Wales' and some of the main policy recommendations were influenced by the review. This included mainstreaming the Welsh language across ministerial portfolios and Assembly Sponsored Public Bodies, and establishing a Government Welsh Language Unit responsible for monitoring the plan's implementation. In November 2002, Randerson announced an additional £26.8 million support for the language over three years channelled through the Welsh Language Board and the Welsh Books Council (NAW, 2003a).

There were opportunities for a variety of interests to input into the Culture Committee's Policy Review of the Welsh Language. However, the committee's review informed Welsh Assembly Government policy rather than forming the basis of policy itself. This emphasized the limitations of attempting to influence the committee and the importance of directly interacting with the Welsh Assembly Government in order to have any serious influence.

CYMDETIHAS YR IATITH AND CYMUNED IN THE POLICY REVIEW

Most organizations related to the Welsh language participated in the review. Cymdeithas's preliminary involvement with the review was threefold. Firstly, it maintained that it was partly responsible for initiating the review. Christine Humphries's amendment to the plenary debate was based on Cymdeithas's proposals for a new Welsh Language Act. This paved the way for Elin Jones's accepted amendment calling for the review. Secondly, Cymdeithas attempted to influence the review's agenda through a meeting with Jenny Randerson and Rhodri Morgan in December 2000 following the Partnership Agreement. Thirdly, during the review's early stages in April and May 2001, Cymdeithas arranged public meetings around Wales to present their arguments and to raise awareness of the review. Randerson, Delyth Evans (deputy minister), Rhodri Glyn Thomas, and the Welsh Language Board contributed to these meetings.

In terms of their formal contribution to the review, Cymdeithas submitted written evidence and made oral presentations to the Culture, Housing and

Local Government and Education Committees. During their presentation to the Culture Committee, Cymdeithas highlighted a number of issues and advocated legislative responses: a Property Act, and a new Welsh Language Act (NAW, 2001f; 2001g). In their presentation, they referred to their documentation on these topics (Cymdeithas yr Iaith Gymraeg, 1998, 1999, 2001). It seemed that some committee members perceived this formal contribution as the totality of Cymdeithas's involvement. However, the organization regularly e-mailed bulletins of evidence to committee members relating to their discussions. These received mixed responses. Cymdeithas developed a comprehensive response to the committee's position paper early in January 2002. It argued that the committee was not giving adequate attention to a new Language Act (Cymdeithas yr Iaith Gymraeg, 2002: 13).

Cymdeithas also attempted to influence the committee's work by lobbying some politicians. In addition to a meeting with Evans and Randerson, the most important meetings were with Plaid Cymru AMs, Rhodri Glyn Thomas, Owen John Thomas and Dafydd Wigley. Cymdeithas particularly benefited from connections with Wigley. He had extensive experience and utilized the evidence from Cymdeithas bulletins in committee discussions on housing and planning, and on the Welsh Language Act. During the committee's drafting process in May 2002, Wigley made a number of contributions on the current 1993 Language Act and provided a list of its inadequacies (NAW, 2002e). A majority on the committee had previously responded that it was too late into the review to reintroduce ideas. According to the *Western Mail*, 'His criticisms of its failure to demand a new Welsh Language Act were thrown out by members' (Betts, 2002c).

In addition, to exert pressure on the committee, Cymdeithas engaged in direct action. In February 2002, members broke into the offices of Randerson and Evans to draw attention to their demands and urge the committee to discuss new legislation, specifically to consider proposals for a new Welsh Language Act. Randerson and Evans had made clear that they thought that a new Act was of little relevance. In addition, the government refused to accept a 1,500-signature petition calling for a new Act, subsequently presented to Glyn Thomas as chair of the committee (*Western Mail*, 2002b; Brooks, 2002b). One member explained:

> We undertook direct action to emphasize the seriousness and its importance [*of a language Act*]. And I'm reasonably certain that it succeeded. You will notice that during one period there was a fair amount of action in the Language Act campaign and they started to discuss a Language Act more seriously.[7]

Following direct action, a number of Labour committee members stated that they did not want to receive further correspondence from the society. The committee chair was quoted in the *Western Mail*: 'when the committee discusses a new Welsh Language Act in April, members could be forgiven for questioning whether they should give in to intimidation' (T. Mason, 2002). During the review, Cymdeithas continued to protest and in June criticized the lack of legislation arising from the review. After the committee's report was published, Cymdeithas continued action for legislation and criticized the Assembly Government for not taking legislative measures.

Overall, Cymdeithas felt they had some influence on the review. In terms of their broader effect, they felt their activities and press coverage raised awareness and expectations surrounding the review. More significantly, Cymdeithas had campaigned for the language to be treated holistically at the Assembly's inception. During the review, this approach was recommended by the Welsh Language Board and included in the final report (NAW, 2002h: 7). To Cymdeithas members, their main campaigning objective, a new Language Act, was not achieved. A number of Assembly Members, the Counsel General and the Welsh Language Board made clear during the review that in their view a new Act was not necessary (NAW, 2000d; NAW, 2001e).[8] However, in conjunction with influencing Dafydd Wigley, they felt that campaigning and direct action put pressure on the committee, and some evidence supports this. The minister, through secondary legislation powers, expanded the existing Language Act to require more organizations to submit language plans. In July 2001, twenty-five new organizations were brought under its scope, with another seventeen organizations in May 2002 (NAW, 2001h; 2002f). Furthermore, the committee suggested that the Richard Commission examine the possibility of giving the Assembly powers to allow it to reform the 1993 Act (NAW, 2002h: 13).

Cymuned was not included on the list of proposed consultees in May 2001, as it simply was not established at this point. However, the high-profile media coverage of Cymuned made their engagement in the review inevitable. In terms of Cymuned's formal interaction with the review, it presented a written submission and appeared before the Culture Committee. Cymuned's submission was the basis of their presentations to the Culture and Housing and Local Government Committees on 7 November 2001, four months after their establishment (Cymuned, 2001e). It was comprehensive and included evidence on the housing situation and 170 researched policy recommendations. Before the Culture Committee, Cymuned called for policy advances in statutory education, integrating non-Welsh-speaking adults, facilitating the use of Welsh in the community, changes in the governance of Welsh-speaking communities and assisting local people in buying houses (NAW, 2001g).

To Cymuned members, its approach to the consultation was similar to that of any professional body. However, they argued that they didn't receive a real hearing or fair play by the Culture Committee. The main reason was that on the morning of their presentation, the *Welsh Mirror*'s front page exclusive story was that two Labour AMs, Lorraine Barrett and Huw Lewis, intended to 'ask the Home Office for a ruling on whether the proposals constitute a breach of new race-hate laws' (Cymuned, 2001d). The *Mirror* quoted the allegations that Cymuned's document was 'illegal and likely to whip up racial tensions', and that they intended to confront the group on its appearance (Cymuned, 2001d). Members of Cymuned were angered by the article and subsequently submitted a formal complaint to the *Welsh Mirror* in accordance with the Press Complaints Commission guidelines. In addition, Huw Lewis AM attended the committee session as a substitute for another Labour member. Lewis's negative attitude towards the Welsh language was previously made apparent during the policy review of higher education undertaken by the Education and Lifelong Learning Committee.[9]

Despite the negativity felt by Cymuned, there were positive reactions. The Minister stated that though she did not agree with all of their recommendations, she was interested in the novelty of Cymuned's ideas (Cymuned, 2001b). Furthermore, in response to Cymuned's discussions with the Local Government and Housing Committee in January 2002, Delyth Evans expressed 'her appreciation of Cymuned's constructive contribution to the discussion on housing and the Welsh language' (NAW, 2002a). Following their appearance before the Culture Committee, Cymuned transcribed the questions asked by members, prepared fuller written responses, corresponded and held meetings with AMs (Cymuned, 2001b). Cymuned felt that their greatest influence over the committee's report was in the detailed discussions that ensued. This included responding to a committee position paper in January 2002 and later pressing for further proposals to strengthen the report. After publication, they responded to the report and government statement and published their responses in a document titled *Equality and Justice* (Cymuned, 2002c).

Fundamental to Cymuned's strategy in the review was contact with Assembly Members. However, they received mixed responses to requests for meetings. During the period of the review, out of sixty AMs, Cymuned met with 23 politicians including 10 Plaid AMs and 6 out of 27 Labour AMs. Two members of the Culture Committee, Lorraine Barrett and Alison Halford, refused to meet with the group. The group did however have one informal and two formal meetings with the minister and deputy minister. Wigley was another important contact, and they discussed the housing situation. Cymuned's Annual General Meeting in March 2002 called on Culture Committee members not to endorse the report and to produce a minority report that included recommendations on housing (Cymuned, 2002b). The committee aimed to achieve cross-party consensus in its final report. Cymuned felt that they influenced Wigley and in March 2002, he asked the committee to consider the issue of migration and Evans backed this. During the final drafting stages in May, as with language legislation, Wigley made concerted moves to strengthen the report by including proposals on planning and housing (NAW, 2002e). According to the *Western Mail*, 'he succeeded in winning support on other housing and planning issues after the intervention of deputy minister Delyth Evans, Labour's leading thinker on the language question' (Betts, 2002c). As a result, seven housing recommendations were included in the committee's final report. A statement that inward migration was having a detrimental effect on the sustainability of Welsh-speaking communities was also inserted into the report (NAW, 2002h).

The National Assembly was not the only political forum where Cymuned presented evidence relating to the review. Cymuned's international department subcommittee gained official accreditation for Cymuned to attend a United Nations Working Group on Minorities at the end of May 2002. This was the first time the Welsh language was raised in an official UN context and they contended that the Welsh and UK governments were not addressing how Welsh was being undermined as a community language. They contended that, in accordance with international law, 'the government must encourage conditions for the promotion of the Welsh language and intervene in the housing market in order to protect the integrity of the local traditional community' (Cymuned, 2001c). The group felt that this put some pressure on the Assembly as it gained publicity in the press.

Overall, Cymuned's influence on the review was evident in the insertion of recommendations relating to housing in the committee's report. However, these recommendations were not included in the government's policy statement. As a result, the group felt that while they successfully influenced the committee's review, they failed to instigate actual policy change. In terms of their broader effect, the group felt that they generated public awareness of a rural housing emergency and the situation of 'Welsh' as a community language.

When considering Cymdeithas yr Iaith and Cymuned's involvement in the Policy Review of the Welsh Language, both groups utilized different channels to interact with the Culture Committee. The main channel tended to be the formal public consultation and during the course of the review, both groups engaged with some influential AMs. However, their subsequent contact with Welsh Assembly Government Ministers and civil servants involved in government policy formulation was limited. Both felt that the main issues they raised were not given sufficient attention and though the report's recommendations were an improvement, they remained inadequate.

CYMDEITHAS AND CYMUNED POST-DEVOLUTION

Cymdeithas and Cymuned's involvement with the review reflected the operation of the organizations, their relationship with the National Assembly and broader policy network surrounding the Welsh language post-devolution. First, the openness of the Assembly's committees provided opportunities for the organizations to participate in its work. Committee proceedings were held in public and documentation was available on the Assembly's website, providing transparency. Organizations could shadow committee proceedings and make presentations. In addition, the ease of contacting Assembly Members via e-mail facilitated their input into the review. This contrasted with the previous situation of closed discussions between civil servants and ministers that characterized Welsh Office policy-making when language campaigning organizations were largely excluded. The involvement of organizations such as Cymdeithas and Cymuned was important to the review. Their expertise and experience contributed to overcoming problems such as the review's broad remit, the differences in competences of committee AMs on language issues, and the Culture Committee's small secretariat. Some argued, however, that despite the openness of the review, the potential for change was very limited in any formal consultation, as the dominant policy direction was already determined. Referring to the review, a member of Cymuned stated: 'I suppose this part of the process was all that a public consultation should be . . . There wasn't any real political will for change . . . The only comments that get any real hearing are those that fit the strategy that's already been decided'.[10]

Examining Cymdeithas and Cymuned highlighted a number of issues that suggested the relative 'outsider' status of the groups in the Assembly's work. First, the review highlighted the resource implications and challenges for small voluntary organizations post-devolution. Both organizations focused on the committee's review. Their actions do not suggest that they adequately recognized that in order to gain meaningful influence on government policy, interacting with Welsh Assembly Government Ministers and civil servants was vital. This suggested that their voluntary basis meant they did not have the capacity to partake in informal lobbying, develop contacts with civil servants and be fully aware of the shift towards executive policy-making. Otherwise, they would have taken account of the distinction developing between the Welsh Assembly Government and the National Assembly and the increasingly limited influence to be gained through structures such as the Assembly's committees during the first term of devolution.

Cymdeithas's dependence on voluntary financial contributions meant that the society's resources were limited. The employed officer's time was spread across a number of campaigns, often related to different levels of government. Some Cymdeithas members cited the resource problem to explain that they were unprepared for devolution and had found it difficult to adapt. One member stated:

> I think it's been a matter of lack of resources to employ people that have prevented us from allocating someone to concentrate fully on the Assembly as an institution. Because there is really a tension between that sort of work and work related more generally to campaigning.[11]

Wyn Jones suggested that Cymdeithas was not adapting well to devolution and particularly to political lobbying (2002: 10). It seemed that their origins as a protest movement and financial constraints made adapting difficult.

Cymuned experienced similar capacity disadvantages in engaging in constitutional lobbying. By the end of the review, responding to government press releases and reports required a rapid response, and with limited resources this was difficult. Only a small team liaised with politicians, and two individuals on a voluntary basis undertook the technical work, developing and responding to documentation. One Cymuned member stated: 'Voluntary organisations are disadvantaged . . . We're relatively strong in terms of what we organise on the local branches level particularly in some areas. What we are lacking in are individuals at the centre able to do the complex work'.[12] The group's lack of resources and its dependence on voluntary contributions and fund-raising meant that during the Assembly's first term they employed only one part-time administrative officer and made a conscious decision not to prioritize their resources to lobbying the Assembly.[13]

The second element that Cymdeithas and Cymuned's involvement in the review highlighted was the difficulties in interacting with Assembly Members. As a result, the media was important to gain public attention and exert influence on the Assembly and Welsh Assembly Government. Overall, both groups had mixed experiences with the political parties. Both organizations benefited from connections with Plaid Cymru and particularly Dafydd Wigley. This reflected Cymdeithas's continuing links with Plaid post-devolution. This contrasted with Cymuned, which Plaid viewed suspiciously, and as a threat. Cymuned members contended that the tactical mistake was not to make sufficiently clear to Plaid their decision not to form as a political party.[14] As a result, informal contacts within the party were more important.

Cymdeithas and Cymuned had contact with the minister and deputy minister during the review, and these were important actors. Therefore both groups targeted ministerial channels. It could be argued that this was done in the context of the committee's review and they didn't partake in subsequent dialogue with ministers and civil servants to influence government policy. More broadly post-devolution, Cymdeithas continued to meet with some politicians from across the spectrum, but relations with the Conservative Party remained weak. However, Cymdeithas's commitment to civil disobedience seemed negative due to the response of a number of Labour AMs following direct action. In addition, Edwina Hart, Minister for Local Government and Housing was reluctant to meet with Cymdeithas.

Cymuned's experience also varied. Cymuned seemed to have some influence on the review as housing recommendations were included in the final report. This suggested that they presented well-researched evidence and were extremely active in lobbying when politicians were forthcoming. Their contact with Edwina Hart and relevant officials relating to housing during the same period as the review supports this. However, some AMs were openly hostile to the group with accusations that Cymuned was a racist movement.[15] These accusations were supported by the press, namely the *Welsh Mirror* (McGuiness, 2003). In addition to the difficult relationship with Plaid Cymru, some Labour Party members perceived Cymuned as extremist, as is evident in the statements of politicians during the review. This uneasy relationship with some members of the Labour Party was particularly problematic. Indeed, it reflected the negative attitude of a faction within the party towards the Welsh language. In reference to the language debate's re-emergence, Fowler remarks:

> During 2001, the political-intellectual agenda gradually slipped away, without reply, from politicians ... from academic research ... into the hands of a small, anti-interventionist, and unrepresentative wing of basically four Labour Party members in Wales; Huw Lewis (AM, Merthyr Tydfil and Rhymney); Llew Smith (MP, Blaenau Gwent); Don Touhig (MP, Islwyn) and Alun Pugh (AM, Clwyd West). (2002: 7–8)

Ron Davies emphasizes negative attitudes towards the language in the Wales Labour Party during its internal devolution debate in the 1990s. While Davies's departure from that party must be taken into account, he states:

> The bitterest opposition came from those who, for whatever reason were uncomfortable with the idea of a distinctive Welsh identity being expressed assertively and were most certainly uncomfortable with the Welsh language being seen as anything other than a cultural relic. (2003: 2)

This study has drawn attention to the effects of this minority in the Labour Party on the engagement of some organizations with the National Assembly.

Thirdly, the negative attitude of some politicians from all political parties to both groups distinctly contrasted to the experiences of other organizations post-devolution, particularly those that received state funding. As an Assembly Sponsored Public Body, the Welsh Language Board was central to the review and subsequent WAG policy. Its *Vision and Mission* document set the agenda and the board had a significant impact on the review's direction and its final recommendations (WLB, 1999). Therefore the board retained its expert position on Welsh language policy-making, similar to its situation pre-devolution. Post-devolution, the board was closely linked to the Assembly, its source of funding, and the Language Board was responsible for administering government funding.

Post-devolution, the majority of civil society organizations related to the Welsh language, around forty overall, such as Mentrau Iaith, National Eisteddfod, Mudiad Ysgolion Meithrin and Urdd Gobaith Cymru, gained Welsh Assembly Government funding via the Welsh Language Board. These organizations were better placed to influence policy-making. They had full-time staff that resulted in closer, informal and more meaningful contacts with the Welsh Assembly Government and its civil servants.[16] This meant that contributing to the committee's review was less important. They became the main implementers of *Iaith Pawb* along with the Language Board, and they received greater Assembly Government funding. Moreover, the review suggested that funding arrangements could negatively affect organizations' propensity to move outside the consensus and provide alternative ideas. At the end of August 2001, Rhodri Glyn Thomas expressed concern at the quality of submissions to the review. Betts explains: 'Some submissions have been disappointing – with some of the most important Assembly-sponsored public bodies submitting evidence which said nothing about how policies needed to be changed, instead telling members what the organisation had been doing during the past 12 months' (2002a). In addition, only three organizations, Cymdeithas, Cymuned and the Mentrau Iaith, discussed the need for a new Welsh Language Act during their presentations to the review (NAW, 2002c; 2001i). This reflected a lack of cooperation within the language movement that contrasted with the coalition-building pre-devolution over issues such as Welsh-medium schools, the education curriculum and the 1993 Welsh Language Act. A possible reason for this lack of cooperation was that some groups were reluctant to be publicly associated with Cymdeithas. Perhaps more significant is the impact of the Welsh Language Board and funding ties. It has been argued that legislation protecting the language culminating in the 1993 Welsh Language Act de-politicized the language and lessened the impetus to campaign for the language (C. H. Williams, 1998: 102). Rhodri Williams, then Chair of the Welsh Language Board stated in 1998: 'Any thought of a battle for the Welsh language is certainly over. The battle that was between Welsh-speakers and the authorities for greater provision of services in Welsh have largely been won' (Phillips, 1998b: 13). Moreover, as was the case during the review, the close relationship with the board seemed to have deterred organizations from raising alternative policy ideas. Policy networks suggested partnership between organizations, and that they shared the same policy ideas and formed a consensus around these.[17] Interrelated to this, it could be argued that the organizations did not want to threaten their funding status. One Cymdeithas member noted:

> the Welsh Language Board has created a big difference in relation to campaigns for 'Welsh' . . . It has inhibited a lot of debate and undermined the contribution that a number of bodies made in the past and has in recent years made them reluctant to make public contributions . . . These organizations are supportive in principle but they can't be publicly active due to their dependence on the Language Board for funding.[18]

Another sector that weakened Cymdeithas and Cymuned's influence on the review were private sector organizations lobbying against a new Language Act that sought to impose requirements of bilingual working practices on the private sector. Organizations including CBI Wales and FSB Wales directly lobbied the committee, lobbied through the Economic Development Committee and received support from a number of influential bodies such as the Wales Tourist Board (NAW, 2001j, 2001k).

Therefore, Cymdeithas and Cymuned's contribution to Welsh language policy-making was more limited than other organizations and they were disadvantaged compared to the main actors in the Welsh language policy network. A number of organizations in receipt of government funding had greater capacity, stronger contacts with government and could gain meaningful influence on the Welsh Assembly Government. This highlights that Cymdeithas and Cymuned were more peripheral compared with other civil society organizations with an 'inside track' to the Welsh Assembly Government. Nevertheless, in contrast to the partnership and 'insider' status that could potentially compromise the autonomy of organizations and their scrutiny ability to raise alternative ideas and be critical of government, they were amongst a minority of organizations with autonomy due to their financial situation. This provided them with the potential to discuss alternative ideas and challenge government policies.

Also the policy review raised questions regarding methods of engagement with the National Assembly and its response to more controversial groups. Initially, Cymuned undertook constitutional lobbying rather than direct action. This was influenced by an awareness of the post-devolution context and the Assembly's aims to be 'inclusive'. Members of Cymuned had been critical of Cymdeithas yr Iaith for protesting and committing direct action rather than engaging with politicians. However, the unwillingness of some AMs from all political parties to be lobbied by Cymuned frustrated their efforts. Indeed, these politicians paradoxically spurred its decision to undertake non-violent civil disobedience as a course of action where appropriate (Brooks, 2002b). A policy resolution was passed in their Annual General Meeting in 2002 that 'calls upon Cymuned to continue to campaign through constitutional and community methods at every opportunity, at national and branch level . . . non-violent civil disobedience has its appropriate place in a political system where the rights of minorities are disregarded' (Brooks, 2002b). This reflected the diversity of viewpoints in the movement on the issue including the concern of some members that civil disobedience could affect public support. Cymuned did not undertake direct action during the review, but the *Western Mail* quoted the minister's response to their decision: 'what right had an organisation which had become part of the political process, she asked, to threaten law-breaking when . . . the Assembly's culture committee review of Welsh language policies – was far from being completed' (Box 5.1) (Betts, 2002b).

Cymdeithas's dual strategy of political lobbying and civil disobedience, not to be exercised by Cymuned by 2003, raised questions whether these were complementary strategies to influence policy change. Within Cymdeithas, the effectiveness of direct action in promoting policy change by democratically elected devolved institutions received little internal questioning. It was ironic that Cymuned encountered stronger opposition from some politicians while attempting to lobby than did Cymdeithas when it committed civil disobedience. Some reasons that might explain this irony have already been discussed. Cymdeithas was well established, had greater acceptance in Plaid Cymru, but faced some opposition from across the political parties. Cymuned was newly established in the midst of a re-emergence of the language debate, and this raised uncertainty around its intentions and direction. It led to a problematic relationship with Plaid Cymru but more significantly it resulted in hostility and accusations that it was an extremist and racist movement by some factions in the Labour Party, the dominant party in government. Questions can be raised whether protest and civil disobedience were appropriate in the policy-making process post-devolution. One side would contend that devolution brought some self-governance to Wales together with a consensual style of politics that did not comfortably accommodate civil disobedience. This argument was made by an Assembly Member:

> I think the big dilemma for the protest movement now is how the protest movements specifically related to the Welsh language react to a political

---

Box 5.1: *Western Mail Report,* **20 April 2002**

<u>Campaign of civil disobedience urged</u>

THE Welsh-language pressure group Cymuned is holding its first annual general meeting today, with a debate expected on whether it should begin a campaign of civil disobedience.

So far the group has focused on a political lobbying campaign to achieve its aim of protecting the Welsh-language heartlands, including meetings with AMs and giving evidence to Assembly committees.

The leadership has consciously sought to avoid the kind of tactics employed by Cymdeithas yr Iaith Gymraeg.

But with the membership expected to vote in favour of civil disobedience it now appears that the consensus within the group has broken down and there is a move to raise the profile of the organisation.

The motion to be voted on at Harlech today reads, 'Cymuned believes that civil disobedience is justified in a political system where minorities, and the right of a minority to exist, are ignored. Bearing this in mind, the annual general meeting is of the opinion that Cymuned should be prepared to consider adopting civil disobedience when appropriate.'

If it does begin a campaign of lawbreaking it can expect to lose a great deal of political clout in Cardiff Bay.

First Minister Rhodri Morgan said, 'There is an issue that condemnation of a threat of civil disobedience, however obscure the group involved, is something that all political parties should give. I condemn it totally. It is the way to wreck the chances of the survival of the language into the twenty-first century.'

However, Cymuned founder member Simon Brooks has admitted that his policy of political lobbying has been a failure even before the Assembly publishes its long-awaited strategy on the Welsh language.

He said, 'The political class in Wales have to understand that if they want a moderate Welsh-language pressure group, and a move away from the direct action of the past forty years, they have to engage with it.

'Unless this happens I cannot credibly defend political methods.'

---

institution in Wales that has accepted responsibility for the Welsh language and where there is a government … I think that there are major questions facing the protest movement and they need to act in relation to the situation that has spawned from devolution to Wales.[19]

The language movement's counter-argument maintained that the limitations of the devolution settlement and the reluctance of some AMs to engage with groups strengthened civil disobedience's standing as a legitimate feature of any democratic polity. Cymuned's experience suggested that attempting to adapt and to work within the political structures to exert pressure on government was not always possible when 'inclusiveness' was lacking and politicians were unwilling to engage, and were indeed hostile. Brooks, one of the then leading figures of Cymuned, explained:

> The political class in Wales have to understand that if they want a moderate Welsh-language pressure group, and a move away from the direct action of the past 40 years, they have to engage with it. Unless this happens, I cannot credibly defend political methods. (*Western Mail*, 2002a)

While Cymdeithas and Cymuned's capacity to influence the Assembly and Assembly Government was limited by the number of reasons outlined above, both organizations demonstrated a potential to promote engagement and participatory norms post-devolution. A number of the features of their internal structures, such as the composition of their main decision-making bodies and broader opportunities for membership engagement in decision-making and campaigning could potentially promote bottom-up participation. Moreover, Cymdeithas promoted the engagement of young people. In its initial stages, Cymuned was active in local community activity. By spring 2004, there were some signs that the strength of dense community activity was waning, in terms of more limited numbers willing to be involved in activities such as picketing (Brooks, 2004: 2). Nevertheless, both organizations demonstrated the potential to make a specific contribution to improving the quality of democracy by incorporating groups viewed as more challenging to involve in the political process.

In addition to difficulties reflected in their interaction with the Culture Committee's review, both organizations' involvement with the Assembly was affected by the complexity of the devolution settlement. Cymdeithas and Cymuned targeted policy areas such as housing/planning where powers were divided between Westminster, the Assembly and local government. The lack of clarity in where functions and responsibilities lay put further pressure on existing capacity issues. Cymdeithas expressed this in its evidence to the Richard Commission:

> Although it [the Assembly] has powers in important fields such as education and health, these fields are only partially devolved. So in view of such a horizontal division of power, understanding the true powers of the Assembly is a very difficult task. (NAW, 2003b: 2)

Nonetheless, both organizations made the Assembly their main political target and contributed to deepening devolution. Cymdeithas and Cymuned expressed their continuing dissatisfaction with the devolution settlement and called for greater powers and for legislative advances, such as a new Welsh Language Act and a Property Act. Cymdeithas's written evidence to the Richard Commission stated: 'It is not possible for the institution to make meaningful use of those powers which it does possess, as it is expected to operate on the basis of a complex and ineffective constitutional settlement' (NAW, 2003b: 1).

Finally, examining Cymdeithas and Cymuned and the Policy Review of the Welsh Language illustrated the effects of devolution on *Welsh civil society* organizations. Devolution was envisaged as a catalyst in the development of *Welsh civil society*. Cymdeithas's situation suggested that some well-established organizations experienced difficulties in adapting to devolution. While devolution was not the central stimulant in the establishment of Cymuned, the new political context influenced its efforts at constitutional lobbying. Cymuned's greater propensity to use multiple channels to influence the Assembly's work suggested greater flexibility in the structures of an organization established post-devolution. The negative experiences of both organizations with some AMs suggested that devolution was both a deterrent and a catalyst to the development of these organizations. However, devolution increased the relevance of these *Welsh civil society* organizations. Despite their limited policy development capacities owing to their low financial base, devolution made their Wales-only policies more relevant due to increased policy-making attuned to the needs of Wales, in Wales. Examining these organizations led to identifying some of the characteristics associated with what is 'Welsh' about *Welsh civil society*. These were that organizations' policy-development capacities were located in Wales and focused on Wales; that the National Assembly was their main political target; and that organizations called for greater powers for the devolved institution.

CONCLUSION

Cymdeithas yr Iaith and Cymuned highlighted that organizations campaigning for the recognition of the Welsh language made the National Assembly their main campaigning target and attempted to engage in its work. However, in contrast to the other cases where organizations were better resourced and more professionalized, being smaller and voluntary meant that a lack of resources and financial capacity challenged their interaction with the Assembly, as did the hostile attitude of some AMs.

The Culture Committee's Policy Review of the Welsh Language and Cymdeithas yr Iaith and Cymuned's involvement highlighted a number of aspects of the dynamic between civil society and devolution. It illustrated that the committee structure of the National Assembly brought greater transparency to policy-making. As Rawlings referred to the review, 'Upward pressure and responsiveness simply unimaginable for Wales in the Westminster context; it is a very practical rendition of the new opportunities and challenges of interest-group politics post-devolution' (2003: 218). However, it also identified that as the committee was only contributing to policy development, targeting Welsh Assembly Government ministers and civil servants was essential. Cymdeithas and Cymuned's focus on the committee itself suggested that limited capacities made it difficult to be aware of shifts towards the predominance of the executive policy-making in the Assembly during the first term.

The appropriateness of Cymdeithas's dual strategy of political lobbying and civil disobedience in relation to the National Assembly was questionable due to the negative reaction of politicians. However, the opposition and, at times, open hostility of politicians from all political parties, and particularly by some members of the dominant party, directly affected Cymuned's decision to adopt the principle of civil disobedience as a means of influencing the Assembly. This paradoxical situation raised difficult questions regarding methods of engagement of these groups and demonstrated exceptions to the 'inclusiveness' of the National Assembly. The theoretical literature in Chapter 2 suggested that civil disobedience can be deemed legitimate if it is self-limiting and in response to insufficient channels for civil society to influence political society, the latter including political parties and parliaments (Cohen and Arato, 1999: 602). Wilson commented that groups would take alternative action of this type as they felt an inability to be heard by policy-makers (1990: 71).

Cymdeithas and Cymuned played a more limited role in the Welsh language policy-making network compared with a range of other organizations that received government funding and gained increased funds because of the Assembly Government's policy. They had closer relations that were potentially more exclusive with the Assembly and Assembly Government. This situation reflected the neo-corporatism literature's argument that exclusive relations develop between privileged groups and the state that can constrain the engagement of other organizations in the political system (Wilson, 1990: 69). Furthermore, during the review, those organizations that received Welsh Assembly Government funding contributed little to advancing policy ideas. This suggested that organizations did not want to threaten their close relationship with the Language Board and Welsh Assembly Government. It seemed that the Welsh language policy network created a context that minimized disagreement and differences in policy ideas, and organizations accepted the status quo. This situation also reflected the assertion in the neo-corporatist literature that partnerships lead to consensual relations with the state that threaten organizations' ability to hold the state accountable (Wilson, 1990: 69). In this context, their relative 'outsider' status did mean that Cymdeithas and Cymuned possessed greater autonomy that potentially enabled them to scrutinize government and hold government accountable. The experiences of Cymuned and Cymdeithas with some Assembly Members was somewhat reminiscent of the language movement before devolution, when Cymdeithas's relationship with the Welsh Office as an 'outsider' contrasted with organizations that received government financial support (Thomas, 1997: 327).

This chapter suggests that the experiences of both organizations contrasted with the more general experiences of civil society in post-devolution Wales. Ironically, these organizations in the area of the Welsh language, the area where the Assembly had the greatest power, faced opposition from within the Assembly. This contrasted with the partnership experiences of the other organizations examined active in devolved and non-devolved areas of power. It highlighted the degree to which the Welsh language was an issue of renewed political contention within the National Assembly and the negative attitudes in a section of the Welsh Labour Party during the first term. The further development of the Assembly's policies in relation to the language will demonstrate whether Cymdeithas and Cymuned's experiences was an exception or indicative of an uneasy relationship between the Welsh Assembly Government and protest groups for the Welsh language post-devolution.

6

Non-Devolved Redistribution:
Oxfam Cymru and Make Trade Fair

The previous two chapters discussed the engagement of civil society organizations active in policy areas previously under the remit of the Welsh Office that have been devolved to the National Assembly for Wales. The next two chapters also consider issues of redistribution and recognition, but examine civil society organizations involved in non-devolved policy areas that remained UK central government responsibility during the first term of devolution. This chapter examines Oxfam Cymru's contribution to the Oxfam International Make Trade Fair Campaign.

Foreign policy issues such as international treaty negotiations and international development fall under the remit of UK central government after devolution. Indeed, foreign affairs was one of the areas in which the National Assembly has least formal power. The Assembly's main potential to act on international matters was through Section 33 of the Government of Wales Act 1998. This states that 'the Assembly may consider, and make appropriate representations about, any matter affecting Wales' (HMSO, 1998b). This allowed the Assembly to 'operate as a voice for Wales: whether the matter is devolved or not' (Rawlings, 2003: 381). It could be argued, of course, that international policy was precisely that kind of 'high policy' area in which central government would seek to maintain its exclusive prerogatives. It would be unrealistic, in other words, to expect an enhanced role for 'regional' government. However, there stands a long tradition of civil society campaigning for peace and social justice issues in Wales, and civil society was a basis for activity on international issues in Wales. If and how civil society organizations active in this field reacted to devolution thus provides interesting pointers to the broader impact of devolution on civil society in Wales post-devolution.

One UK-wide civil society organization that forms part of the international development sector involved in Wales since the 1970s is Oxfam. This chapter examines the extent to which devolution has impacted on its presence in Wales by analysing the pre-devolution Oxfam in Wales and the post-devolution, Oxfam Cymru. In order to do this, the chapter focuses on Oxfam Cymru's role in the first year of Oxfam International's major three-year Make Trade Fair (MTF) campaign launched in April 2002. The impetus for this campaign was the increasing global disparities in wealth between North and South.

Following a relatively successful campaign to cancel the debts of some Third World states, a number of international development organizations, including Oxfam International through Make Trade Fair, targeted the rules of international trade and campaigned for greater economic redistribution to Third World states. It is fair to state that it is difficult to establish a direct link between the impact of the campaigns undertaken by any organization and policy changes by governmental or international institutions. This is exacerbated when attempting to assess Oxfam Cymru's role in a broader Oxfam International campaign. However, Oxfam Cymru's role in Make Trade Fair provides a focus for investigating what effect, if any, devolution has had on Oxfam Cymru. Make Trade Fair centred on international trading rules, state governments and international institutions that have the power to promote greater economic redistribution. It clearly targeted areas where functions were not devolved to the National Assembly. The case study therefore provides an ideal example of the extent to which devolution has impinged on a civil society organization in Wales active in a non-devolved policy area.

The first section of the chapter provides the background to Oxfam's work in Wales before devolution to identify changes in Oxfam Cymru post-devolution. The second section outlines the main features of Make Trade Fair. Oxfam Cymru's role in Make Trade Fair is then investigated. The main section of the chapter examines what the previous discussion tells us about the broader impact of devolution on Oxfam Cymru. It argues that Make Trade Fair highlights how devolution had a profound impact on Oxfam Cymru that transformed its capacities, its interaction with political structures and its identity as an organization.

CHARTING OXFAM'S PRESENCE IN WALES

This section provides some of the pre-devolution background to Oxfam Cymru and locates its development as part of Oxfam GB. Oxfam GB is currently one of the largest and best-known charities in the UK. Despite this, secondary literature on Oxfam GB is rather limited. Such literature as does exist tends to focus on Oxfam's overseas work and discusses little of its organizational and campaigning structures in the UK (Black, 1992). In this context, charting the evolution of Oxfam's presence in Wales is rather difficult.

Oxfam was established in 1942, initially as the Oxford Committee for Famine Relief, as part of the effort to counter food shortages facing European occupied countries during the Second World War (Black, 1992: 9). Oxfam's remit and work overseas expanded and by the 1960s it was recognized as a development agency. Oxfam's organizational structures in the UK have developed to promote campaigning, fund-raising and information campaigns. In 1965, the charity had twenty regional staff and 400 Oxfam groups across the UK. In Wales, without regional staff, Oxfam was dependent upon volunteers (Gwynn, 1993: 4). In 1979, a Campaigns Department was established that strengthened Oxfam's staffing structures and its ability to establish volunteer supporter networks (Black, 1992: 299). This development strengthened Oxfam's campaigning potential and increased its presence in different areas of the UK including Wales. At the end of the 1970s, a Public Affairs Unit was established in London to enhance Oxfam's lobbying capacity by fostering links with Members of Parliament, trade unions and professional bodies (Black, 1992: 206).

Oxfam has expanded beyond the UK and by 2002 there were twelve autonomous Oxfam development agencies (Oxfam International, 2002a: 271). In 1996, these joined as a confederation to establish Oxfam International (OI) (Stephen, 2001: 107). The formation of Oxfam International facilitated closer working and there is 'regular collaboration between the members and they are involved in joint campaigning, fund-raising, programme planning and lobbying activities' (Stephen, 2001: 107). This demonstrated that Oxfam, as a non-governmental organization (NGO), has the capability to be a major player on the international level.

Oxfam in Wales – Oxfam yng Nghymru

During the 1970s Oxfam employed campaigns staff in Wales. However, within Oxfam's internal organization, Wales was not treated as a single entity. For instance, north Wales was initially administered from the Chester office, then from Cardiff but later returned to Chester's administration. By the beginning of the 1990s, Oxfam's presence became known as Oxfam in Wales. This provided a more distinct Welsh identity and delineated from Oxfam in the north-west and south-west. Oxfam's regional office in Wales was based in Cardiff and campaigns officers worked in north and south Wales. However, Oxfam in Wales operated largely on the same basis as English regional offices with campaigns officers managed by the Campaigns Department in Oxford. Oxfam GB campaigns were developed and coordinated there. Where possible, organizers from Wales amended plans to suit the Welsh context in terms of targets and events within campaigns. This is demonstrated below in the case of fair trade campaigns. One distinct difference was that materials such as newsletters were bilingual: a recognition of the need to broaden Oxfam's appeal in Wales.

Oxfam began selling products from Third World producers in the 1960s. In 1992, promoting fair trade products such as coffee in Oxfam shops and supermarkets gained momentum. In Wales, a tour by a Dominican Republic coffee producer supported Oxfam's promotion efforts (Oxfam in Wales, 1992: 1). Oxfam in Wales encouraged the establishment of local groups to contribute to campaigns on fair trade. This reflected their emphasis on grassroots work within Oxfam in Wales to strengthen their local campaigning network (Oxfam in Wales, 1993: 2; Oxfam in Wales, 1992: 2). By 1994, these efforts led to the establishment of campaign groups in seven towns in Wales enabling joint action, raising the profile of campaigning issues and facilitating fund-raising through local events (Oxfam in Wales, 1994: 1). Overall, Oxfam in Wales' contact with the public sector was limited. Following local government reorganization in 1996, Oxfam contacted all local authorities requesting that they adopt fair trade policies and promote fair trade outlets but these efforts were largely unsuccessful (Oxfam in Wales, 1996a: 3).

There were other aspects to Oxfam in Wales's campaigning. It supported the annual Oxfam GB fasting event and held fund-raising activities in Wales including rugby matches. Oxfam in Wales integrated its campaigns into its attendance at national events such as National Eisteddfodau and the Royal Welsh Agricultural Show. It also produced campaigning cards to be sent to Welsh MPs (Oxfam in Wales, 1996a: 7).

Although Oxfam in Wales had good contacts with some political actors, Oxfam GB maintained overall responsibility for directly lobbying politicians. Oxfam in Wales attended party conferences in Wales and arranged fringe meetings. A novel initiative in the run-up to the 1997 General Election campaign was to sponsor a motion on global poverty at party conferences, and this gained the support of all political parties (Oxfam in Wales, 1996a: 2; 1996b: 1). Oxfam in Wales engaged informally with politicians, at both Westminster and European levels, that supported Oxfam's work raising awareness and gaining local press coverage (Oxfam in Wales, 1997: 3). Occasionally, staff and volunteers in Wales undertook more high-profile activities if government ministers visited Wales (Oxfam GB, 1997: 4). However, more extensive links had been developed by the UK level with MPs and party activists earlier in the 1990s (Oxfam GB, 1993: 4). Oxfam GB were responsible for the Constituency Contact Scheme, with support to specific individuals coming from the Wales staff. As part of the scheme, supporters in Wales actively lobbied Welsh MPs to gain support for Oxfam campaigns (Oxfam in Wales, 1997: 1). Overall, Oxfam in Wales's engagement with and lobbying of politicians was limited, as this was the remit of the Oxfam GB Parliamentary Team.

Box 6.1: Oxfam Cymru Vision Statement

<u>Oxfam Cymru vision</u>

History

In 1998 Oxfam GB decided to '*establish a stronger local identity in Wales and in Scotland in order to maximise the opportunities presented to Oxfam by political devolution*'. A thorough process that involved information gathering, consultation with Oxfam staff, volunteers, and external stakeholders in Wales, culminating in a 3-day conference at Barry was set up. This led to the 'Oxfam Cymru' initiative that began in May 2000.

Key Aspects of Oxfam Cymru Vision

Identity

Oxfam Cymru is an integral and contributing part of Oxfam GB

Oxfam Cymru is rooted and grounded in Wales and in the realities of the Welsh context

Oxfam Cymru will increasingly be recognized as a leader and contributor in Wales

Oxfam Cymru will increasingly be seen as an agency which works cooperatively with a range of strategic partners in addressing the challenges of Global and Welsh poverty

Purpose

To be an excellent communicator of Oxfam's messages, campaigns and programmes

To maximize the potential of the Welsh political, media, NGO and commercial sectors at Wales, UK, Euro and Global levels in the fight against poverty and suffering

To stimulate, attract and channel the concerns of people in Wales about poverty and suffering into effective action

To make a distinctive contribution to the developing Welsh civic nationhood which is inclusive, participatory and externally focused

Relationships

If we are to succeed in our vision we shall need to develop strong relationships in three key areas. These relationships will be the foundation for what we achieve.

1. External Wales Relationships

This is identified as the key to our developments. Our profile as Oxfam Cymru needs to be increasingly established, promoted and developed through the entire range of our activities. We need to be seen as a dynamic contributor to Welsh life through our relationships with politicians, the media, NGOs, Trade Unions, academics, target membership organisations and key partners.

2. Internal Oxfam Cymru Relationships

Given the nature and size of Wales, and of our team, it's vital that we maximize the benefits and synergies of the four dimensions of Oxfam Cymru's work.

Cooperative ways of working are essential between Trading, Development Education, UK Poverty Programme and Communications/Campaigns team.

3. Wider Oxfam Relationships
We are an integral part of Oxfam GB, which is a member of Oxfam International. This reality is to be made real in the ways we work. Certain target departments in Oxfam GB are prioritized for relationship-building. We, and they, need to identify added value ways of working together. In addition, we are building relationships with parts of Oxfam's global programme. We have unique opportunities as amongst the small Oxfam Cymru team we have people from the three Oxfam GB Operating Divisions [Trading, Marketing and International].

(Oxfam Cymru, 2001a)

The year 1998 was a turning-point for Oxfam's presence in Wales. With devolution to Scotland and Wales imminent, Oxfam GB prepared for the new political context. In 1998 Oxfam GB decided to 'establish a stronger local identity in Wales and in Scotland in order to maximise the opportunities presented to Oxfam by political devolution' (Oxfam Cymru, 2001a). A conference held in Barry brought together Oxfam staff, volunteers, external stakeholders in Wales and an input from Oxfam GB Directors to discuss how to take this forward in Wales (Oxfam Cymru, 2001a). From 1998 to 2000, gradual changes took place. A new post was created – head of Oxfam Cymru – in preparation for staff restructuring in 1999, the number of campaign staff was reduced from two to one all-Wales officer. Work continued on development education and Oxfam's poverty programme, established in 1996, was extended to Wales in 1999. Two additional posts were appointed in 2001 (policy and media officers) and a campaigns officer was appointed in 2002, to complete the restructuring of the team.

The main changes in Oxfam's structures in Wales were fully implemented in May 2000 with their rebranding as Oxfam Cymru. Oxfam Cymru's Vision Statement (Box 6.1) outlined the relationship between the different levels, 'Oxfam Cymru, firmly rooted in Wales, is an integral part of Oxfam GB and Oxfam International' (Oxfam Cymru, 2001a). At the same time, Oxfam Cymru stated it was establishing a stronger *local* identity and also acknowledged the need to recognize Wales as a nation in its structure. Furthermore, Oxfam located itself in the peace and justice movement in Wales and identified new opportunities in post-devolution Wales to work on social justice issues (Oxfam in Wales, 1999: 2).

Previously, Oxfam in Wales operated on the same basis as English regional offices and had limited autonomy. When appropriate, it adapted UK-wide campaigns to the Welsh context through its use of existing national events, engaging political actors and production of bilingual materials. Oxfam in Wales's main contribution to campaigns was its local group activity. Its contact with the public sector was limited and those contacts that existed were not utilized to their optimal advantage to affect policy change. Supporters in Wales contributed to Oxfam GB efforts to lobby politicians that supported Oxfam GB's parliamentary contacts work. The plans instigated at the establishment of devolution therefore suggested significant changes in Oxfam's presence in Wales.

THE MAKE TRADE FAIR CAMPAIGN

Over the years, Oxfam's campaigns for fair trade expanded from the initial focus on product promotion and culminated with the Make Trade Fair campaign. There was a gradual realization that tackling trade inequalities required campaigning on the policy practices of international trade itself. In Make Trade Fair, Oxfam contended that while participation in world trade had the potential to reduce poverty, the nature of the international economic system meant that inequalities between rich and poor have increased. Oxfam argued that the rules and practices of international trade needed to be reformed to assist the poor out of poverty (Oxfam International, 2002a: 6). The intellectual background to the campaign was provided by *Rigged Rules and Double Standards: Trade, Globalization and the Fight against Poverty*, an Oxfam International report. It provided Oxfam's analysis of the main difficulties facing developing countries caused by the international trading system (Oxfam International, 2002a). It described the current rules of world trade, presented Oxfam's case for change and its policy recommendations. According to Oxfam, 'The problem is not that international trade is inherently opposed to the needs and interests of the poor, but that the rules that govern it are rigged in favour of the rich' (Oxfam International, 2002a: 3).

As an overarching campaign, Make Trade Fair incorporated various aspects of Oxfam's campaign on trade issues, and over the three years of the campaign these were divided into different campaigning stages. As an Oxfam International campaign, all Oxfam agencies were involved in decision-making, and as a 'corporate priority' all members were expected to channel the majority of their resources into Make Trade Fair (Oxfam GB, 2002f). *Rigged Rules and Double Standards* explained that Oxfam's approach to the campaign was 'to work with the many organisations and individuals around the world who are already campaigning to ensure that trade makes a real difference in the fight against global poverty' (Oxfam International, 2002a: 1). The intention was to create international public action and to 'seek to build the kind of movement that has brought an end to apartheid, banned the use of landmines, and made real progress in reducing Third World debt' (Oxfam International, 2002a:1).

The first stage of Make Trade Fair focused on the dependence of the world's poorest countries on primary commodities as their main exports earnings (Oxfam International, 2002a: 11). Oxfam argued that coffee was amongst those commodities most affected by structural over-supply, and was an example of how countries have become overdependent on one commodity. It called for a commodities institution to manage global commodity markets and a new system of commodity agreements. It called on transnational corporations (TNCs) to be more socially responsible in their purchasing and the creation of a World Trade Organization (WTO) working group on trade and commodities (Oxfam International, 2002a: 170). The coffee campaign was launched in September 2002 to illustrate primary commodity dependence.

The second stage of Make Trade Fair was the dumping campaign. It drew attention to the lack of market access for developing countries as an example of unfair trade rules. It highlighted the high tariff barriers used by northern governments to restrict exports from developing countries (Oxfam International, 2002a: 3). Oxfam called for measures including a comprehensive ban on export dumping and recognition of the rights of developing countries to protect agriculture in the same way as rich countries (Oxfam International, 2002a: 120). Agricultural dumping was used to highlight the problems arising from subsidies and export dumping by rich countries.

The third stage to Make Trade Fair campaigning was labour rights. Make Trade Fair targeted transnational companies, the motors of globalization. Oxfam claimed that they have failed to spread the benefits of globalization in poor countries (Oxfam International, 2002a: 12). It recommended strengthening the International Labour Organization's (ILO) standards and state governments' adherence to these, and WTO Trade Policy Reviews to report on trade-related employment standards by TNCs (Oxfam International, 2002a: 205). Oxfam's campaign focused on women as an example of how weak employment standards affect people in poor countries.

The main target of Make Trade Fair was the World Trade Organization. Oxfam contended that the disproportionate influence of rich countries and bias in favour of large corporations in the WTO made it a 'governance system based on a dictatorship of wealth' (Oxfam International, 2002a: 15). Oxfam criticized the WTO's international trade rules and specifically the trade-related aspects of intellectual property rights (TRIPS) and General Agreement on Trade in Services (GATS). TRIPS has provided uniform implementation of WTO intellectual property rights around the world while disregarding disparities in development. In contrast, Oxfam recommended reform to accommodate different levels of development. It claimed that the GATS agreement, under which governments should provide a free market in all services, threatened developing countries and empowered TNCs (Oxfam International, 2002a: 224, 229). Oxfam called for strengthening the WTO's provisions for the differential treatment of developing countries to enable their governments to protect some sectors and regulate foreign investment (Oxfam International, 2002a: 238). Stopping Aids and the price of medicines in developing countries were the focal point for campaigning in this stage of Make Trade Fair.

In order to influence key decision-makers on policies that affect poor countries, high-level advocacy was central to Make Trade Fair. Oxfam's main channels were the OI Advocacy Office in Washington, its offices in New York and Geneva that liaised with the World Bank, the International Monetary Fund and the United Nations. In addition, the confederate parts of Oxfam influenced state governments. In the UK, the Oxfam GB Parliamentary Team targeted MPs sitting on the International Development Select Committee, and liaised with ministers and the Department for International Development. Oxfam Cymru's ability to instigate policy change was limited. Cutting out a role for Oxfam Cymru in Make Trade Fair would be challenging.

OXFAM CYMRU AND MAKE TRADE FAIR

Popular campaigning

On Make Trade Fair's international launch in April 2002, Oxfam Cymru held a 'trans-Cambrian' road show. A van with the MTF logo travelled from Bangor to Cardiff stopping in main towns and collecting signatures in support (Oxfam GB, 2002a). The launch in Wales contrasted with Oxfam GB's main launch when a big event was held in London involving a shipping container. Differences between the launches suggest that from the onset, Oxfam Cymru had some autonomy. The coffee campaign launch held on 18 September 2002 underscores this point. In contrast to the Oxfam GB launch in London, Oxfam Cymru held all-Wales launch events with coffee mornings held at Oxfam shops to highlight the fate of the coffee industry. Oxfam Cymru also extended Oxfam in Wales's practice of taking campaigns to events such as the National Eisteddfod. As part of Make Trade Fair, it attended a range of events and festivals, and this was extended further in 2003. Such activities aimed to raise public awareness of trade justice issues and gain local and national media coverage.

Oxfam Cymru was also involved in Oxfam GB efforts to gain popular support for Make Trade Fair. Oxfam GB continued to be mainly responsible for interacting with constituency contacts in Wales, through the Activists Team, supplemented with support to individuals from the Wales campaigning and policy officers. This contributed to MTF as visits to MPs were arranged in pursuit of the coffee campaign in November 2002. E-campaigning was relatively new to Oxfam. In Make Trade Fair, signing up online to the 'Big Noise' e-campaigning initiative was described as 'innovative, interactive campaigning action' and all members of Oxfam International participated (Oxfam GB, 2002f: 2). Oxfam Cymru encouraged people to sign up but 'Big Noise' mailings were sent from Oxfam GB. Oxfam Cymru was yet to use mass e-mailings to contact supporters in Wales, though it was suggested that this could be undertaken in future.

During Make Trade Fair, Oxfam Cymru attempted to expand support for its campaigns by building closer partnerships with other organizations. One campaign alliance was with the National Union of Students Wales. Oxfam Cymru's campaigns coordinator attended fresher fairs in universities and higher education colleges around Wales promoting campaigns, generating support for the 'Big Noise' and encouraging the establishment of student groups (Oxfam Cymru, 2002e). In addition, as part of its alliance programme, Oxfam Cymru was actively involved in establishing the Trade Justice Movement (TJM) Wales, a coalition of around thirty organizations including development and environmental organizations. The TJM movement in England had been established for a number of years. In Wales, early work on developing Trade Justice Movement groups centred on Cardiff, and Oxfam promoted groups in other towns and cities. Joint action with the TJM, including a Fairtrade Conference in February 2003 and the TJM week of action at the end of June 2003, contributed to Make Trade Fair.

Advocacy strategies

The second facet of Oxfam Cymru's role in Make Trade Fair was influencing policy change. One of Oxfam Cymru's successes in MTF related to Iceland, the frozen food company with its headquarters in north Wales. Through examining Jubilee 2000 debt campaign research, Oxfam Cymru discovered that Iceland was demanding a £12m debt claim from the Guyana government.[1] Oxfam approached the company and requested a meeting. TJM campaigners such as Christian Aid and the Jubilee Debt Campaign protested outside Iceland's headquarters, and its parent company, The Big Food

Group, dropped its compensation claim (*Daily Post*, 2003; Oxfam Cymru, 2003a). Oxfam's previous success, when Nestlé dropped a similar claim against the Ethiopian government, doubtless strengthened their hand. Oxfam lobbying, in conjunction with popular pressure by TJM activists, led to a successful policy change in accordance with the aims of Make Trade Fair.

Oxfam Cymru's main contribution to securing policy change in Make Trade Fair by 2003 was via its engagement with politicians. Make Trade Fair fed into Oxfam Cymru's presence at the Welsh party conferences. For example, at Plaid Cymru's conference in Colwyn Bay, a coffee cooperative leader from Guatemala participated at their fringe meeting. This was more high profile than under Oxfam in Wales. External observers remarked that this was extremely professional and effective in gaining support for Make Trade Fair.

Oxfam Cymru's advocacy strategies in Make Trade Fair targeted the National Assembly for Wales and the Welsh Assembly Government. Days after the launch of Make Trade Fair on 17 April, the 'Wales and the World' conference held in Cardiff was co-hosted by Oxfam Cymru, WWF Cymru and the Assembly. Its purpose was to discuss Wales's response to the World Summit on Sustainable Development held in Johannesburg in August/September 2002. Amongst the 300 delegates were Assembly Minister Sue Essex and First Minister Rhodri Morgan. Furthermore, Oxfam briefed Rhodri Morgan before the Johannesburg Summit where he called for trade reform that supported Oxfam's aims. In Johannesburg, he also visited an Oxfam partner's treatment action campaign for Aids. In addition, Oxfam cooperated with the Welsh Assembly Government and called for establishing a global network of devolved government regions on sustainable development. The Welsh Assembly Government became the co-founding member of the international Network of Regional Governments for Sustainable Development (NRG4SD).

In their interaction with the Assembly, Oxfam Cymru developed advocacy strategies relating to Make Trade Fair campaigns. Milk was identified as the most relevant case to Wales in the dumping campaign. In a presentation to the Assembly's Agriculture Committee, Oxfam Cymru discussed the impact of dumping on the international dairy industry. Moreover, it received an assurance from the Agriculture Minister that Common Agricultural Policy (CAP) reform would be raised when opportunities arose. Furthermore, it had contact with the Assembly's Sustainable Development Unit on these issues and made representations in conjunction with the Farmers Union of Wales (FUW) to key Assembly Government civil servants and ministers.

A number of policy recommendations concerning Make Trade Fair were included in *A Call for an Outward Looking Wales*, a manifesto proposal for the National Assembly for Wales 2003 election. The manifesto compiled by Oxfam Cymru on behalf of a coalition of twenty-four organizations was launched with Assembly cross-party support. It called on the Assembly to act on domestic and international issues (Oxfam Cymru, 2003a). First, regarding the dumping campaign, it called on the Assembly Government to use its influence in the European Union to urgently reform the CAP (Oxfam Cymru, 2003b: 2). Secondly, it called for the Assembly Government to fund a Wales fair trade development officer to assist Wales in becoming the first fair trade country (Oxfam Cymru, 2003b: 1). The Welsh Assembly Government made a commitment to becoming a fair trade country and its Sustainable Development Action Plan published in 2004 stated they would work with partners to develop proposals to achieve this aim over the following two years (Welsh Assembly Government, 2004b: 21). Thirdly, it requested the insertion of a number of ethical and environmental require-ments in the Assembly's Voluntary Procurement Code on supplying fair trade goods, working standards and environmentally sustainable alterna-tives (Oxfam Cymru, 2003b: 1). Finally, it called on the Welsh Assembly Government to make a commitment to an all-Wales strategy to improve the working conditions and profile of home workers in Wales (Oxfam Cymru, 2003b: 2). While home working was a serious problem in poor countries, a report commissioned by the UK Poverty Programme also identified its relevance in Wales (Oxfam GB, 2002c). After inviting the National Group on Homeworkers to brief Assembly Members and gaining the support of AMs such as Dafydd Wigley to lobby Edwina Hart, Oxfam Cymru succeeded in ensuring Assembly Government part-funding for the two-year Wales Homeworking Project (NAW, 2003c).[2]

As a global campaign, Make Trade Fair was decided according to Oxfam International priorities. This offered little flexibility for Oxfam Cymru. Nevertheless, through a combination of popular campaigning and effective advocacy work, Oxfam Cymru succeeded in making a contribution to Oxfam GB's role in Make Trade Fair. It used different channels to generate popular support for Make Trade Fair. Most significant were its strategies which successfully targeted the National Assembly and in particular the Welsh Assembly Government to attempt to influence other levels of government and to make commitments and take action in areas that formed part of Make Trade Fair.

OXFAM CYMRU POST-DEVOLUTION

Considering the capacities of Oxfam in Wales before devolution, Oxfam Cymru's involvement in Make Trade Fair suggests a transformation in Oxfam's presence in Wales.

First, Oxfam Cymru made its greatest contribution to Make Trade Fair through its interaction with the National Assembly and particularly the Welsh Assembly Government. This reflected Oxfam Cymru's extensive engagement with devolved government structures during the first term of devolution. One reason for this was the accessibility of the Assembly's structures, evident in the opportunities to make presentations to committees as part of Make Trade Fair. Oxfam Cymru's interaction with the Welsh Assembly Government complemented Oxfam GB's work. It encouraged government politicians to use party channels and intergovernmental relations to influence UK Government and European Union-level policy, for example on CAP reform. Oxfam Cymru's influence on Rhodri Morgan's contribution to the World Summit in Johannesburg demonstrated that Oxfam Cymru's unprecedented access allowed it to directly influence his agenda at this international level. These opportunities did not exist in Wales before devolution and were more open than at the UK level due to the potential for greater access to high-level politicians and a deeper emphasis on personal relationships in Wales. One officer stated that 'devolution has given us other opportunities not just specifically Welsh ones and generally push the issue quite hard and get more access than on a parliamentary level'.[3] Further evidence is that an Oxfam Cymru official had the opportunity to question Tony Blair on his visit to the Assembly during the Afghanistan war. Referring to influencing politicians during the Johannesburg Summit, an Oxfam GB officer stated:

> We went to the Earth Summit in Johannesburg in August and whereas we had quite a lot of difficulty in getting access to some of the world leaders that we wanted to get to, Oxfam Cymru were able to influence Rhodri Morgan quite successfully . . . and were able to get him to do stuff for us in Johannesburg which we wouldn't have been able to get ourselves, to get access that we couldn't get.[4]

Moreover, Oxfam Cymru's extensive interaction with the Assembly contrasted with the more limited involvement of other organizations in this study including those in devolved areas of power.

Oxfam Cymru's contribution to Make Trade Fair was facilitated by its increased capacity since devolution. This enabled it to take advantage of the opportunities afforded by devolution and to build on Oxfam GB's lobbying experience at Westminster and EU levels. Its staffing structure positively affected Oxfam Cymru's contribution to Make Trade Fair. The campaigns coordinator could focus strategically on the campaigning aspects of Make Trade Fair. Other officers in their expert areas interacted with the media in Wales, raised the profile of Oxfam Cymru and engaged with Welsh politicians. The importance of contacts with the Welsh Assembly

Government to Oxfam Cymru's input to Make Trade Fair reflected the vital appointment of a policy officer in 2001 dedicated to liaising with the Assembly. It improved Oxfam Cymru's political lobbying and development of a political strategy. The new staffing structure, adopted as part of the restructuring in 2000, demonstrated Oxfam's foresight at the outset of devolution and commitment to take advantage of the new opportunities. As one Oxfam Cymru officer stated, 'Oxfam GB are taking us seriously . . . We've got more people in the team, Oxfam GB have made more resources available to us . . . So they're giving us the tools to do the job we're here to do.'[5] Make Trade Fair illustrated how this structure provided Oxfam Cymru with a professionalized campaigning and lobbying capacity to make an impact in Wales and in international campaigns. This contrasted with more poorly resourced organizations within civil society generally that were less well equipped to interact with the Assembly post-devolution.

Secondly, Make Trade Fair provided clear evidence of the strategic role that Oxfam Cymru developed during the first term as a result of formal and informal access to the Assembly Government. These more exclusive channels were vital to gaining influence. Most significantly, the head of Oxfam Cymru formally participated on the Voluntary Sector Partnership Council as the representative of the international development sector. This provided high-level access to ministerial politicians and senior policy advisers. Referring to the Partnership Council, an Oxfam Cymru officer made the following revealing comment:

> That's a position of influence. You get to meet people, you get to know who they are, not just politicians but senior policy advisers. As part of the Partnership Council and the Voluntary Sector Scheme there is an established pattern of ministerial meetings that take place every year.[6]

Oxfam's alliances with organizations such as the Wales Council for Voluntary Action and key development organizations such as the Welsh Centre for International Affairs was central in gaining its position on the council, reflecting strategic alliances that Oxfam developed within civil society in Wales post-devolution. In sum, Oxfam Cymru established itself as the main international development organization with regard to liaison with the Welsh Assembly Government and as a representative of the sector in Wales. It worked in partnership with the Assembly on devolved issues, such as receiving WAG co-funding to develop projects for homeworkers in Wales and incorporated non-devolved areas into its interaction with the Assembly. Therefore, despite its predominant involvement in non-devolved issues, Oxfam's interaction with the political process was transformed as a result of devolution. According to an officer, the most effective channels of influence were 'the personal relationships that we've got with the politicians and the policy advisers. Because in a sense it very much isn't Westminster and the way you use the structures are dependent on good personal relationships.'[7]

Thirdly, Make Trade Fair illustrated the weakened situation of Oxfam Cymru's campaigns base. The strength of Oxfam in Wales's campaigns revolved around the activities of members in localized areas. This activity diminished, and Make Trade Fair illustrated Oxfam Cymru's development of an alternative campaigns base, in particular fostering partnerships with Oxfam shops and alliance-building.[8] One of the reasons for developing these alternative campaign structures was Oxfam Cymru's low base of activists in Wales compared with the size of the movement. Large-scale events such as the van travelling across Wales to launch Make Trade Fair compensated for limited numbers of activists. One interviewee remarked on the launch: 'it was quite spectacular and quite ambitious but at the same time it didn't require us to have that many bums on seats, people on the ground'.[9] In contrast with the pre-devolution period, 'there's more activity across a wider area but of course the downside is the level of activity in what were previously areas of very high activity has come down as well'.[10] Oxfam Cymru therefore faced the costs of decreased local activity, limiting bottom-up opportunities, and gained the advantage of greater all-Wales activity as a result of the new constitutional arrangements.

Considering Oxfam's international reputation and its abilities in high-level advocacy during the first term of devolution, it might be expected that developing its supporter base would not be a priority. Oxfam had a strong structure of individual supporters that participated in campaigns via the Constituency Contact Scheme, Activist Team, e-campaigning and the provision of financial support. Essentially, Oxfam GB was responsible for these. However, Oxfam Cymru's structures for promoting active participation in decision-making on policy issues were limited. One Oxfam supporter remarked: 'There's no groups for people to come together to cooperate and support each other. They've been focusing on a structure of individuals lobbying and groups haven't been important to them.'[11] Make Trade Fair's priorities were determined globally by OI, and campaigning decisions were taken within Oxfam GB. Where space for differentiation existed in the campaign, Oxfam Cymru staff decided. Overall, this reflected the top-down structures of decision-making within Oxfam as a whole. Supporter engagement opportunities identified were bi-annual Oxfam Volunteer Forums in north and south Wales and Oxfam Cymru's nomination of four supporters to attend the Oxfam GB Assembly every eighteen months (Oxfam GB, 2002e). Therefore, while its structures for supporter campaigning were, as part of Oxfam GB's campaigning structures, relatively solid, there was less scope for supporters to participate directly in decision-making on policy objectives and campaigns. To a degree, this was inevitable as Oxfam was an international organization that worked to address international issues and priorities. It must be acknowledged that Oxfam's activities did promote participation – its gender-participatory projects and its work with Anti-Poverty Network Cymru and in promoting global citizenship education in schools promoted participation and targeted exclusion. Nevertheless groups and structures that promoted a 'bottom-up' approach could enhance Oxfam's campaigns and promote greater participation.

Fourthly, Oxfam Cymru's contribution to Make Trade Fair highlighted its recognition of the Assembly's potential as an important political voice on non-devolved issues. This spurred Oxfam to highlight limitations to the Assembly's powers and expressed interest in greater devolved powers for the Assembly. Oxfam Cymru's ability to gain Assembly and Welsh Assembly Government support in Make Trade Fair reflected how Oxfam as a whole benefited from devolution, regardless of the Assembly's limited remit in international affairs. Oxfam targeted Assembly Members for support:

> They will often act as spokespeople for us, they might not be able to make policy change in the Assembly on issues but they will speak on the media, and they will speak within their party structures and in the Assembly on these issues.[12]

The commitment of the majority of Assembly politicians to peace and international social justice issues was evident in the all-party group on International Development that was coordinated by Oxfam Cymru's political officer. Paradoxically perhaps, the lack of clarity surrounding the Assembly's powers broadened Oxfam's lobbying opportunities. A specific example was Oxfam's encouragement for Assembly Members to make Statements of Opinion (Section 33 of GoWA) to support Oxfam campaigns. Of greater significance, where words were supported by actions, was Oxfam's lobbying of the Welsh Assembly Government to use its influence within party structures and other levels of government. The Welsh Assembly Government under the leadership of Rhodri Morgan was keen to have a greater voice on international issues and the lack of clarity surrounding its powers enabled it to engage and support the campaigns of organizations involved in international issues.

In order to build on its successes during the first term, Oxfam Cymru has supported increased powers for the Assembly. The reasons for this are apparent from the comments of one officer: 'it's very empowering working in civil society in Wales although obviously the restrictions of powers under the Assembly kind of hold that back to a level, but it does give us much greater voice and ability to interact with decision-makers'.[13] Greater powers would expand opportunities to raise political issues within political institutions and party structures, make campaigns more relevant to Wales and increase its contribution to Oxfam campaigns. Formally, Oxfam Cymru expressly supported a greater international voice for the Assembly. In launching *A Call for an Outward Looking Wales*, its policy officer argued that such a development was crucial to the success of the Assembly: 'Wales must have a greater impact in the world . . . unless the Government of Wales involves itself in global issues, its plans are doomed to fail' (Oxfam Cymru, 2003a). In interviews, the attitude of some Oxfam staff was clearer:

> It's frustrating that they [the Assembly] don't have more devolved powers . . . that's the biggest hindrance. You have the feeling that if as Welsh politicians within Wales with an international remit, they would be saying much more radical things and speaking much more in terms of global social justice issues.[14]

Another stated: 'I think as an organisation, whilst we're not a political organisation, we've seen the benefits of devolution and I think we'd be pleased if the Assembly had more powers.'[15] Therefore, it has called for a more international agenda for the Assembly, thus implying further powers for the institution. One interviewee spoke of Oxfam's contribution in the following terms: 'Part of our mission is to help devolution along, not in the political sense, but to create an outward looking Wales.'[16]

Finally, Oxfam Cymru's role in Make Trade Fair reflected how devolution shifted Oxfam Cymru towards a stronger sense of *Welsh civil society* and also paradoxically affirmed its *civil society in Wales* characteristics. The changes surrounding Oxfam Cymru strengthened liaison with Oxfam GB. Make Trade Fair illustrated Oxfam Cymru's stronger coordination with departments in Oxfam GB and the increased formal and semi-formal con nections since devolution. For example, cooperation and information-sharing on advocacy strategies between the Parliamentary Team and the policy officer in Oxfam Cymru increased. This was rather surprising, considering that changes in Oxfam Cymru's management structures afforded it a greater status within Oxfam GB's structures. The head of Oxfam Cymru (previously Regional Campaigns Manager) was now managed by the Deputy Director of Oxfam GB. The line management of this post at a directorate level was therefore more strategic. Following changes in mid-2003 in Oxfam GB structures, the head of Oxfam Cymru became managed by Oxfam GB's Director of Campaigns and Policy.

From Oxfam Cymru's inception, integrating into Oxfam GB's work was viewed as a means to increase the effectiveness of campaigns and promote greater awareness of Oxfam Cymru. Continuing *civil society in Wales* characteristics were evident in Oxfam Cymru, as it was 'firmly rooted in

Wales, is an integral part of Oxfam GB and Oxfam International' (Oxfam in Wales, 1999).

Paradoxically, Oxfam Cymru's integration into Oxfam GB's work sat with the greater Welsh outlook it developed that reflected *Welsh civil society* characteristics. This was evident in Make Trade Fair when opportunities existed for flexibility in campaigning and Oxfam Cymru's approach differed from those of other UK regions. This included different campaigning events, the use of Oxfam shops in campaigns, greater bilingual materials (Oxfam Cymru, 2000). With Make Trade Fair, Oxfam Cymru became more responsive to the Welsh context, and its increased capacity facilitated developing policies and campaigns for Wales in Wales. Again, the focus on the National Assembly as their main political target and the manifesto for the Assembly Elections 2003 were strong examples of Oxfam Cymru's capacity to attempt to influence the domestic Welsh agenda. Oxfam GB supported these developments, evident in Oxfam Cymru's status, since 2000, as a small-nation programme rather than a regional office. These changes reflected a shift towards *Welsh civil society* and highlighted that devolution was the main factor in promoting this greater Welsh outlook. The previous title, Oxfam in Wales, suggested a UK organization in Wales. Oxfam Cymru was a strong rebranding statement that promoted greater Welsh values within the organization. As one interviewee stated: 'we had to be seen as a Welsh institution within the institutional life of Wales'.[17] Therefore while some *civil society in Wales* roots remained evident, Oxfam Cymru has located itself as part of *Welsh civil society* as an organization intent on 'making a distinctive contribution to the creation of a Wales with a strong sense of civic nationhood that is inclusive, participatory and externally focused' (Oxfam Cymru, 2001a).

CONCLUSION

the big idea being that we're a Welsh organisation, that we're here to take advantage of devolution, that is the reason why we're bigger than Oxfam in the south-west of England even though population-wise we are smaller than the London region.[18]

This chapter has examined the evolution of Oxfam's presence in Wales from its pre-devolution existence to the robust organization developed during the first term of devolution. Make Trade Fair demonstrated that even when considering an international Oxfam campaign that was distinctly non-devolved, Oxfam Cymru was able to make an effective contribution. The key feature of Oxfam Cymru's ability to contribute to Make Trade Fair were opportunities provided by political devolution to Wales and the consequent changes in Oxfam's presence in Wales.

The strategic review in 1998 encouraged Oxfam GB to take devolution seriously, and it committed resources to ensure that Oxfam Cymru could be a major player in the civil society of post-devolution Wales. As a result, while other organizations within civil society continued to be poorly resourced, its new professionalized staffing structure transformed its capacities to take advantage of the opportunities provided by devolution. Oxfam Cymru's engagement with the Assembly's structures was extensive and it developed more exclusive relations than some organizations due to its high-level access with Welsh Assembly Government ministers and civil servants. Indeed, it was viewed as the main international development organization and an important partner of the Assembly. Oxfam Cymru viewed the Assembly as an important political voice on non-devolved issues. It was strongly supported due to its contribution to the Assembly's work and because of the Assembly's own aims for greater powers on these issues. The achievements of the first term of devolution implied that Oxfam Cymru would welcome greater powers for the Assembly.

'Oxfam in Wales' in pre-devolution Wales characterized the organization as *civil society in Wales*, a UK-wide organization based in Wales. Oxfam Cymru strengthened its relations with Oxfam GB but also developed a greater Welsh outlook. This suggested a duality in Oxfam Cymru's situation in continuing to be an integral part of Oxfam GB but also being rooted in Wales: 'we hold those two things in tension and it is a question of holding them in tension'.[19] The rebranding as Oxfam Cymru and its work during the first term of devolution suggested that despite this duality, it developed as it intended. It established itself as a Welsh organization in the institutional life of Wales, 'an organisation which is part of Welsh Civil Society ... working for Social Justice and the overcoming of poverty on the international stage' (Oxfam in Wales, 1999: 2). All this serves to underline the effects of devolution in changing the context within which organizations operate, boosting the 'Welshness' of organizations, regardless of whether they are predominantly involved in devolved issues. The effects on Oxfam Cymru is therefore a particularly significant finding, considering its predominant emphasis on a non-devolved policy area.

7

Non-Devolved Recognition: Stonewall Cymru and Section 28

Chapter 5 examined civil society organizations engaged with the National Assembly which were concerned with the devolved issue of recognition for the Welsh language. Thus it examined the sector of civil society most actively involved in identity politics in Wales. In contrast, here we focus on issues of recognition that remain non-devolved, namely the recognition of sexual orientation, an element of the politics of identity that had a relatively low profile amongst the organizations of civil society in Wales before devolution.

As with a large amount of equality of opportunity legislation applying to Wales, the main responsibilities and functions relating to sexual orientation remain with Westminster following devolution (Chaney and Fevre, 2002b: 5).[1] Many contend that lesbian, gay and bisexual (LGB) people have been subject to legislative discrimination. Section 28 of the Local Government Act 1986, amended in 1988, was widely cited as a key example. It prohibited local authorities from intentionally 'promoting homosexuality', or promoting the view that homosexuality was acceptable as a 'pretended family relationship' in teaching (HMSO, 1988). In effect, some argue that Section 28 legitimized and institutionalized homophobia: 'clause 28 placed the principle that homosexuality was socially undesirable and inherently inferior to heterosexuality on the statute book in an explicit form for the first time' (Jeffrey-Poulter, 1991: 236–7).

Organizations campaigning to ensure recognition of sexual orientation were weak in pre-devolution Wales. In part, this was a reflection of the general weakness of LGB groups throughout the UK as a whole, with the exception of a few metropolitan centres. Since 1989, the year following the introduction of Section 28, one increasingly high-profile lobbying organization for lesbian, gay and bisexual rights in the UK was Stonewall.

This chapter focuses on the involvement of Stonewall Cymru (initially Lesbian, Gay and Bisexual Forum Cymru/Stonewall Cymru), established in 2001, in issues surrounding Section 28.[2] Section 28 was a non-devolved issue where the Assembly had no power of repeal. On its third attempt, the Labour government succeeded in repealing Section 28 in Westminster as part of the Local Government Act 2003. This provided a key setting to assess whether devolution affected an organization in Wales concerned with non-devolved issues of recognition. Moreover, Stonewall Cymru's part-funding from the Assembly made it the first government-sponsored LGB organization in the UK, even though issues of sexual orientation remained largely non-devolved. It is therefore a particularly interesting example of the Assembly's efforts to achieve 'inclusiveness' and of the impact of funding on civil society–state relations. In addition, the dual influence of the Assembly and Stonewall on Stonewall Cymru raises interesting questions regarding Stonewall Cymru's autonomy and identity post-devolution.

Here we firstly examine LGB organizations before devolution in order to develop a comparison with LGB groups post-devolution. The second section establishes the context for examining Stonewall Cymru's involvement in issues surrounding Section 28. The following section investigates Stonewall Cymru's attempts to influence issues surrounding Section 28. The final section draws on the preceding discussion in order to make clear what this illustrates of the impact of devolution on Stonewall Cymru. It highlights the centrality of Stonewall Cymru's status as an Assembly consultative body in providing it with unprecedented levels of access to the Assembly and Assembly Government and the potential effects of the Assembly and Stonewall's funding on its independence and identity post-devolution.

THE LESBIAN, GAY AND BISEXUAL (LGB) MOVEMENT BEFORE DEVOLUTION

This section examines LGB organizations in the pre-devolution period in order to provide a comparison by which to examine Stonewall Cymru post-devolution. It firstly contextualizes LGB groups in Wales within the broader UK situation and discusses Stonewall's establishment. Then, it examines LGB groups in Wales before devolution and it identifies that their small size, funding difficulties, a lack of networks and their non-engagement with governmental structures were the main factors that explained the weaknesses. Finally, the key processes that contributed to founding LGB Forum Cymru in 2001 and its main structures are outlined.

Section 28 and Stonewall

According to Wise:

> Of the major 'new social movements' working for civil rights from the end of the Second World War on in the UK, the lesbian and gay movement has been

the least successful in terms of influencing and establishing change at the social policy and statutory levels. (2000: 1–2)

However, the progress of Clause 28 through Parliament suggested that a significant change was in the offing. 'Stop the clause' campaigns were established and campaigning groups, including more militant direct action groups, sprang up across the UK (D. T. Evans, 1995: 113). Indeed analysts suggest: 'Never had there been such a proliferation of lesbian and gay activities simultaneously and nationwide' (Stacey, 1991: 301). In the absence of an organization representing LGB interests, the introduction of Clause 28 had largely caught the LGB population unaware. The ease by which the clause became legislation also suggested that the 'community' could not depend on political parties to fight their cause (Healey, 1994). Overall, 'the new threats highlighted by Section 28 . . . was encouraging the emergence of alternative campaigning initiatives' (Jeffrey-Poulter, 1991: 245).

As other organizations lost momentum, Stonewall was established in May 1989. It aimed for legal equality and social justice for lesbians, gay men and bisexual people. It was founded as a professional parliamentary and legal lobbying non-partisan organization that was funded by individual donors. It intended to monitor gay and lesbian issues in legislation and establish an all-party parliamentary working group to liaise with sympathetic politicians (Jeffrey-Poulter, 1991: 245–6). It filled the vacuum where no lobbying group had existed to represent LGB interests in the context of Clause 28. Stonewall was run by a self-selecting management committee. It was not a membership organization, neither did it claim to represent the 'community'. This meant that Stonewall determined its own agenda and did not have to be accountable to its supporters. Jeffrey-Poulter argues:

> By rejecting the need for mass membership and keeping decision-making in the hands of a small elite committee containing essential expertise, Stonewall has built in a safeguard against the debilitating factional infighting which has damaged and restrained almost every other gay campaigning organisation. (1991: 256)

By the 1990s, Stonewall was the main pro-gay lobby organization and it had developed highly professional lobbying capabilities.

Labour's accession to power in 1997 led to optimism amongst the LGB 'community' due to the cooperation that had taken place with Labour in opposition (Wise, 2000). Stonewall launched its 'Equality 2000' campaign in 1997 that targeted five areas of discrimination and aimed to achieve change by 2000 (Wise, 2000: 2). Stonewall played a key campaigning role in cases where legislative changes enacted under Labour have given greater recognition to sexual orientation. These included removing the ban on lesbians and gay men in the armed forces, changes in immigration rights for same-sex partners, and a reduction in the age of consent through the Sexual Offences (Amendment) Act 2000 to bring it in line with heterosexuals. Stonewall's campaigning methods expanded to include greater grassroots involvement, for instance engaging with MPs to support lobbying (Palmer, 1995: 36).

LGB issues in Wales before devolution

Many parallels can be identified between Wales and the UK situation in the nature and development of LGB organizations. Though some activity related to LGB issues in Wales such as helplines commenced at the end of the 1970s, most activity developed during the 1980s and 1990s. Section 28 politicized the LGB movement in Wales and activity increased. Individuals from Wales participated in UK-wide rallies and Aberystwyth was the location of a protest against Section 28.

One of the effects of Section 28 was the establishment of Cylch (Cymdeithas Y Lesbiaid a Hoywon Cymraeg eu Hiaith: *Association of Welsh-speaking Lesbians and Gays*) in 1990. Cylch mostly centred on Aberystwyth but operated on an all-Wales basis with local groups, for example in Bangor and Lampeter, and it depended on its membership for funding. The organization's key political aims were to secure the status of the Welsh language within the gay and lesbian scene and to ensure the place of lesbians and gay men amongst Welsh-speakers. Consequently, it undertook high-profile campaigning and targeted organizations such as the Evangelical movement and Cymdeithas yr Iaith. In terms of the public sector, Cylch contacted county councils to inquire whether sexual orientation was included in their equal opportunities policies. Their campaigning methods included public action that gained substantial media attention, publishing a magazine and pamphlets, and having a stall at the National Eisteddfod. Cylch came to an end in 1996/7 and a member reflected that its openness was part of the reason for this: 'We'd pretty much gone to the extreme in terms of being open. In hindsight, it wasn't an impetus for new people to join the organization.'[3]

LGB Forum Cymru has regarded Cylch as the only all-Wales organization that was established before devolution. However, a diversity of LGB groups was active around Wales and some common characteristics can be identified. Organizations were predominantly small, operating in specific geographical areas within Wales. They tended to be support services rather than tackling discrimination more broadly: for instance, support groups for young gay people; for parents of gay people; help lines; health issues; housing issues (North Wales Lesbian Line, 2001). Activity was more dense in urban areas such as Cardiff, but in other areas such as Dyfed no organizational activity or support services existed. Groups also experienced funding difficulties and depended on internal donations. For example, in 2001 half of the help-lines had no funding and around 75 per cent of other organizations had well below £10,000 turnover.[4] Furthermore, there was very little contact or networks between organizations. One Stonewall Cymru member explained that 'There is very little communication between LGB groups themselves in regions or across Wales and very little communication between the LGB groups and other equality groups, or the general community.'[5] The 'hidden' aspect to sexual orientation contrasts with most civil society organizations. Compared with those covered by other equality organizations, the LGB 'community' is not visibly identifiable, nor does homophobia encourage openness: 'LGB communities and groups need to make it possible for people to access them so that they can deal with their sexual orientation. But there is also a guarded element in it because we have great fear of discrimination and homophobia.'[6] Before devolution, there was little interaction between LGB groups in Wales and governmental structures. Cylch's interaction with local government was a rare example. Avenues for engagement were lacking, and groups tended to distrust governmental structures and had low expectations of what could be achieved if they did engage. This reflected the experiences of other equality campaigners:

> Women, disabled people, members of ethnic minority communities and other groups have faced longstanding patterns of inequality. These have been compounded by the marginalisation of these groups from formal decision-making structures, and notably, government in Wales. (Chaney & Fevre, 2002b: 4)

As an academic explained that to the Welsh Office, LGB issues were 'not on the radar screen'.[7]

Establishing LGB Forum Cymru

The situation of LGB groups in Wales before devolution meant that the resources, networks and capacity necessary for an all-Wales LGB organization to engage with the National Assembly were lacking. However, a number of processes contributed to LGB Forum Cymru's establishment in August 2001. Greater interaction within the LGB community in Wales since 1997 created an awareness of the benefits of joint working. Initially, this resulted from the establishment of LGB police liaison groups post-1997. LGB groups worked with police authorities to establish lesbian and gay policing initiatives as the police conformed to requirements set by the Home Office to address diversity issues. All-Wales conferences on homophobia held in Cardiff in three consecutive years pushed cooperation between groups further and were an impetus to form an all-Wales political group on LGB issues. One Stonewall Cymru member explained:

> once the Labour Party came into power in 1997, there was quite a momentum in the north to try to form some structure between the lesbian and gay communities due to the requirement to work with the police. Through that work I realized that there was a space for a structure throughout Wales to get lesbian and gay people together to cooperate.[8]

Devolution meant that organizations realized the potential for engaging with the National Assembly and groups contacted Edwina Hart as Chair of the Equality of Opportunity Committee regarding recognition of sexual orientation (NAW, 2000e). From the outset, the committee was clear that it intended to consider all equality issues including sexual orientation and required an organization with which to consult.[9] At the same time, it was aware that current LGB structures were inadequate and was receptive to promoting capacity-building in order to facilitate developments towards an all-Wales organization with which it could consult. In this context Stonewall was keen to influence the National Assembly. A Stonewall Scotland office established in Glasgow in April 2000 had allowed it to influence the Scottish Parliament. In terms of the Assembly, Stonewall's executive director made representations to the Equality of Opportunity Committee (NAW, 2000f; 2000i).

These factors overlapped and members of groups in Wales approached Stonewall about establishing a branch in Wales. Consultative meetings were organized with Stonewall's support. The Assembly's Equality Unit became involved, and the Equality of Opportunity Committee and its minister supported establishing LGB Forum Cymru. It was decided that LGB Forum Cymru would work in partnership with Stonewall with shared financing between the Assembly and Stonewall (LGB Forum Cymru, 2002a).[10] In February 2001, a steering group was established composed of members of different groups and observer status was granted to other institutions.[11]

LGB Forum Cymru was officially launched in August 2001. In January 2002, two part-time officers were appointed. One political development worker based in Cardiff was charged with engaging with the National Assembly and acted as coordinator of Stonewall Cymru. A community development worker was based in Bangor and was coordinator of LGB Forum Cymru. At its inaugural conference in April 2002, an Executive Committee was elected by the membership of LGB Forum Cymru. This main decision-making body was charged with determining the overall strategic direction of the organization. A chair and a deputy chair were appointed. In voting for the Executive Committee (subsequently Stonewall

Cymru Council), members were encouraged to ensure that the committee's composition reflected and incorporated the diversity of the LGB 'community' in Wales. The ballot paper stated: 'We ask you to bear in mind that LGB Forum Cymru seeks to ensure inclusion and encourages: regional representation, cross-party representation, gender parity, minority communities representation, Welsh language representation, professional association and trade union representation' (LGB Forum Cymru, 2003). In addition, to further promote diversity, 75 per cent of the Council were elected members and 25 per cent were co-opted without voting rights. In terms of the interrelationship with Stonewall, a member of the LGB Forum Cymru Executive Committee was on Stonewall's Executive Board, and staff in Wales were line-managed by Stonewall in London. In April 2003, the organization's name was changed from LGB Forum Cymru to Stonewall Cymru.

SECTION 28

Stonewall Cymru's activity around Section 28 is examined in two ways: first, we consider the Section 28 legislation and identify how subsequent legislation has affected its status and narrowed its remit. Secondly, we focus on the successful repeal of Section 28 through the Local Government Bill 2003. It is worth noting that the Scottish Parliament repealed Section 2A (the Scottish equivalent) through the Ethical Standards in Public Life Act 2000 in June 2000 (Stonewall, 2003a: 1). For England and Wales, previous Labour government attempts to repeal Section 28 as part of the Local Government Bill (1999) and the Learning and Skills Bill (2000) were unsuccessful (see Wise, 2000; Waites, 2001).

Clause 28 was introduced as an amendment to the Local Government Bill in December 1987 and was supported by the Conservative government. Consequently, Section 28 of the Local Government Act 1988 inserted a new section 2A to the Local Government Act 1986 under 'prohibition on promoting homosexuality by teaching or publishing material'. It states that:

2A (1) A local authority shall not –
a) intentionally promote homosexuality or publish material with the intention of promoting homosexuality;
b) promote the teaching in any maintained school of the acceptability of homosexuality as a pretended family relationship. (HMSO, 1988)

One of the main concerns with Section 28 was the lack of clarity created by the legislation. It was widely believed that it led to confusion in schools about discussion of sex education, sexuality and addressing homophobia.

While Section 28 aimed to control sex education in schools, it applied directly to local authorities. The Conservative government reiterated the point in subsequent legislation. As a result of the Education Act 1993, guidance was published in 1994 on sex education in schools. It emphasized that Section 28 did not apply directly to schools. Responsibility for sex education was transferred to the governing body of a school itself (Waites, 2001: 497). As a result, Section 28 had less direct implications for sex education in schools than previously was the case.

Under Labour, the Learning and Skills Act 2000 regulated sex education and as a result influenced issues surrounding Section 28. It clarified that local authorities were not responsible for sex education and that the Secretary of State was under statutory duty to issue guidance on sex and relationship education. This was to ensure that pupils 'are protected from teaching and materials which are inappropriate having regard to the age and the religious and cultural background of the pupils concerned' (Waites, 2001: 499). In addition, new Sex and Relationships Guidance was published in July 2000 that addressed gay sexuality for the first time. Sections dealt with homophobic bullying and the needs of young lesbians, gay men and bisexuals:

> It is up to schools to make sure that the needs of all pupils are met in their programmes. Young people, whatever their developing sexuality, need to feel that sex and relationship education is relevant to them and sensitive to their needs. (Stonewall, 2003a: 2)

This was therefore the second legislation to emphasize that local authorities had no role in sex education. Rather, the governing body and head teacher of a school were responsible for sex education regulated by the Secretary of State, who issued guidelines on sex education, which included issues of gay sexuality. All this served to underline that as a result of subsequent legislation, Section 28 had become outdated, or at least had been bypassed.

Repeal

Three years later, Section 28 was successfully repealed as part of the Local Government Act 2003. Consultation on the bill commenced in June 2002 and the first full debate on the bill was introduced in January 2003. Repeal of Section 28 was initiated through an amendment tabled as a new Clause 121. The amendment received cross-party support at committee stage in the Commons and was passed by 19 votes to 2. Subsequently, in a Commons debate on 10 March 2003, it was supported by 356 votes to 127 (Stonewall, 2003e). The then Conservative leader, Iain Duncan-Smith voted against repeal as did others from the Conservative Party (Stonewall, 2003e). The

Minister for Local Government and the Regions, Nick Raynsford, explained the government's position in the Commons debate:

> Section 28 is an unnecessary measure that many people find deeply offensive, because it stigmatises certain lifestyles. We are committed to tackling actual and perceived discrimination on the grounds of sexual orientation, and section 28 is widely perceived as discriminatory. (Commons Hansard, 2003b)

Another of the main arguments made for repeal of Section 28 as part of the Commons debate in 2003 was its obsolescence, evident in the effect of subsequent legislation outlined above. During the debate, Chris Bryant MP stated: 'at the moment, the section is obsolete. It only exists as a declamatory law and it makes people feel all right about being prejudiced against homosexuals in society' (Commons Hansard, 2003a).

The debate moved on to the House of Lords on 3 April 2003, when it held its first debate on repeal of Section 28 in England and Wales (Stonewall, 2003h). After a House of Lords committee considered it, the House debated the bill. An amendment was tabled that attempted to allow for repeal on the condition that parents had a greater role in determining the content of sex education in schools in order to protect children (Stonewall, 2003n). However, in the final vote on Clause 121, repeal of prohibition on promotion of sexuality, peers voted 180 to 130 in favour of repeal on 10 July 2003 (Stonewall, 2003n).

STONEWALL CYMRU AND SECTION 28

In its first year, LGB Forum Cymru did not campaign against Section 28. This was partly deliberate as there was concern that Stonewall's campaign at the end of the 1990s had focused excessively on schools. As noted above, schools were outside the remit of Section 28 legislation. One member explained this concern:

> Stonewall's tack on addressing Section 28 was always coming back to what was happening in schools, and how children and young people were being deprived of that kind of education, which was an absolute fallacy and was confusing a lot of the work in education.[12]

However, at LGB Forum Cymru's inaugural conference in April 2002, attendees decided the organization's key strategic objectives. Section 28 was raised as a priority area. This gave LGB Forum Cymru a mandate and it cooperated with Stonewall.[13] Stonewall Cymru's input into the Stonewall campaign against Section 28 took two forms. As a member of Stonewall

Cymru's Executive Committee was a member of Stonewall Executive Board, it contributed to shaping the policy message of Stonewall's campaign. The campaigning shifted to emphasize the inappropriateness of the outdated legislation and its offensive language. In addition, Stonewall Cymru officers were involved in Stonewall decision-making on the nature and messages of the public campaign.

In 2003, Stonewall Cymru contributed to campaigning to repeal Section 28 by promoting the 'No to Hate – Let's Nail Section 28' campaign in Wales. This included engaging with the press to generate public awareness. Stonewall produced petition postcards to be sent to the leaders of the political parties urging them to support the repeal of Section 28, and a similar petition was placed on their website (Stonewall, 2003a: 3). Stonewall Cymru officers expanded this campaigning to Wales. Postcards and posters were produced in English and in Welsh for the first time and were disseminated to groups and venues to gain support, but they faced a difficult campaigning terrain as there was no existing campaign infrastructure. Stonewall Cymru did not invest heavily in popular campaigning. Previous attempts at repeal had led to questioning the value of strong public campaigning and suggested that behind-the-scenes lobbying and the targeting of specific peers was more likely to prove effective. As a member stated at the time of the repeal:

> I'm not clear any more how much campaigning has to happen to effect that change ... I almost wonder whether if energy and time was spent trying to convince one or two people, we might be doing far better, because it's a handful of people that are blocking it now.[14]

Due to its extensive expertise and capacity, Stonewall in London was responsible for direct lobbying, and advocacy on issues surrounding Section 28. Its policy officers led the main lobbying, and Stonewall Cymru officers were updated on developments through Stonewall's internal briefings. However, Stonewall Cymru undertook some advocacy work. At the annual party conferences in Wales, its officers liaised with politicians, promoted the postcard campaign and raised awareness of the importance of Section 28 in Wales and Stonewall Cymru's efforts to monitor voting. In addition, they attempted to gather information on supportive and sympathetic politicians. A number of Welsh peers were subsequently contacted, and this work intensified as the legislation was discussed in the Lords.

More significantly, Stonewall Cymru engaged with the National Assembly on repealing Section 28. The Welsh Assembly Government was consulted by central government and supported the move to repeal Section 28. More broadly, there was support within the Assembly to repeal Section 28. During the attempt at repeal in 1999, Assembly Members raised

Section 28 through the Statements of Opinion procedure and two statements were made in support of repeal and another pressed for the retention of Section 28.[15] In order to capitalize on the support, in 2003, Stonewall Cymru encouraged AMs and Ministers to promote repeal through party mechanisms. As part of its role as a consultative body to the Equality of Opportunity Committee, Stonewall Cymru made presentations to the committee. One stated that:

> LGB Forum Cymru was not confident that the amendment to repeal Section 28 would be passed by the House of Lords and would be speaking to Assembly Members over the coming week for advice on how to reach Welsh Lords who might be sympathetic to voting in support of the amendment. (NAW, 2003f)

Stonewall Cymru's main success in political advocacy surrounding Section 28 was not related to repeal *per se*, but was arguably even more significant. One Stonewall Cymru member stated the case in the following terms:

> specifically the Section 28 campaign in the Lords, in the House of Commons, Stonewall Cymru has probably played a very small role. If we talk about what Section 28 does or what it doesn't do, or what impact it has on education and talking about sexual orientation in schools, then I think we have had a huge impact with the Sex and Relationships in Schools Guidance.[16]

Due to its devolved responsibility for education and consequently sex education guidance for schools in Wales, the National Assembly's Education Department revised the Sex and Relationships Education in Schools Guidance in 2002. This was to replace the Sex Education in Schools guidance issued by the Welsh Office in 1994, taking account of the requirements of the Learning and Skills Act 2000. As an Assembly consultative body, Stonewall Cymru participated in the consultation on a draft of the guidance. Its input to the Guidance was highly relevant as three members of its steering group worked in education and two were experts in sex and relationships education. They formulated the response to the consultation and provided evidence to support their recommendations. A member stated that the response was 'taking it way beyond where we thought the Assembly would go because we knew that in the end it would be a compromise'.[17] Members subsequently participated in meetings with Education Department civil servants and provided extensive expertise to policy-making. They felt that their input was seriously considered.

The guidance was issued in July 2002. For the first time, it included a section on sexual identity and sexual orientation and addressed concerns about Section 28. It states that 'Section 28 of the Local Government Act

1988 does not prevent the objective discussion of homosexuality in the classroom, and schools can provide counselling, guidance and support for pupils' (NAW, 2002l: 11). It also states:

> the National Assembly is clear that teachers should be able to deal with these issues honestly, sensitively and in a non-discriminatory way . . . It is important that young people develop an understanding and respect for others regardless of their developing sexual orientation. (NAW, 2002l: 11)

This guidance provided 'the most clear-cut statement of any government agency in the UK regarding education issues referring to same sex issues',[18] and suggested the strong influence of Stonewall Cymru on its development. Assembly Ministers Jane Davidson and Jane Hutt launched it in January 2003. Lorraine Barrett AM tabled a Statement of Opinion on 27 February 2003 welcoming the guidance (NAW, 2003h).

STONEWALL CYMRU

On the basis of the preceding examination of Stonewall Cymru's contribution to issues surrounding Section 28, this concluding section seeks to draw some broader conclusions regarding the organization's development and the degree to which devolution has affected Stonewall Cymru.

First, Stonewall Cymru's main contribution to issues surrounding Section 28 resulted from taking advantage of its working relationship with the National Assembly for Wales and Welsh Assembly Government based on its status as a consultative body. Stonewall Cymru's contacts contrasted with the marginalization of LGB organizations from governance structures in Wales before devolution. It developed a relationship with the Equality of Opportunity Committee that was highly supportive of establishing and financing LGB Forum Cymru. Its standing invitation to the committee as an adviser placed Stonewall Cymru on an equal footing with the three statutory commissions relating to issues of discrimination – gender, race and disability (NAW, 1999a: para. 2.9). This reflected how the Assembly's committee structure promoted openness to external actors.

More significantly, Stonewall Cymru's direct involvement with civil servants developing the Sex and Relationships Education in Schools Guidance emphasized the extensive relations it developed with the Welsh Assembly Government in a relatively short time. This high-level access illustrated the status afforded to the organization in being supported by the work of the Equality Unit and invited to respond to consultations issued by all government departments (Stonewall Cymru, 2003). Consultative-body status provided opportunities to influence political decisions and directly engage in policy formulation on a range of subjects. Contact with the Welsh Assembly Government was further exemplified at the first LGB Forum Cymru conference when Assembly Members from all political parties were present and Rhodri Morgan stated: 'the importance of a Forum, which can reach out to the lesbian, gay and bisexual communities across Wales, cannot be underestimated' (LGB Forum Cymru, 2002b).[19]

Secondly, in addition to the opportunities open to Stonewall Cymru, its resources assisted it in taking advantage of these opportunities. The appointment of a part-time political development officer certainly facilitated the development of relationships with Assembly Members, Assembly Government Ministers and civil servants. However, despite the increased resources, many of the pre-devolution difficulties affecting LGB groups in Wales persisted. In its first year, the pressures of developing the organization without employed staff made undertaking public campaigning impossible. Once Stonewall Cymru's two part-time officers were in place, establishing the organization was the main priority. One member explained: 'Wales has needed something like this for so long that as soon as it came along there was a ton of things coming in to be dealt with.'[20]

Infrastructure difficulties meant that Stonewall Cymru faced the challenge of initiating cooperation between groups and attempting to empower organizations to contribute to determining the organization's direction, and to engage with the Assembly. According to a Stonewall Cymru member: 'I think that the Assembly was wide open – I was absolutely surprised. The challenge that we have got is actually much more about mobilizing lesbian and gay people to take their rightful place because the door is open to take it.'[21] No quick fixes could achieve this, as 'within the groups, there isn't any particular awareness of engagement with the Assembly. Us standing up as a community and expecting anything, there is no great expectation of service within the Assembly to LGBs.'[22] The staffing resources of two part-time staff working at opposite ends of Wales were not sufficient to realize this. Nonetheless, Assembly funding played a major part in effecting change. According to a member:

> Without resources, it's very difficult to bring the whole of Wales together ... That's not easy to do unless there is some finance to support that. Without someone who is like an organisation who is willing to be spoken to and willing to hear us, that might have been difficult.[23]

This highlighted the difficulties facing organizations dependent on volunteers and with limited financial resources in post-devolution Wales.

Thirdly, the relationship between Stonewall Cymru and the Assembly signified a transformation in the climate towards LGB issues in governance structures in Wales. This was clear in Stonewall Cymru's unique status as the only government-sponsored gay and lesbian organization in the UK (NAW, 2002j: 7.1; Stonewall Cymru, 2003). Section 120 of the Government of Wales Act 1998, which placed a statutory duty on the National Assembly to ensure equality of opportunity to all the people of Wales, was central in ensuring this. The clause is unique amongst devolution statutes. Chaney and Fevre state: 'the Welsh equality duty is singular in its non-prescriptive phrasing and all-embracing scope. It is an *imperative* that applies to *all* people and *all* functions of government' (2002b: 8). As with Oxfam Cymru, this case demonstrated that organizations active in non-devolved issues have benefited from engaging with the Assembly as it used its existing powers to tackle issues such as discrimination on the grounds of sexual orientation that were largely non-devolved.

Many respondents felt that the statutory equality duty was pivotal in establishing the organization. A Stonewall Cymru representative stated that 'Stonewall Cymru wouldn't have happened if the Assembly wasn't there; if the Assembly wasn't established on the basis of equality to all'.[24] The funding relationship established Stonewall Cymru as a single consultative body to represent the whole LGB community (LGB Forum Cymru, 2002c: 8). It was also charged to work in partnership with agencies, organizations and statutory bodies, and this facilitated joint working. Stonewall Cymru was also elected to the board of Wales Council for Voluntary Action (WCVA). Its status as a government-funded body therefore assisted its engagement with other bodies. A member stated:

> Once we got members of staff, the fact that LGB Forum Cymru was half funded by the Assembly gave our staff an entrée to meet these people that they wouldn't previously been given an entrée to, e.g. people in local authorities, people in police services.[25]

Overall, Stonewall Cymru's status as a consultative body in receipt of Assembly funding created a close relationship with some departments of the Welsh Assembly Government. As previous chapters demonstrated, this was very important to gain meaningful influence on the Assembly. Stonewall Cymru fulfilled the Assembly's requirement of having one organization that could represent and be consulted regarding LGB issues. The theoretical literature in Chapter 2 highlighted the potentially negative democratic implications of appointing one organization to represent diverse interests if this created privileged relations between one group and the state. Stonewall Cymru's advantageous position provided seemingly greater leverage over the Assembly and Assembly Government's policies than other organizations had. Considering the discussion in the theoretical literature, such a situation could be seen as detrimental to democracy as it could potentially exacerbate the inequalities that existed between organizations in their capacity and influence with government. The Assembly's part-funding of Stonewall Cymru illustrated many dilemmas surrounding the funding of organizations. Though Stonewall Cymru, with the input of LGB community in Wales, developed a business plan in order to determine its own agenda rather than responding to funding, it was unclear whether its funding agreement with the Assembly would compromise its autonomy.[26] Stonewall Cymru had a unique status, and during the first term of devolution, the relationship with the Assembly was positive and no situation of strong disagreement was experienced. However, an Assembly Member pointed out that this would almost certainly not remain the case indefinitely:

> A point will come and it's sure to arise, where the membership of the Forum want to say things that the Assembly Government don't want to hear. It will be interesting to see how easy it will be for the Forum's staff and officials to take those issues on strongly with the Assembly.[27]

Therefore, the full implications of the funding arrangements remained unclear. It must, however, be acknowledged that the lack of infrastructure and capacity of LGB organizations before devolution, and continuing problems post-devolution, highlighted the severe difficulties in developing LGB representation at an all-Wales level. While questions surrounded the sponsoring of organizations by government, in this case it was essential in attempts to reverse marginalization and involve isolated groups in government.

Fourthly, though Stonewall Cymru faced difficulties in engaging its membership in decision-making, its structures were conducive to promoting participation. This was evident in relation to Section 28. Stonewall Cymru campaigned on Section 28 following a mandate from members. Overall, efforts were made to engage the 600–700 members in determining the direction of the organization and to be responsive to their needs.[28] In addition to the membership electing Stonewall Cymru Council, members were consulted via mail shots on aspects such as Stonewall Cymru's strategic objectives and other key decisions. Locating staff in north and south Wales also reflected its effort to include the LGB 'community' in its work. The bottom-up nature of Stonewall Cymru's internal decision-making was in stark contrast to Stonewall's own operation, and the former's structure demonstrated its potential to promote participation and be representative of the LGB community. These features were essential considering its role as an all-Wales umbrella body for the diverse LGB 'community'. The low base of activity of LGB groups in Wales meant that Stonewall Cymru's participation structures were yet to be fully developed, and its popular campaigning structures were in their initial stages. It could be argued that the success experienced by Stonewall Cymru during devolution's first term and its status as a consultative body diminished the need to develop popular campaigning. Indeed, its strong ability to engage directly with the Assembly may mean that it could be counter-productive for it to resort to extensive popular campaigning, for instance to the same levels as Cymdeithas and Cymuned. Nevertheless, its bottom-up internal structures demonstrated its efforts to promote participation and its potential to make a specific contribution to enhancing democracy.

Assembly support for repeal of Section 28 and the advances made in recognizing sexual orientation in the guidance highlighted how the Assembly, in partnership with Stonewall Cymru, ventured into non-devolved areas of power post-devolution. The Assembly could not repeal Section 28, but 'the Assembly's change to schools guidance to allow discussion of sexual identity and orientation were seen as the next best thing to repealing Section 28' (NAW, 2002k: 2.1). The near-unanimous consensus within the Assembly to repeal Section 28 if it possessed the powers, reflected the commitment of many AMs to LGB issues.[29] Through the guidance, the Assembly, acting in close cooperation with Stonewall Cymru used its existing powers to advance on Westminster policies and counter the effects of non-devolved legislation in Wales. This was also the case with other areas such as new employment legislation protecting the LGB community from discrimination in the provision of goods and services (Stonewall Cymru, 2003). The Assembly's eagerness to address these issues and engage Stonewall Cymru in its work suggested that it desired to have a voice on these non-devolved issues.

Paradoxically, Stonewall Cymru's success in influencing the Assembly and Assembly Government during the first term served to highlight the limited nature of the Assembly's current powers regarding LGB issues. In its evidence to the Richard Commission (see Appendix 1), Stonewall Cymru noted that 'the Welsh Assembly Government has been unable to promote equality of opportunity for lesbian, gay and bisexual people in Wales to the extent that it would wish because of reserved powers held at Westminster' (NAW, 2003i). To address this, it called for amending the Government of Wales Act so that tackling discrimination would be included in the Assembly's equality of opportunity duty, and for further devolution of equality of opportunity powers (NAW, 2003i). Its 2003 National Assembly election manifesto also called for amending the Assembly's Standing Orders to formalize the relationship between Stonewall Cymru and the Equality of Opportunity Committee (Stonewall Cymru 2003). Furthermore, it called for representation of LGB issues on the Voluntary Sector Partnership Council (Stonewall Cymru, 2003). Stonewall Cymru, as a body consulted by the Assembly, drew attention to the limitations of the Assembly's powers and called for greater powers for the devolved institution while also advocating greater status for itself within the Assembly's structures.

Finally, Stonewall Cymru presented a case of shifts in the identity of an organization post-devolution. Campaigning surrounding Section 28 highlighted Stonewall Cymru's cooperation with Stonewall in lobbying and inputting into policy-making on non-devolved issues. This was seen as beneficial to Stonewall Cymru. A member noted: 'because Stonewall has great access and is a respected organisation on this issue, and its high profiling campaign, our influence has been I think quite good for us in Wales'.[30] Stonewall had long-standing links with politicians and government departments, and Stonewall Cymru had only developed *ad hoc* links with Welsh MPs, but expected to expand on this. A member stated: 'there's a great deal of value in working with Welsh MPs possibly in tandem with Stonewall where appropriate or independently where there's a specific Welsh issue'.[31] In addition, Stonewall Cymru adopted the popular campaign developed by Stonewall suggesting that it was yet to develop its own campaigning strategies. The nature of the campaign to repeal Section 28 and the relatively recent establishment of Stonewall Cymru limited its contribution and increased its dependency on Stonewall. However, the strong cooperation between them reflected *civil society in Wales* tendencies.

In some respects, the rebranding of the organization from LGB Forum Cymru to Stonewall Cymru in 2003 suggested that a shift was taking place towards increased *civil society in Wales* characteristics. Initially, in 2001, the impetus for setting up the organization was devolution, and the Assembly's support for its establishment was vital. Stonewall on a UK level was also instrumental. However, it was decided not to form a branch of Stonewall in Wales as there were concerns within some LGB groups that Stonewall before devolution was an overtly London-centric organization. Therefore, the decision to establish LGB Forum Cymru which had a partnership with Stonewall UK consciously located itself as part of *Welsh civil society*. A member explained the situation:

> We created this fudge. Stonewall was putting loads in, so we had to formalise the relationship with Stonewall. We formalised what we called a partnership agreement which said the name of the organisation was LGB Forum Cymru but implicit in that name was that this was a partnership between Stonewall and LGB Forum.[32]

The Executive Committee unanimously agreed the shift to Stonewall Cymru. Some interviewees within Stonewall Cymru and within the Assembly pointed out that the rebranding as Stonewall Cymru reflected that the status of the organization and its relationship with Stonewall called for greater clarity. However, a more deep-seated change within the organization could also be discerned. In 2002, the idea of partnership was clear in LGB Forum Cymru's business plan: 'Stonewall, the UK wide gay and lesbian rights organization, works in partnership with the Forum in Wales's (LGB Forum Cymru, 2002b:2). By 2003, a closer bond with Stonewall UK was expressed, 'Stonewall Cymru is part of Stonewall UK' (Stonewall Cymru, 2003). Thus, the strengthening of the relationship with Stonewall, evident in Section 28, suggested a shift towards a stronger sense of *civil society in Wales*. The short time between the rebranding and the end of devolution's first term meant that the full implications of the changes were unclear.

While developments surrounding the rebranding of Stonewall Cymru suggested stronger *civil society in Wales* characteristics, a number of aspects reflect *Welsh civil society* characteristics. Many interviewees contended that the foundations and Welsh basis established for LGB Forum Cymru would ensure that Stonewall Cymru retained its Welsh identity. These included that the National Assembly was its main political target; Stonewall Cymru Council as the main decision-making body ultimately determined its direction; its offices in north and south Wales; its conscious adoption of bilingualism to include the Welsh-speaking LGB community. There were some concerns that Welsh-speaking lesbians and gay men did not perceive Stonewall Cymru to be their voice and this demonstrated the difficulty of incorporating the diversity within the LGB community. The Welsh nature of the organization was explained:

> your first responsibility is to the LGB, the population, a specific part of the population in Wales. Now the engagement is with the administration of that population and that you have the means to articulate the voice of that population to a wider community in the UK.[33]

Stonewall Cymru seemed to be subject to a difficult balancing act with potential dual influences arising from its relationship with Stonewall and the National Assembly and Welsh Assembly Government. This highlighted the crucial role of the Stonewall Cymru Council in balancing the relative influence of both funding sources. In terms of Stonewall's standpoint, a Stonewall Cymru member noted: 'I think it is happy for the Welsh operation to have quite an indigenous existence – to set priorities in Wales for what it wants to achieve and for Stonewall to bring expertise and help facilitate that.'[34] Others emphasized the importance of securing Stonewall Cymru's autonomy as it was not clear whether Stonewall's priorities on a UK level were the same as the priorities of people in Wales. A member stated: 'if Stonewall Cymru is to represent the voice of gay and lesbian people in Wales, then it needs to be very, very careful that it holds the London influence in check'.[35] Stonewall Cymru illustrated how the identity of organizations can evolve towards a sense of *civil society in Wales*. The complexity of its identity was evident: 'it's a Welsh-based organisation with an office in the UK. Because whereas the capacity is all in the UK, the drive is in Wales, the motor is in Wales'.[36]

CONCLUSION

The examination of Stonewall Cymru's involvement in issues surrounding Section 28 illustrated the transformation of organizations relating to recognition for sexual orientation post-devolution. This contrasted to the weaknesses of LGB groups and their limited involvement with government structures before devolution. Stonewall Cymru's unique status as an Assembly Government-funded consultative body facilitated its influence on the Sex and Relationships Education Guidance issued by the Welsh Assembly Government, which served to counter the effects of non-devolved legislation in Wales.

Stonewall Cymru's status demonstrated Assembly efforts to consult and fund structures to represent groups most subject to inequality. Questions could be raised whether this is legitimate. The organization's dependence on Assembly and Stonewall funding certainly served to illustrate the complex situation of such organizations and the dilemmas that arise from their 'dependent' status. It also suggested that government funding can deepen inequalities of capacity and influence between civil society organizations. In addition, though Stonewall Cymru's structures promoted membership engagement, the Assembly's requirement for a single organization to represent the whole LGB 'community' for consultation purposes was potentially problematic. It could be argued that this could hinder democracy as Stonewall Cymru's ability to represent the diversity of interests within the 'community' could be questioned.

Nevertheless, Stonewall Cymru was faced with persisting difficulties in terms of lack of infrastructure, capacity and networks. It had the onerous task of addressing the distrust and low expectations of government extant in the LGB community, and in encouraging this community to engage with the Assembly. Assembly funding was crucial to this work, and such support could be seen as promoting democracy by developing a more participative policy process and addressing a culture of marginalization.

The far-reaching effects of the statutory equality duty in the Government of Wales Act facilitated the Assembly Government and Assembly politicians to pursue their support and interest in addressing non-devolved issues of discrimination such as sexual orientation. Following its successes during the first term of devolution, Stonewall Cymru highlighted the restrictions on the Assembly's powers in relation to LGB issues, promoted greater powers for the Assembly and its own status in the Assembly's structures. This was more significant due to Stonewall Cymru's predominant involvement in non-devolved issues.

Stonewall Cymru also highlighted the shifts in the identity of an organization post-devolution. Other chapters identified how organizations that were previously characterized with stronger *civil society in Wales* tendencies illustrated greater *Welsh civil society* characteristics post-devolution. In contrast, Stonewall Cymru's rebranding arguably shifted the organization towards *civil society in Wales*. Stonewall was the main channel of influence for the organization to input at the Westminster level and it seemed that a non-devolved area such as sexual orientation necessitated a direct partnership and effective sharing of resources with a UK-level organization. Stonewall Cymru's main decision-making body was the Stonewall Cymru Council, and other aspects reflected continuing *Welsh civil society* tendencies. However, the shift from LGB Forum Cymru to Stonewall Cymru suggested that Stonewall at the UK level had a strengthened influence over the organization's direction.

From the experience of marginalization from governmental structures in pre-devolution Wales, Stonewall Cymru's involvement in Section 28 issues highlighted the transformation of the fortunes of LGB participation in policy-making after devolution, even if the recognition of sexual orientation remained a non-devolved issue.

APPENDIX 1

Written Evidence to Richard Commission, May 2003

Introduction

Stonewall Cymru welcomes the opportunity to give evidence to the Richard Commission. Our response to the draft questions for the equal opportunities evidence session are set out below. First we have provided a few words of explanation about Stonewall Cymru.

About Stonewall Cymru

The purpose of Stonewall Cymru is to provide an all Wales organisation that will work individually and in partnership with other agencies, organisations, statutory bodies and individuals to:

- promote the human rights and equal treatment of lesbian, gay and bisexual people;

- challenge discrimination against lesbian, gay and bisexual people;
- articulate the needs and interests of lesbian, gay and bisexual people and represent these to the National Assembly for Wales and other appropriate bodies;
- consolidate and develop the infrastructure with lesbian, gay and bisexual communities across Wales to enable them to contribute to and have representation in policy developments.

The overall strategic direction of Stonewall Cymru is determined by a Council of fifteen members, which is elected by the membership of Stonewall Cymru. Stonewall Cymru has two offices – in Bangor and in Cardiff. Stonewall Cymru is part of Stonewall UK.

Powers of the National Assembly

Are the powers of the Assembly in relation to equal opportunities adequate and effective?

Section 120

Section 120 of the Government of Wales Act 1998, which sets out the Assembly's duty with regard to equality of opportunity, has been widely interpreted – by the Assembly and outside organisations – as going further than the statutory requirements placed upon other UK public bodies. The Assembly has taken a pro-active approach and sought to promote equality of opportunity in its work. One example of this positive approach has been to fund consultative bodies, such as Stonewall Cymru (previously the Lesbian, Gay and Bisexual Forum Cymru), which is one of the first government-funded consultative forums of its type in the UK. Stonewall Cymru believes the current equality of opportunity duty, as it has been interpreted over the last four years, is strong and adequate. Indeed we would argue that such a positive duty to promote equality should be introduced across the UK. However we would be concerned if recent anecdotes prove to be true – that lawyers have advised the Assembly that it is currently going beyond its powers under Section 120. If there is ambiguity about the extent of the Assembly's powers to promote equality of opportunity for all across Wales we would strongly support clarification in any revisions to the Government of Wales Act so that a proactive duty is clearly established.

Standing Orders

The *Standing Orders* of the National Assembly for Wales set out the procedures for the operation of the Assembly. Standing Order 14, which concerns the Committee on Equality of Opportunity, gives particular priority to three equality strands:

The Committee shall also have particular regard to the need of the Assembly to avoid discrimination against any person on grounds of race, sex or disability. (Standing Order 14.1)

Stonewall Cymru asks that the Standing Orders be amended to give equal priority to tackling discrimination on the grounds of sexual orientation. The Standing Orders should be amended in light of new European legislation outlawing discrimination in employment on the grounds of age, sexual orientation and religious belief; the forthcoming establishment of a Single Equality Body covering at least six equality strands; and the Assembly's duty to have 'regard to the principle that there should be equality of opportunity for all'. The current priority given to just three areas of discrimination creates a hierarchy of equality. Whilst it must be said that the work of the committee during its first term has been broader than just these three equality areas, and has included the appointment of a representative of the Stonewall Cymru as an adviser to the committee, this may change if the political climate alters. Stonewall Cymru calls for the Committee's Standing Orders to be changed so that tackling discrimination on the grounds of sexual orientation, as well as age and religious belief, is given equal status to race, sex and disability. Stonewall Cymru also supports the recommendation made in the Absolute Duty report that the role and functioning of the new Assembly-sponsored consultative forums, such as Stonewall Cymru and the Wales Women's National Coalition, be formalized and enshrined in the Standing Orders. This would strengthen the committee's links with key marginalized communities and help ensure the effectiveness of the Welsh Assembly's statutory equality duty.

How do these powers interact with UK equal opportunities legislation?

Equality of Opportunity is a power that remains with the UK Parliament. The Assembly's equality duty applies to all functions devolved to the National Assembly, including health, education, social services and housing. The interaction between UK legislation and the Assembly's powers is currently not satisfactory. The organisations that enforce and/or promote UK equality legislation – the CRE, DRC, EOC and Welsh Language Board – do not have formal links with the National Assembly for Wales. Discussions about a new Single Equality Body in Wales have highlighted how the interaction could be improved. Some of the suggestions arising from discussions involving voluntary and statutory equality organisations across Wales are that:

- the Single Equality Body in Wales should have formal links with the National Assembly for Wales, as well as the UK government;
- the body should play a role in advising and monitoring the equality aspects of the Government of Wales Act (Section 120 and Section 48);
- the Assembly should play a role in appointing the Wales Commissioner;
- the SEB in Wales needs sufficient autonomy and flexibility to be able to respond to equality priorities in Wales (and to the political priorities of the Assembly).

What problems have been raised in relation to these powers?

The Welsh Assembly Government has been unable to promote equality of opportunity for lesbian, gay and bisexual people in Wales to the extent that it would wish because of reserved powers held at Westminster. Even in devolved areas the Assembly has been limited in its influence.

Example 1: Section 28
The Welsh Assembly Government recently published new guidance on developing sex and relationships education policy. In relation to Section 28 the guidance clearly states:

> Section 28 of the Local Government Act 1988 does not prevent the objective discussion of homosexuality in the classroom, and schools can provide counselling, guidance and support for pupils. (p. 11, *Sex and Relationships Education in Schools*)

However our experience of helping and encouraging schools to apply the sexual identity and sexual orientation part of the new guidance is Welsh schools are unwilling or fearful because of Section 28. Many are still unclear about what Section 28 means. Contrary to myth, Section 28 does not apply to schooling or the way that schools teach sex education or other issues relating to homosexuality. Section 28 states clearly that it only applies to local authorities in England and Wales – it never applied to schools themselves. The Learning and Skills Act 2000 *removed any local authority control over sex education*. Despite clear and unambiguous support for the repeal of Section 28 from three of the four main political parties in Wales, and in spite of clear guidance for schools, the National Assembly is prevented from providing equality of opportunity for lesbian, gay and bisexual young people in Wales. The Scottish Parliament has already repealed Section 28.

Example 2: Employment Legislation

In efforts to reduce discrimination faced by lesbian, gay and bisexual people the Assembly has been prevented from acting because of the limits to its powers. New legislation will soon make it illegal to discriminate against someone because of his or her actual or perceived sexual orientation. Unlike legislation on race, gender and disability, the rules will not apply to goods and services. So lesbian, gay and bisexual people will continue to be discriminated against, without the possibility of legal redress, in the provision of insurance, health and many commercial services for instance. The Welsh Assembly Government's response to the Equality and Diversity: Making It Happen consultation makes clear its wish to bring the three new strands of sexual orientation, religion and belief, and age up to the level of protection as existing strands through a single equality act. This would effectively provide lesbian, gay and bisexual people in Wales with protection from discrimination in the provision of goods and services. The UK government has decided not to do this at the current time. Thus despite widespread political support in Wales for measures to help bring about equality for lesbian, gay and bisexual people the Assembly is constrained by the limits of its powers.

What has been the impact of Section 120 of the Government of Wales Act and how has it been implemented?

The National Assembly has driven forward the equality agenda in Wales for lesbian, gay and bisexual people. As a direct result of Section 120 the National Assembly has helped to fund Stonewall Cymru as a consultative body representing lesbian, gay and bisexual people in Wales. The Assembly's Equality of Opportunity Committee has also invited a Stonewall Cymru representative to sit as an adviser to the committee on issues of sexual orientation. The impact of this support has been widespread, with Stonewall Cymru participating in the formulation of policy on a wide range of subjects, including employment, health and well-being, older people and housing.

What improvements in the present arrangements would you like to see?

Our suggested improvements are included throughout this report. We ask that:

- Section 120 continues to be interpreted as a positive duty to promote equality of opportunity;
- equal status be given to tackling discrimination on the grounds of sexual orientation in the Standing Orders of the Equality of Opportunity Committee;

- the role and functioning of the Assembly-sponsored consultative forums be formalized and enshrined in these Standing Orders;
- the Single Equality Body in Wales should have formal links with the National Assembly for Wales and this role should include advising and monitoring the equality aspects of the Government of Wales Act and influence in the appointment of the Wales Commissioner;
- further devolution of equality of opportunity powers to ensure a coherent and more effective approach to policy implementation;
- the lesbian, gay and bisexual voluntary sector in Wales be included as a category of interest on the Wales Voluntary Sector Partnership;
- continued financial support to the lesbian, gay and bisexual voluntary sector in Wales to enable it to fully participate in the democratic process in Wales.

Electoral Arrangements

How adequate/effective are the electoral arrangements of the National Assembly from an equal opportunities perspective?
No comment to make.

What changes would make the Assembly more representative and inclusive?
There are currently no openly lesbian, gay or bisexual members of the National Assembly. Whilst massive progress has been made to improve gender balance, there has been little progress towards ensuring representation in the Assembly chamber from ethnic minorities or from lesbian, gay or bisexual people. The Assembly has provided funding to Stonewall Cymru to improve its consultation processes with lesbian, gay and bisexual people in Wales. This is a hugely positive step, which must continue. We believe that a further improvement would be for the lesbian, gay and bisexual voluntary sector to be represented on the Voluntary Sector Partnership Council, in the same way that umbrella organisations in the race, gender, disability and religious sectors are represented.

Stonewall Cymru's written evidence to the Richard Commission
(NAW, 2003i)

8

Conclusion

This conclusion returns to the questions outlined in the Introduction to examine the findings regarding the impact of devolution on civil society during the Assembly's first term. The final section then draws out some of the broader implications of the study for devolution in Wales and for civil society theory.

CIVIL SOCIETY AND THE POLITICAL PROCESS POST-DEVOLUTION

The Introduction raised a number of questions regarding civil society's ability to revitalize democracy. One aspect was the extent to which civil society became involved with the Assembly and the democratic implications of this engagement. In examining the relations between civil society and the National Assembly in its first term, it was clear that devolution transformed the engagement of organizations with the political process with mixed consequences for democracy. Devolution created a shift as it led to new and more extensive opportunities to interact with government structures in Wales (see also Chaney et al., 2007). Civil society organizations took advantage of these opportunities and contributed to improving the quality of policy-making, thus playing an important role in demonstrating that devolution 'made a difference'. The Assembly's policy process was conducted according to a 'team Wales' approach by engaging the expertise of external actors including civil society to develop 'made in Wales' policies. Civil society engagement with the Assembly has thus been important to the devolution project.

However, examples of inclusive and 'new politics' working practices were overshadowed by a more complex picture. The findings were that some organizations had closer and more exclusive relations with the National Assembly, with potentially negative democratic implications. One key factor was that disparities existed between organizations. Some restructured, professionalized and expanded their resources, and this increased their capabilities to lobby, both formally and informally, Assembly Government Ministers and civil servants. They also had the capacity to develop high quality and expert policy submissions on a par with the public sector. Others had limited capacities and depended on voluntary financial contributions, which affected their ability to engage with the Assembly. These exclusionary aspects and the major inequalities in power and influence between organizations, arising from financial differences, resonate with the theoretical literature's assertion that civil society can exacerbate inequalities of power that places limits on its democratic potential (Whitehad, 1997; Ehrenberg, 1999). Findings on the inequalities within civil society concur with the research into the voluntary sector and women's organizations' interaction with the Assembly (Chaney et al., 2000: 9; Dicks et al., 2001: 111; Chaney and Fevre, 2001c: 152–3; see also Chaney et al., 2007).

The case studies provided evidence that the Assembly and Welsh Assembly Government exacerbated existing inequalities by developing more exclusive relations with some organizations. Although the Assembly had arguably the greatest power in relation to the Welsh language, some controversial groups active on Welsh language issues were unacceptable to some actors in the political process and particularly to a section within the dominant party. Some also viewed civil disobedience negatively. The theoretical literature discussed in Chapter 2 argued that civil disobedience was legitimate in a democratic polity if organizations had insufficient channels to influence political society, that is political parties and parliaments (Cohen and Arato, 1999: 602). Cymdeithas' and Cymuned's situations suggested that groups active in some areas were less acceptable to the ruling Welsh Assembly Government compared with most civil society organizations post-devolution. Furthermore, it showed that the 'democratization' of government in Wales was not complete as the case relating to the Welsh language identified limits to the Assembly's 'inclusiveness'. Rawlings's comments in relation to another episode relating to the Welsh language were again relevant: 'what price – it may be asked – inclusiveness, in the sense of the Assembly listening to all sides of (lawfully expressed) opinion?' (2003: 216).

In addition, the Assembly's internal structures, with the potential to promote 'inclusiveness', were downgraded with the shift towards a cabinet structure during the first term. The findings on Cymdeithas and Cymuned reflected the Assembly committees' limited role and the importance of direct engagement with the Welsh Assembly Government. The predominance of executive policy-making during devolution's first term heightened the importance of having expertise and being well resourced. These were prerequisites to having access to high-level formal and informal contacts with Welsh Assembly Government Ministers and civil servants and a meaningful influence on policy-making. Other channels that secured high-level engagement included Voluntary Sector Partnership Council membership and Assembly consultative-body status. The most significant factor in creating stronger ties between the Assembly and some organizations was, however, receipt of funding. Those organizations that received, either directly or indirectly, some Assembly funding in devolved and non-devolved areas had stronger contacts with the Welsh Assembly Government.

Therefore, the Assembly and Welsh Assembly Government perpetuated and exacerbated disparities between the ability of organizations to influence the Assembly. This finding concurs with Chaney and Fevre, who cautioned that the Assembly's actions heightened inequalities and potentially threatened democracy (2002a: 903). As was the case with Chaney and Fevre's work on equality organizations, the case studies confirmed the relevance of the neo-corporatism literature to the Welsh case (2001a: 38; 2001c; 2002a: 903). The significance of the receipt of Welsh Assembly Government funding in potentially establishing more exclusive relations with some organizations reflected the neo-corporatism literature that warns of the potentially negative democratic effects by creating elitism and marginalization within civil society (Wilson, 1990: 69). Cymdeithas and Cymuned's limited role in Welsh language policy-making contrasted with a range of other organizations that received government funding with potentially more exclusive relations with government. Neo-corporatism also asserts that partnerships lead to consensual relations with the state and to assimilation that threatens organizations' ability to hold the state accountable (Wilson, 1990: 69). During the policy review of the Welsh language, organizations receiving Welsh Assembly Government funding contributed little to advancing policy ideas, suggesting that they were unwilling to step outside the consensus.[1] This suggested, in accordance with neo-corporatism, that funding and policy networks could affect the scrutiny ability and relative autonomy of organizations. Therefore, Cymdeithas and Cymuned were amongst a minority of organizations with financial autonomy that potentially enabled them to discuss alternative ideas and hold governmental structures accountable.

Other cases raised similar concerns regarding the effects of strong relations and partnerships between civil society and the Welsh Assembly Government. Stonewall Cymru was the most interesting case due to its unique status as an Assembly Government-sponsored network. The establishment of exclusive relations between one group representing LGB issues and the state could be viewed as creating inequalities between organizations. The requirement for one organization to represent the whole diversity within the 'community' raised a third aspect of the literature on neo-corporatism in which the relationship with the state can affect the representativeness of organizations and damage their accountability to their membership. Again, the funding agreement suggested that the Assembly Government could impact on Stonewall Cymru's direction and autonomy. However, in this case, funding was essential to establishing LGB representation at an all-Wales level. On a more analytical level, it provided an example of state agency in developing civic capacity. Future development of Stonewall Cymru will demonstrate whether the Assembly's initiative provided a sufficient boost to the organization, thus enhancing democracy.

The relevance of the neo-corporatism literature was evident in other cases as it seemed that funding and policy networks created key partners and had similar effects on Assembly–civil society relations. Central issues raised were the importance of the WCVA during devolution's first term and the role of the Voluntary Sector Partnership Council. WCVA's status was based on its prominence in the five years before devolution. During the first term, it was a dependable partner with expertise to contribute to the Assembly's work and it presented itself as the representative of the voluntary sector in Wales. The Voluntary Sector Partnership Council's membership, key organizations from each facet of the voluntary sector, again suggested that the Assembly promoted exclusive relationships with specific organizations and that these groups gained a privileged status with the Assembly. A problem, which the Partnership Council itself was aware of, was that it was unclear to what extent they were representative of the sector as a whole. This format was beneficial to the Assembly and Assembly Government. It was more 'efficient' in bureaucratic terms as, in accordance with the neo-corporatism argument, it increased levels of participation and provided government with expertise without having the task of interacting with a multiplicity of interests (Wilson, 1990: 69). Overall, however, these types of partnership practices, evident in a number of cases, placed some organizations in a more powerful position as 'representatives'. This situation had potentially negative democratic consequences in reinforcing exclusion and marginalization within civil society, threatening the representativeness, but more clearly the autonomy of organizations.

Therefore examining the extent of civil society organizations' involvement with the Assembly during devolution's first term highlighted that priority was placed by the Assembly and the majority of civil society organizations on building partnerships. This accorded with *A Voice for Wales*'s emphasis on the role of the voluntary sector as a partner to the National Assembly (Welsh Office, 1997: 15). This strongly suggested that, as Day et al. contend, the 'Third Way' approach was adopted by the Assembly (2000: 27). In some cases, the Assembly revitalized civil society organizations, evident in the Assembly-sponsored structures. Some positive democratic effects were evident, assisting the Assembly to address its difficulties and improving policy-making. However, the nature of some partnerships and the complex funding situation of a number of organizations in post-devolution Wales suggested exclusive relations with some organizations. It confirmed the relevance of the neo-corporatism literature in the Welsh context and raised concerns regarding the effects on civil society's ability to develop the kind of scrutiny capacities that are usual in a vibrant democracy.

CIVIL SOCIETY AND THE QUALITY OF WELSH DEMOCRACY

Due to the expectations that civil society could promote a participatory democracy, another aspect was its internal democratic potential to encourage greater participation. In practice, there were differences in the degree to which organizational structures encouraged further active participation and civic engagement. This reflected differences between traditional and more contemporary organizations. As a more contemporary organization, Oxfam Cymru had opportunities for individual supporter participation in campaigns, but comparatively more limited opportunities for active supporter engagement in decision-making on policies and priorities. Its highly professionalized structures, however, provided it with the greatest capacity to influence the Assembly and Assembly Government. It tended to reflect top-down internal processes of decision-making and a focus on high-level advocacy, but this was inevitable as it was an international organization working according to an international agenda. As a result, the opportunities for supporters to participate actively in its decision-making on policy issues and campaigns were more limited than other organizations examined in the study. This tended to suggest that despite its role in promoting supporter participation in campaigning, its project work and activities that promoted participation, there were some limits to Oxfam's potential to promote broader democratic involvement.

Cymdeithas', Cymuned' and Stonewall Cymru's internal structures reflected traditional associational ties that suggested a greater propensity to promote civic engagement. Their main decision-making bodies were formed from and elected by their membership and they promoted membership involvement in decision-making and campaigns. Cymdeithas and Cymuned had less capacity to engage with government structures, making popular campaigning essential to raise public attention and to exert pressure on government structures. Organizations that promoted engagement, including Groundwork, could potentially make a specific contribution to improving the quality of democracy by incorporating more 'challenging' groups to involve in the political process, e.g. young people and marginal-ized communities. The sentiment of one Cymdeithas member reflected the potential contribution of organizations to improve the quality of democracy by promoting participation:

> you have a commitment to participatory democracy that is more than voting every five years. I'd like to think that civil society plays a role in that sense by providing opportunities for people to participate ... the role of our movement as part of civil society is to provoke and provide opportunities for people to think politically.[2]

More generally, differences in the opportunities for active membership participation within some organizations raised potential questions regarding civil society's ability to enhance democracy. The contrasts nevertheless highlighted that groups operate differently and through internal structures or activities could promote participation. A group may not have horizontal internal decision-making structures conducive to promoting participation, but its activities and projects could generate participation and tackle exclusion. Some organizations clearly had the potential to encourage further civic participation. The most conducive were those with democratic and horizontal structures that provided active membership opportunities in decision-making and campaigning, thus potentially promoting participatory democracy ideals.

CIVIL SOCIETY LEGITIMIZING AND DEEPENING DEVOLUTION

A final aspect regarding civil society's potential to revitalize democracy was the question of whether organizations' activities served to legitimate devolution. One matter to be investigated was concern that the complexity and lack of clarity of the Assembly's legislative competence would have a negative effect on civil society's engagement with the Assembly. The findings suggested it had dual effects on the interaction of civil society organizations with the devolved institution. The complexity detrimentally affected some organizations involved in devolved areas, namely Cymdeithas and Cymuned. This reflected the research findings regarding the effects on voluntary sector and equality organizations with limited resources (Chaney et al., 2000: 213). Cymdeithas stated in its evidence to the Richard Commission (see Appendix 2):

> Although it [the Assembly] has power in important fields such as education and health, these fields are only partially devolved. So in view of such a horizontal division of power, understanding the true powers of the Assembly is a very difficult task. (NAW, 2003b: 2)

The stark paradox was however that the complexity worked to the advantage of adequately resourced organizations primarily involved in non-devolved policy areas and facilitated their engagement with the Assembly. Though Oxfam Cymru and Stonewall Cymru were predominantly involved in non-devolved issues, they saw the Assembly as an important political voice. Their lobbying promoted the Assembly to take action on non-devolved issues and to use its influence within party structures and other levels of government. This included encouraging AMs to utilize Section 33 to make Statements of Opinion on LGB issues and on international issues. More significantly, Section 120, the equality of opportunity duty, justified the Assembly's support for establishing consultative networks such as Stonewall Cymru to address non-devolved issues in the current devolution settlement. Therefore, in contrast to the politics of recognition of the Welsh language, which generated hostility within the Assembly, these cases emphasized the political commitment within the Welsh Assembly Government and by Assembly Members to have a voice on these non-devolved issues. The Assembly was subsequently willing to advance beyond the unclear boundaries of the devolution settlement. Therefore, the lack of clarity in the Assembly's powers enhanced both the efforts of civil society organizations and the Assembly to advance these agendas.

Overall, considering civil society's limited role in the devolution process, have organizations legitimized devolution? Most civil society organizations involved in devolved and non-devolved areas contributed to legitimizing the Assembly as they adopted the devolved institution as their main political target. Organizations assisted in overcoming difficulties faced by the Assembly in its first term and thus contributed to making devolution work. Furthermore, organizations examined in both devolved and non-devolved issues, to differing degrees, highlighted the limitations in the National Assembly's powers and advocated amending the Government of Wales Act 1998. For organizations primarily involved in non-devolved matters, the current settlement restricted the Assembly in their respective areas and the first term provided an impetus to call for greater devolved powers. For instance, in its evidence to the Richard Commission, Stonewall Cymru highlighted limitations in the Assembly's current powers to address LGB issues:

> the Welsh Assembly Government has been unable to promote equality of opportunity for lesbian, gay and bisexual people in Wales to the extent that it would wish because of reserved powers held at Westminster. Even in devolved areas, the Assembly has been limited in its influence. (NAW, 2003i)

Thus, civil society attempted to influence and deepen the direction of devolution. This development is in line with Paterson and Wyn Jones's speculation that this would be a consequence of the settlement (1999: 192).

It suggested a process of 'spill-over' where organizations' engagement in one area of the Assembly's work promoted involvement in other areas. Whereas civil society made only a limited contribution in the achievement of devolution, its role in legitimizing and deepening devolution suggested that devolution has been a force of empowerment and revitalization.

WELSH CIVIL SOCIETY AND CIVIL SOCIETY IN WALES

In addition to the research questions associated with civil society and democratic development, two questions related to civil society and identity in post-devolution Wales remain. One aspect focused on the *civil society in Wales / Welsh civil society* distinction to examine what impact devolution had on the identity of organizations. Utilizing this distinction highlighted a number of key issues. It assisted in understanding that *civil society in Wales* and *Welsh civil society* were not either/or categories: viewing them as two opposites on either end of a spectrum provided greater clarity. Key attributes to assess the identity of organizations were the effects of the location of power and decision-making on their autonomy. Examining Cymdeithas and Cymuned highlighted some of the 'Welsh' characteristics of *Welsh civil society*. Key attributes included the National Assembly seen as their main target; policy-development capacities and decision-making structures located in Wales and focused on Wales; calls for greater powers for the devolved institution.

With regard to organizations examined in this study with greater *civil society in Wales* characteristics, ties with UK-wide organizations still persisted, but, to differing degrees, organizations restructured on a more Welsh basis and shifted towards *Welsh civil society*. This concurs with the expectation that devolution would increase the presence of British-orientated organizations in Wales and would simultaneously 'Welshify' them (Paterson and Wyn Jones, 1999). From examining Oxfam Cymru, it seemed that a number of international development organizations, like Amnesty International and Save the Children, developed a presence in Wales following devolution. These primarily related to non-devolved issues and suggested a broader trend of an increased presence of *civil society in Wales*.

Other evidence highlights that these shifts were not reflected throughout civil society in Wales. Stonewall Cymru's case demonstrated that the identity of *Welsh civil society* organizations can potentially shift more towards *civil society in Wales* post-devolution as changes in 2003 strengthened the relationship with Stonewall. Furthermore, one of the most high-profile events relating to civil society during devolution's first term was the Children's Society's withdrawal of its operations from Wales. The charity had fourteen key projects in Wales working with vulnerable children and young people, and received part-funding from the Assembly and local authorities (T. Mason, 2001). As a result of this action the Assembly and the WCVA held a seminar with the heads of UK voluntary organizations working in Wales to 'discuss the implications of devolution for their current decision-making processes and accountability to Wales' (NAW, 2001n). In addition a working group on the issue was established, and *Working within Wales: Shared Principles*, the Code of Principles for UK voluntary organizations working in Wales (Box 8.1), was developed (WAG, 2006). Therefore, though the findings identified a shift in the identity of organizations, devolution did not have such a significant impact on the identity of some *civil society in Wales* organizations.

Nevertheless, how can we understand the shift towards *Welsh civil society*? It could be argued that many organizations were being opportunistic in their response to the new opportunities resulting from devolution. However, the degree of structural changes within organizations in the Assembly's early years facilitated their contribution to the devolution project and suggests that organizations were also principled in their actions. The most minimal and symbolic shift in the identity of organizations was evident in a change in name. More substantial changes were greater autonomy from the UK level and the subsequent internal organizational changes. Restructuring in many cases led to establishing a more high-level managerial staff in Wales compared to the pre-devolution period and more strategic staffing structures. The result of these changes was that organizations were able to develop a strengthened Welsh outlook, increase their recognition of Wales as being different and become more responsive to the Welsh institutional context. Organizations therefore developed decision-making and policy-making structures to design policies for Wales and made the National Assembly their main political target. Groundwork Wales explained: 'now our response and the way we choose to develop our organisation is about responding to Welsh issues'.[3] A number of these aspects reflected the Welsh Assembly Government's Code of Principles for UK voluntary organizations (WAG, 2006). A further step was that these changes were supported in many cases by expressing a commitment to being a 'Welsh' organization. The changes in Oxfam Cymru intended to locate it as part of *Welsh civil society*, 'as a Welsh institution within the institutional life of Wales's (Oxfam in Wales, 1999).

Overall, the effects of devolution on the relationship between civil society and identity were significant. Changes in the Welsh institutional context promoted greater recognition of Wales and involvement with its political institutions, thus increasing a Welsh outlook amongst the organizations of civil society.

Box 8.1: Welsh Assembly Government Code of Principles for UK Voluntary Organizations in Wales

Working within Wales: Shared Principles

Aim of the Code of Principles

> *The aim of the Code of Principles is to maintain and strengthen good working relationships between the Welsh Assembly Government, UK voluntary organisations working in Wales and other key stakeholders. It aims to provide a basis for increased dialogue and understanding, to ensure that the voluntary sector and the Assembly work together to achieve shared aims.*

The Code of Principles will not replace the Voluntary Sector Scheme, which sets out how the Assembly will promote the work of the voluntary sector in Wales, but aims to recognize the particular role that UK voluntary organisations play in Wales. Organisations are invited to endorse the Code of Principles as the basis of a mutually advantageous relationship.

Code of Principles for working in Wales

Welsh Assembly Government
The Welsh Assembly Government is committed to the following principles in relation to the voluntary sector:

*   recognising, valuing and promoting the work of the voluntary sector in Wales;
*   consultation with the voluntary sector on policy changes and new policy developments;
*   delivering services on the basis of 'who does what best' – that is, a commitment to identifying where the voluntary sector might take the lead in or contribute to the implementation of new policies, and ensuring that there are appropriate funding mechanisms in place;
*   prior discussion and reasonable notice before any policy changes or decisions which would lead to withdrawal or significant reduction in grants;
*   recognising that voluntary and community organisations are independent organisations, which determine their own priorities and manage their own budgets;
*   valuing the skills, experiences and ideas that UK voluntary organisations bring to Wales through their work in the rest of the UK and beyond;
*   ensuring that local government in Wales engages with voluntary organisations in a fair and equitable way and will establish indicators to monitor their effectiveness.

UK voluntary organizations
[Name of Organisation] is committed to the following principles in relation to its work in Wales:

- recognising that Wales is a distinct nation with its own democratically elected government and unique social, economic, political and cultural circumstances;
- recognizing that Wales is a bilingual country and therefore treating the English and Welsh languages on a basis of equality;
- establishing appropriate mechanisms of accountability for services and policies in Wales, including devolution of functions and management structures where possible;
- ensuring that decision-making processes for services and policies in Wales are informed by service users or members in Wales, or have an evidence base in Wales;
- early consultation with funders, stakeholders and service users in advance of any decisions to withdraw, reduce or significantly alter services for people in Wales.

(WAG, 2006)

CIVIL SOCIETY AND CIVIC IDENTITY

Finally, in examining the question of civil society's contribution in the interaction between devolution and national identity, there were some tentative suggestions that civil society's interaction with the Assembly contributed to developing a strengthened civic sense of Welsh national identity. In many respects, it is premature to assess the impact of devolution on Welsh identity and this is an under-researched area in the literature on post-devolution Wales. A full examination of the interrelationship between civil society and national identity was not undertaken in this study. Some initial evidence was however developed through combining the case study evidence with quantitative data. It can be tentatively argued that civil society has taken initial advances towards promoting a greater civic sense of Welsh identity.

Quantitative research surveys from 1997 to 2003 suggested that a greater civic sense of national identity developed in post-devolution Wales. While a note of caution needs to be sounded regarding survey questions on national identity (McInness, 2004), the data on national identity (see Table 8.1) suggested that following devolution there was an increased sense of Welsh identity and a decrease in numbers who identify with a British sense of identity.

The survey question on constitutional preferences was not entirely adequate in considering the degree of civic sense of Welsh identity post-devolution, but as a possible proxy variable, it provided some useful

Table 8.1: National identities in Wales (%) 1997–2003

National Identity	1997	1999	2001	2003
Welsh, not British	17.2	17.7	24.6	22.4
More Welsh than British	25.7	20.7	23.5	28.5
Equally Welsh and British	34.3	38.3	29.4	30.0
More British than Welsh	10.4	7.8	11.2	8.8
British, not Welsh	12.4	15.5	11.3	10.3

Table 8.2: Constitutional preferences in Wales (%) 1997–2003

Constitutional Preference	1997	1999	2001	2003
Independence	14.1	9.6	12.3	13.9
Parliament	19.6	29.9	38.8	37.8
Assembly	26.8	35.3	25.5	27.1
No elected body	39.5	25.3	24.0	21.2

Sources: Welsh Referendum Survey, 1997; Welsh National Assembly Election Survey, 1999, 2001; Wales Life and Times Study; Welsh National Assembly Election Survey, 2003.

suggestions (see Table 8.2). The steady decrease of nearly 20 per cent from 1997 to 2003 in the number of respondents that opposed to the Assembly and the growth in support for an elected body in Wales could be understood as a tentative measure of increasing allegiance to some form of political institution in Wales. The very kind of affiliation that is viewed as central to the civic as opposed to ethnic aspects of national identity. In conjunction with the increased expression of a greater sense of Welsh identity in the previous table, quantitative data suggested that a greater civic sense of national identity developed in the early years of post-devolution Wales. This was tempered as the 2003 survey demonstrated that the percentages expressing a preference for an Assembly had returned to the levels of 1997 with the main constitutional preference from 2001 onwards being a Parliament. Certainly, the parliament option is becoming the most popular: 'support for devolution in Wales has grown substantially since 1997, but a significant number of Welsh voters wish the principle of devolution to be taken further' (Wyn Jones and Scully, 2003: 92). This is confirmed by responses to other survey questions that suggest a majority now support the principle of devolution, despite public disappointment in the limited effects of devolution and the Assembly's performance in different policy areas (Wyn Jones and Scully, 2004: 192). The question regarding which level of government people trust to act in Wales's best interest also highlights that a clear majority select the Assembly before the UK government, the EU or local government (Wyn Jones and Scully, 2006: 15; Scully and Wyn Jones, 2006). The quantitative data suggested an increased sense of allegiance to some form of political institution in Wales post-devolution and moves towards a strengthened sense of civic nationhood in post-devolution Wales. The case study findings also suggested that devolution meant that civil society organizations made initial advances towards contributing to developing a civic national identity. Chapter 2 suggested that civil society could contribute to developing a more civic sense of national identity in two ways. Civil society could promote allegiance to civic institutions. It could also contribute to a greater civic sense of nationhood by enabling a plurality of interests to be represented within civil society. The findings identified that civil society encouraged allegiance to political institutions. Issues already discussed were the strong levels of engagement with the Assembly; organizations' contribution to legitimizing devolution, and organizations' advocacy of greater powers for the Assembly. Though the partnership between a number of civil society organizations and the Assembly raised concerns regarding the nature of organizations' allegiance, the interaction between civil society and the National Assembly can be viewed as a significant contribution to the promotion of a stronger civic sense of Welsh identity.

The study's focus on four case studies made assessing civil society's contribution to an expression of civic national identity as a result of increased pluralism within civil society more difficult to examine. Some findings point to indications that pluralism was more evident within civil society. Devolution was certainly a catalyst for the establishment and development of new organizations. This was evident in establishing Stonewall Cymru as an all-Wales organization to represent the LGB 'community'. Cymuned's establishment also illustrated a greater plurality of organizations within the Welsh language movement and it seemed to represent other interests that were previously less well represented. Moreover, organizations themselves expressed a commitment to developing a civic sense of identity. Oxfam Cymru's aims were to make 'a distinctive contribution to the creation of Wales with a strong sense of civic nationhood that is inclusive, participatory and externally focused' (Oxfam Cymru, 2001a). One Oxfam Cymru interviewee explained this sense of civic nationhood:

> It's about citizenship of a country in which a person's history, roots, original
> location geographically, language etc. isn't the primary defining factor but
> whether or not citizens are actively making constructive contributions to the

development of society and societies within that nation. So it's more of an active intent than a historical accident, and it's very much about the institutions of that nation making it possible for citizens to actively participate.[4]

To sum up, tentative initial findings were developed regarding the organizational changes within civil society and its involvement with the Assembly in the interaction between political devolution and national identity. This is an area that requires more detailed research. There was some evidence of civil society organizations' allegiance to the National Assembly and some indications of a greater plurality of interests represented within civil society. This suggests that civil society was developing the capacity to make a valuable contribution to enhancing the civic elements of Welsh identity and potentially stimulated moves towards a strengthened sense of civic nationhood in post-devolution Wales.

After mapping out the main findings of the four case studies, we can now examine the broader implications of this study to devolution to Wales and to civil society theory.

DEVOLUTION TO WALES

Let us begin with Wales, and first focus on what may be regarded as some of the more positive findings. The research has identified that devolution has had a profound and extensive impact on civil society in Wales. Indeed, and somewhat paradoxically perhaps, the case study findings suggested that devolution had a more significant impact on organizations predominantly involved in non-devolved issues where the Assembly's powers were limited. This highlighted that the National Assembly and Welsh Assembly Government were able to generate a much greater influence throughout civil society than might have been expected.

One of the most significant effects of the changes in the Welsh institutional context was the shift in the identity of a majority of organizations towards a strengthened Welsh outlook. This increased Welsh outlook was particularly evident in relation to organizations that previously operated in more British terms of reference: what has been described above as *civil society in Wales*. It seemed highly likely that the findings developed here reflected a broader trend that included civil society, the political parties, private- and public-sector organizations and administrative agencies. Devolution made organizations and institutions more 'Welsh', defined not in terms of language or geography but in terms of interaction with Welsh political institutions and a recognition that Wales was distinct. It may be confidently expected that an expansion of the Assembly's policy divergence from London and enhanced powers could accentuate this trend.

Another positive element in the interrelationship between devolution and civil society related to the case study findings on Welsh national identity. While it was expected that devolution would strengthen Welsh identity, this study tentatively suggested that moves toward a stronger *civic* sense of Welsh nationhood took place during the first term of devolution. As argued in the Introduction, a strengthened sense of identity that had the capacity to encompass the whole of Wales was a highly desirable possible effect of devolution. Changes within civil society and its interaction with the Assembly made some contribution to this development. While it seems premature to contend that devolution definitively and irrevocably established a strong civic sense of Welsh identity, it seems that steps in this direction have been taken.

Finally, and relatedly, civil society organizations' engagement in the Assembly's work was particularly important for the devolution project. As the Assembly faced legitimacy problems in the Welsh Devolution Referendum and the 1999 National Assembly elections because of low voter turnout, civil society's contribution to the Assembly's legitimization was even more important. Moreover, organizations involved in both devolved and non-devolved areas highlighted limitations in the Assembly's powers and called for further powers for the devolved institution. Most interestingly, organizations predominantly involved in non-devolved issues attempted to encourage the Assembly to utilize its existing powers to address non-devolved issues. All this suggested a two-way spill-over process in civil society's engagement with the Assembly. The involvement of organizations in one area of the Assembly's powers seemed to spur other organizations in that sector to engage with the Assembly. It also had the potential to promote organizations to expand the range of policy areas in which they engaged with the Assembly. Civil society organizations therefore contributed to legitimizing the Assembly and were central in advocating a stronger devolution settlement.

However, positive findings regarding civil society were to some extent counterbalanced and overshadowed by other concerns highlighted and investigated in this study. Indeed, the potential concerns discussed here in the context of the first term of post-devolution government in Wales, were likely to be raised even more pointedly during the National Assembly's second term. The 2003 election to the National Assembly saw the establishment of a one-party majority government and the reassertion of the Welsh Labour Party's domination of Welsh politics, thus weakening the Assembly's 'inclusiveness'. This 'inclusiveness' had, of course, been central to promoting extensive civil society engagement. Trends that were well under way during the first term in downgrading 'inclusive' structures, such as the growth of a 'virtual parliament', further solidified during the second term. Amongst the most significant developments were 'large-scale autonomy for what is now called the 'Assembly Parliamentary Service' and a hardening and substantial thickening of the political and administrative core (the "Welsh Assembly Government")' (Rawlings, 2004b: 2). Key implications for civil society's engagement with the Assembly during the second term included a further diminution of the influence of the subject committees, reflected in the reduction of their meetings to a three-week basis (Rawlings, 2004a: 9). Another key development during the second term, viewed by some as the biggest shake-up in Welsh government since the creation of the National Assembly, raises issues for civil society. This is the unexpected decision to merge a number of Assembly Sponsored Public Bodies into the Welsh Assembly Government in April 2006 (Osmond, 2004: 1). The full implications of the abolition of the quangos for civil society were not entirely clear at the time of writing. One obvious change is that an increased number of organizations receive funding directly from the Welsh Assembly Government. Another issue is that advisory panels established to reflect each ministerial portfolio are a central channel for influencing government policies. That a range of civil society organizations has the capacity to gain representation on these boards is a matter of doubt. The potential concerns identified in this research can be summarized as follows.

The study highlighted power inequalities and practices of exclusion within civil society; the stark differences between professionalized organizations and those with limited resources increased post-devolution. This suggested a two-tier civil society, consisting of the 'haves' and the 'have-nots'. This in turn raised concerns about how exactly – indeed, whether – civil society contributed to democratic development. In post-devolution Wales, it seemed that some interests were better equipped to be represented in the political process than others, and that their financial situation was a key issue. Far from widening and enriching democracy, engaging some parts of civil society more fully in the democratic process could potentially merely serve to exacerbate broader inequalities within society.

Patterns of civic participation further exacerbated these concerns. It was precisely those more traditional organizations with limited resources that tended to promote the greatest active membership participation. 'Successful' professionalized organizations tended to provide comparatively fewer opportunities for membership involvement in aspects such as policy decision-making. Contemporary trends of professionalized organizational structures with more limited membership participation were certainly on the increase in the civil society of post-devolution Wales. In the longer term, it could be argued that if inequalities within civil society persisted, its potential to promote participatory norms and enhance democracy in post-devolution Wales must be in real doubt.

When limitations have been raised regarding civil society's democratic credentials, emphasis has been placed on other actors such as the state in the promotion of democracy (McLaverty, 2002: 311). The findings in this book highlighted that the state can also pose a barrier to broad civil society participation in government. Aspects of civil society–Assembly relations raised concerns regarding the nature of democracy in post-devolution Wales, and in particular its much vaunted 'inclusiveness'. The shift to a cabinet system of government and establishing the Partnership Government downgraded the importance of the Assembly's 'inclusive' structures. The report of the Richard Commission added further credence to this interpretation. While commending the subject committees for their inclusivity and accessibility to stakeholders, the commissioners also noted the weaknesses of the committees in influencing Assembly Government policy (WAG, 2004a: 56). A quote from Glyn Davies AM illustrates the point: 'The policy-making role of committees is to a large extent superficial. The committee can develop new policy just as long as it coincides with what the Minister thinks' (WAG, 2004a: 57). Therefore, changes during the first term had mixed effects on the nature of democracy and the type of political culture promoted by the Assembly and Assembly Government. The shifts were positive in addressing the ambiguities of the corporate body status and clarifying accountability within the Assembly. However, there were also negative democratic consequences. These changes limited the Assembly's overall openness, accessibility and transparency, and created disparities between the influence that different organizations were able to exert within the Assembly and particularly on the Assembly Government.

The discussion revealed other limits to the Assembly's 'inclusiveness'. As is also highlighted by the report of the Richard Commission, the study identified how the complexity and lack of clarity of the devolution settlement discouraged some organizations from engaging with the Assembly (WAG, 2004a: 97). The paradox was that the settlement had a positive effect on the engagement of other organizations in predominantly non-devolved areas. In addition, organizations involved in some subject areas were less acceptable to the National Assembly, the paradox here being that, in the case studies, it was those organizations active in the area where the Assembly had the greatest power, that is, the Welsh language, who were most excluded. The organizations most meaningfully involved in the Assembly's work related to non-devolved areas of international development and sexual orientation, areas in which the National Assembly's powers were of course more limited. It could be argued that it is unfair to focus on the Assembly's 'inclusiveness' without also giving due credit to the Assembly's efforts to address the exclusion of marginalized groups and promote capacity-building, particularly through the Assembly-sponsored structures. Yet, even these latter arrangements, as Chaney and Fevre pointed out, raised concerns regarding their mixed democratic implications (2001a). Lack of inclusivity had negative consequences for democracy in Wales that were potentially far-reaching. It suggested that only a limited number of organizations had the capacity to take advantage of opportunities to engage meaningfully with the Welsh Assembly Government. The shift towards a more pluralist and less elitist political culture envisaged at the inception of devolution was not fully achieved.

These conclusions ultimately suggested that the Assembly and Welsh Assembly Government's methods of engagement posed a barrier to promoting democratization in civil society and Assembly relations. The Assembly and Assembly Government's 'inclusiveness' diminished, and as a consequence of weaknesses within civil society the Assembly developed more exclusive relations with some organizations. The strength of 'partnerships' and the weaknesses of other organizations outside the charmed circle raised concerns that there were, possibly, only limited voices with autonomy able to scrutinize government. Considering the weaknesses of other agencies in Welsh society which might be critical of state power, for example the 'Welsh' media, constraints on the ability of civil society to promote accountability can be viewed as a significant democratic concern.

Trends in civil society–Assembly relations during the first term of devolution raised concerns regarding the nature of political culture in post-devolution Wales. It suggested that in reality, beneath the rhetoric of 'bringing government closer to the people', devolution essentially remained 'an affair of the elite' (Rawlings, 2003: 377, 544). If these trends continue, the hierarchy within civil society will be further stratified. The exclusive relations between some organizations and the Assembly Government could dissuade others from engaging with the Assembly and even suppress the development of new organizations. Overall, there is a real dilemma in addressing the weak financial situation and the capacity base of organizations in order to achieve a more level playing-field within civil society. One of the main approaches, Assembly core funding to organizations (either directly or indirectly), raised potential concerns regarding the representativeness and autonomy of those organizations and their role in holding government accountable. Ultimately, if it's all too cosy, this could even threaten the Assembly's legitimacy. The Richard Commission highlighted an interesting, and potentially worrisome, development in this regard: 'We have been struck by the contrast between the enthusiasm of those actively in contact with the Assembly and a seemingly wider public indifference expressed by the particularly low turnout at the two elections' (WAG, 2004a: 255). If a situation developed where only a civil society elite meaningfully engaged with the Assembly while the second tier of civil society, let alone the wider populace, felt excluded and alienated, this would raise deeply troubling questions for the whole future of the devolution project.

The findings therefore highlighted some positive developments arising from the significant impact that devolution has made on civil society. However, there were concerns of potentially negative democratic effects of civil society–Assembly relations arising from the Assembly's political processes and the nature of political culture in post-devolution Wales. Many of these issues are difficult to resolve and there are no quick-fix solutions. Potential policy prescriptions arising from the findings of the study which could address these issues include:

1. Acknowledging that 'partnerships' between the Welsh Assembly Government and individual civil society organizations have the potential to lead to exclusive relations. The potentially negative democratic consequences of such practices need greater recognition by the Welsh Assembly Government and civil society.
2. Making efforts to ensure that receipt of public funding does not create ties that detrimentally affect the scrutiny capacities of organizations. For example, provisions could be included into core funding agreements stating that policy disagreement with the Welsh Assembly Government will not lead to a reduction in co-funding. This is even more important in the assembly sponsored public bodies post-merger context.
3. Ensuring that networks and key organizations that are charged to 'represent' civil society in the Welsh Assembly Government's work beyond the Voluntary Sector Partnership Council can adequately express the viewpoints from the wide range of organizations that they 'represent'. There should be some rotation of the key organizations and individuals selected to represent their sector should rotate. Again, already this takes place on the Partnership Council and the practice should be broadened to other areas. Efforts should be made to address concerns regarding lack of continuity and expertise arising from rotation. Qualitative checks should be undertaken to verify that funding is utilized for consultation processes within sectors of civil society.
4. Establishing processes and capacity-building funding to include a broader range of civil society organizations in the Welsh Assembly Government's policy-making processes. Involving different and less experienced organizations in working groups and task forces can create difficulties. It would, however, help less professionalized groups to develop their internal capacities, promote expertise and foster links within government. For example, checks should verify that a range of organizations are members of groups and task forces that engage in the Welsh Assembly Government's work.

Since this research was undertaken, the Independent Commission Review of the Voluntary Sector was established to advise WAG on reviewing the National Assembly's Voluntary Sector Scheme (WAG, 2004c). While the Commission recommended that the scheme should not be remade, it produced detailed recommendations for the Assembly Government, the WCVA and the Voluntary Sector Partnership Council (WAG, 2004c: 8). Overall, the Commission was positive regarding the scheme and the voluntary sector's involvement with the Assembly and the policy process post-devolution. The Commission identified that the capacity of organizations was an issue, including in relation to policy development (WAG, 2004c: 73). Some of the Commission's recommendations resonate with the potential policy prescriptions discussed above – for example, an emphasis on capacity building and training, and the need for adequate resources to ensure effective and efficient operation of sectoral networks on the Voluntary Sector Partnership Council.

An important recommendation made by the Commission was that WAG should 'work with the sector to promote more vigorously the use of secondments between the Assembly Government and the voluntary and community sectors, as set out in the Scheme' (WAG, 2004c: 74). This development reflects a broader agenda of promoting interchange between staff across the public service, private sector and voluntary sector as part of the Making the Connections public service reform agenda. As a result, WAG is committed to increasing the inward and outward opportunities for interchange between staff from the Welsh Assembly Government and voluntary sector organizations. It is among the most positive innovations. It can strengthen the capacity of voluntary sector organizations and give them an understanding of the Assembly and the sector. The indirect effects of the scheme are to promote and strengthen the networking opportunities in government for individuals working for the voluntary sector, thus improving informal and formal engagement with the Assembly.

CIVIL SOCIETY THEORY

As the study was empirically grounded, it was also interesting to consider the wider implications for civil society theory. In many respects, the study served to confirm that 'civil society' is an analytically useful concept and an important research tool in developing a better understanding of political culture and political systems. However, it also highlighted some of the limitations of the concept. These may be briefly summarized as follows.

First, the unfamiliarity of the concept of 'civil society' in the Welsh context was obvious. Even amongst some individuals who were highly active in a range of 'civil society' organizations, there was sometimes little understanding of the term itself. This reflected the limited usage of civil society in Wales as discussed in the Introduction. One consequence of this lack of understanding was the way in which civil society became a 'catch-all' term. Civil society was used to describe a whole range of different elements of the social world including, for example, local government and the private sector. To some extent, this merely reflected different interpretations within civil society theory itself. However, the point must again be made: how we conceptualize civil society directly affects how its democratic role is perceived. And of course 'civil society' has been popularized on a worldwide basis leading to a great diversity in the meanings attached to the term. If the same lack of clarity and 'catch-all' status characterizes the usage of 'civil society' in other contexts, as in Wales, then this tends to raise doubts as to its utility. Civil society is certainly not an unproblematic term, and utilizing it means that a course has to be steered between competing understandings.

Secondly, utilizing the concept of civil society in an empirical study highlighted some of its fuzziness in a modern liberal capitalist democracy; specifically the blurred boundaries between civil society, the state and economy. At the most elementary level, this meant that it was difficult at times to decide whether some organizations should be categorized as civil society due to their funding status. This also had a more theoretical resonance. The fuzziness arose from civil society organizations' receipt of state funding and their role in implementing government policies. While this highlighted the state's role in revitalizing civil society, it emphasized the increasing interdependencies between the state and 'civil society' that made it difficult to distinguish between them. It also raised concerns regarding the potential effects on civil society's autonomy.

Thirdly, the study confirmed that inequalities of power and influence, characteristic of society as a whole, were evident and indeed exacerbated within civil society. These problems were raised in Chapter 2 where it was asserted that understanding civil society's democratic potential called for focusing on organizations on an individual basis. Some organizations with strong financial resources and better connections with government dominated to the potential detriment of less powerful organizations. Shifts within organizations towards more contemporary trends of membership that led to potentially more limited opportunities for local and active involvement were evident in the Welsh context. Both aspects stressed that civil society organizations can promote democracy in different ways and can perpetuate limitations to democracy.

Overall, the three points made here highlight the need to revisit how civil society is defined and how its democratic potential is perceived. Analysis of relations between the state and society suggested that civil society was becoming increasingly dependent on the state and that its role was shifting towards acting as a partner to the state, improving the state's policy-making and implementation processes. It could also be argued that the corollary of this was that civil society's role in facilitating broader participation and civic engagement, in checking state power and promoting accountable government, was diminishing or at least changing. The study questioned the degree to which civil society organizations served as a check on governmental power in existing western liberal democracies. These key issues arising from empirical research pointed to the need for a two-way relationship between empirical research and theorizing civil society in this area.

Future research directions arising from this study are threefold. First, investigating the impact of devolution on civil society during subsequent terms of devolution to Wales is particularly interesting. There are a number of issues to be investigated in relation to identity. Does devolution continue to influence the identity of organizations and promote further shifts towards a stronger Welsh outlook? Similarly, do developments in civil society contribute to the promotion (or otherwise) of a sense of Welsh civic nationhood? What are the implications of enhanced legislative powers for civil society engagement with the devolved institution? The next step in devolution to Wales, the Government of Wales Act 2006 (Office of Public Sector Information, 2006), implemented following the National Assembly Elections in 2007, suggests positive and negative implications for civil society. The act is viewed as a major development (Trench, 2007: 6). While many details on how the arrangements will work in practice are unclear at the time of writing, some key points can be made. Legally enshrining the separation between the executive and the legislative branches means that the body corporate status disappears and the Act establishes a separate Welsh Assembly Government and a new legal personality, National Assembly for Wales. This legal separation is an important step to provide greater clarity and strengthen accountability. Perhaps the citizens and civil society of Wales will finally realize who is in control.

In addition, Acts of Parliament or Legislative Competence Orders in Council will allow the Assembly to pass Assembly Measures in specific areas. It will therefore be given legal authority by Westminster on a case-by-case basis to pass Assembly Measures in specific areas that form part of the 20 fields of devolved policy areas (as detailed in Schedule 5 of the 2006 Act). These developments can potentially speed up the process of legislating for Wales and incrementally increase the Assembly's powers.

Granting enhanced legislative powers to the Assembly has the potential to promote greater civil society and citizen interest and engagement in the Assembly's legislative process. Furthermore, provisions included in the new Standing Orders (Standing Order 28) deal with procedures for public petitions. It states that the Assembly *must* consider any admissible public petition presented to the Assembly. The Presiding Officer is to refer the petition to a relevant committee to decide on appropriate action (NAW, 2007: 16). This innovation can potentially provide a channel for civil society organizations to try to gain a greater influence on the deliberations and legislation developed by the Assembly.

Other features of the proposals could have negative democratic consequences, however. A key issue is the complexity of the proposals for enhanced powers, particularly the Orders in Council element. This could exacerbate existing concerns regarding the lack of clarity and intelligibility of the Assembly's powers (Rawlings, 2005: 845; Trench, 2006; Richard, 2006). A specific example is continuing the 'jagged edge' or 'jigsaw' patterns of Assembly powers as 'Nothing in the way these proposals are being implemented will remedy the long-standing problem of a high degree of variation in the powers conferred on the Assembly' (Trench, 2007: 15–16). Such a legal labyrinth raises further questions regarding devolution's ability to be inclusive to citizens and civil society. In this context, additional work could also be undertaken to assess civil society's role in the future of the devolution project and whether it retains the important function of legitimizing and advocating greater powers for the National Assembly. Considering the findings of this study regarding civil society–Assembly relations, research into subsequent terms of devolution should allow for further reflection on the implications for democracy. Do these relations continue to be more exclusive thus taking on a 'new-corporatist' form, or is there greater openness to all organizations irrespective of their financial resources or connections with the Welsh Assembly Government?

A comparative study would be extremely valuable in order to understand whether the study's conclusions of the impact of regional government on civil society and political culture are relevant only to Wales or have a wider resonance. Finally, more detailed research is needed, both theoretically and empirically, to understand the interrelationship between civil society and national identity. This is a particularly under-researched aspect of the literature on civil society. The case of Wales deserves particular attention due to the complex and interesting characteristics of national identity in Wales (Hasely, 2005). There is a range of other research issues to be pursued in this area using both qualitative and quantitative techniques in order to gain a better understanding of national identity in Wales post-devolution. Overall, this volume presents a mixed picture. Whether we view this particular glass as 'half full' or 'half empty' may ultimately be a matter of subjective preoccupations and prejudices. From the 'half empty' perspective, the research raised deep concerns regarding civil society, its relations with the Assembly and the political process post-devolution. These concerns were not solely caused by the devolution 'settlement' itself, but have been influenced by broader and deeply embedded aspects of Wales's political culture. Morgan and Mungham pointed out that the nature of political culture could affect devolution to Wales: 'If we have a monist political culture which, deep down, frowns upon debate then this suggests not just a weak political establishment but also a weak civil society because politics reflects civics and vice versa' (2000: 210). Therefore, the 'old' Welsh political culture was more robust and deep-seated than the rhetoric of 'new politics' and 'inclusiveness' would suggest. This included the effects on Welsh politics and political culture of continuing single-party dominance at Westminster and the local level. Another aspect was the more elitist political culture characteristic of the parliamentary model of government at Westminster, also evident in Welsh Office practices. Aspects of this culture resurfaced within the Assembly with the shift to a cabinet system of government. As Rawlings wryly notes, 'the capacity of the Westminster-style parliament tradition to reinvent itself in other settings was grossly underestimated' (2003: 89). From this perspective therefore, many of the concerns raised in the study are intractable and there are few 'quick-fixes'.

Taking the 'half full' view, devolution had far-reaching effects on the positive development of civil society. In many respects, the nature of the devolution settlement created a number of constraints and problems that affected the National Assembly's first term. Their direct effects on civil society were demonstrated in this study. In this constitutional and political context, it was always going to be difficult, if not impossible, to fulfil the unrealistically high expectations regarding devolution and civil society in post-devolution Wales. It might be plausibly argued therefore that the profound effects of devolution on civil society were more extensive than could realistically have been expected. However, if we are to err in this more positive direction, any complacency is wholly inappropriate. In order to secure a positive future for devolution to Wales, the problems and concerns raised in the study regarding civil society need to be recognized. Only then can steps be taken to ameliorate elitist tendencies and gradually build a more pluralist political culture in post-devolution Wales – a political culture conspicuously different from the one Wales has known up to now.

APPENDIX 2

Richard Commission – The Welsh Language Society

Introductory Comments

The Welsh Language Society was established in 1962 following the broadcast of Saunders Lewis's famous radio lecture, *Tynged yr Iaith* (The Fate of the Language). Ever since, the movement has campaigned ceaselessly, using direct and non-violent methods, to ensure a future for the Welsh language. Over the years, detailed policies have been developed in the fields of status, education, housing and planning.

The Welsh Language Society is a movement which wishes to see the development of radical politics in Wales, based on community socialism values. Politics which will, in essence, respond to Wales's needs and which will work to achieve justice for the Welsh language, as well as social and economic justice for the people and communities of Wales.

Therefore the Welsh Language Society naturally welcomed the establishment of a National Assembly, as the process of devolving power has a vital role to play in building the politics described above. The event was identified as one of the main changes in the recent history of Wales. It was also emphasized that the Assembly, despite its weaknesses, had great potential in developing a fair and Welsh government.

However, as we approach the end of the first term, we believe that the experiences of the past years have shown that the Assembly cannot operate effectively as a national body without legislative powers. In many policy areas it is often evident that the muddled and scrambled nature of the constitutional settlement stands as an obstacle to any meaningful and integrated strategy. Furthermore – looking at matters from the specific perspective of our campaigns – it is clear that legislative powers are a must if the Assembly wishes to build a future for the Welsh language in the modern age.

We shall divide our comments into three sections:

1. Some general comments regarding the need for legislative powers.
2. The special relationship between the Richard Commission and the case for a new Language Act.
3. Other proposals regarding the types of legislation for which the National Assembly should have power of implementation.

Section 1: The general case for legislative powers

The Welsh Language Society believes that the present powers of the National Assembly are inadequate and that they do not allow it to have a far-reaching effect on the lives of the people of Wales. Furthermore, it is not possible for the institution to make meaningful use of those powers which it does possess, as it is expected to operate on the basis of a complex and ineffective constitutional settlement. As a result, we call on the Richard Commission to recognize the need for a Welsh Parliament with real legislative powers.

Lack of clear division of power
Problems arise from the fact that the Assembly is a strange concoction of the corporate local government model and a more parliamentary model with a cabinet. Such an arrangement leads to fundamental tensions within the body, raising questions about where exactly power lies or who is answerable to whom.

Indistinct and inconsistent powers
In contrast to Scotland, the National Assembly has secondary powers only. So although it has power in important fields such as education and health, these fields are only partially devolved. So in view of such a horizontal division of power, understanding the true powers of the Assembly is a very difficult task.

The basic problem is that there is no consistent basis as to which powers have been and are being transferred to the Assembly and such insecurity makes it difficult to form any strategy and can cause delay. Of course, in Scotland the problem does not arise as whole areas have been devolved.

Section 2: The relationship between the Richard Commission and the case for a new Language Act

Between spring 2001 and summer 2002, the National Assembly Culture Committee held a detailed review of policies implemented in relation to the Welsh language. In the end, the Culture Committee itself decided not to call for a New Language Act. However, in its final report 'Our language: its future' it said: 'with regard to new legislation, the Richard Commission should look at the possibility of giving the Assembly enabling powers which would allow it to reform the 1993 Welsh Language Act by order.'

As a result, we call on you to pay close attention to this, in addition to the evidence that we present here. We intend to show why the 1993 Welsh Language Act needs to be reformed, and that this reform needs to modify the basis of the present legislation's principle and procedure.

1. The case for reform of the 1993 Language Act
By now, an increasing number of people recognize that there are many weaknesses in the 1993 Welsh Language Act. Since it was passed, it has not succeeded in extending the real rights of Welsh-speakers and it has

not led to the normalization of Welsh language use. We therefore believe that the time has come for it to be reformed and strengthened.

We note here two specific areas which prove the need for reform of the present legislation:

- the lack of any clear statement of the status of Welsh as an official language in Wales;
- the fact that its powers are limited to the public sector.

2. The need for fundamental changes

In discussing the need to reform and strengthen the 1993 Welsh Language Act, we emphasize that fundamental procedural changes are necessary. It is not good enough that the measure, in its current form, is merely amended a little to include the above points. It must be accepted that there are great problems concerning the whole implementation of the act.

Section 3: Specific Proposals regarding the types of legislation that the National Assembly should implement

We outline here another specific area which is central to the future of the Welsh language and the communities of Wales and which once again emphasizes the need for the National Assembly of Wales to have legislative powers.

Housing and planning and the need for a Property Act

The Welsh Language Society calls on the National Assembly to ensure a *Property Act* which will lead to the adoption and implementation of housing and planning policies which will set a firm basis for the future for all the communities of Wales, the Welsh language and the natural environment.

In addition, the Assembly should establish a democratic Housing Forum to represent the interests of local authorities, housing providers and their tenants, as well as others in the sector, in discussions and decisions on national housing and planning policies. Most people by now recognize that there is a housing crisis in the communities of Wales. We see our communities, especially those that were the backbone of the Welsh language, changing fast as local people are pushed out of the property market and richer outsiders take over. So we have two entwined situations – the housing crisis and the communities' and Welsh language crisis. It is the system which permits this that is to blame, not individuals. As a result, a *Property Act* is the only way of ensuring fairness for the people and communities of Wales.

Conclusions

At the end of the National Assembly's first term, there is now an increasing consensus which is of the opinion that the body cannot operate effectively without possessing legislative powers. The Welsh Language Society supports this call, and calls on you to recognize this in your conclusions.

In the specific case of the Welsh language, we believe that it is senseless that Westminster alone has the power to legislate on matters which concern the language. It is likely that neither the expertise nor the time is there to deal fairly and effectively with such matters. Indeed if there is any case that can be said to be unique to Wales – this is it.

The Welsh Language Society March 2003

Excerpts from Cymdeithas yr Iaith's evidence to the Richard Commission (NAW, 2003b)

Notes

Notes to Chapter 1

[1] A range of articles, chapters and papers were produced from the following research projects: 'The effectiveness of inclusive governance: a study of the participation and representation of "minority groups" in the first two years of the National Assembly'; 'Social capital and the participation of marginalised groups in government 2001–04'; and 'Gender and constitutional change: transforming politics in the UK?' The University Of Wales Board of Celtic Studies funded the first study while ESRC grants were the funding sources for the two other projects. The first two projects were undertaken jointly by researchers at the School of Social Sciences, Cardiff University and School of Sociology and Social Policy, University of Wales, Bangor; and Edinburgh University along with collaborators at Queen's University Belfast. University of Liverpool and Cardiff University undertook the third project.

Notes to Chapter 2

[1] For reviews of *Civil Society and Political Theory*, see Pedersen, 1992; Axtmann, 1995; Schmidt, 1993; Weaver, 1993; Alexander, 1993; Baynes, 1993.

[2] For critiques of Putnam's work, particularly *Making Democracy Work*, see Levi, 1993; Laitin, 1995; Tarrow, 1996; Foley & Edwards, 1996; King & Wickham-Jones, 1999; Mouritsen, 2003. These critiques address a number of issues surrounding Putnam's work. The most relevant for present purposes is criticisms for not including social movements and political associations within civil society and for overemphasizing the role of secondary associations in civil society (Foley & Edwards, 1996; Mouritsen, 2003). As this book has adopted the definition of civil society developed by Cohen and Arato, this issue does not necessarily detract from the validity of Putnam's work to this volume.

[3] There are arguments within neo-corporatism regarding how it is to be used and most usefully applied (Moore & Booth, 1989: 3). As part of this, arguments are made regarding differences in the breadth of interest group politics covered by the neo-corporatism theory (Wilson, 1983: 112; Mansbridge, 1992: 495). This book does not intend to discuss this. The chapter focuses instead on the important suggestions that neo-corporatism provides to how relations between

the state and civil society can hinder democracy. As a result, the discussion makes the greatest usage of Wilson's work (1983; 1990).

Notes to Chapter 3

1   Section 48 of the Government of Wales Act 1998 states: 'The Assembly shall make appropriate arrangements with a view to securing that its business is conducted with due regard to the principle that there should be equality of opportunity for all people' (HMSO, 1998c). Section 120 of the Government of Wales Act states:

(1) The Assembly shall make appropriate arrangements with a view to securing that its functions are exercised with due regard to the principle that there should be equality of opportunity for all people.
(2) After each financial year, the Assembly should publish a report containing:
   a) A statement of the arrangements made in pursuance of subsection (1) which had effect during the financial year and,
   b) An assessment of how effective those arrangements were in promoting equality of opportunity. (HMSO, 1998d)

2   In 1998, 2,000 civil servants worked in the Welsh Office. In April 2001, 3,248 civil servants worked in the Assembly and this increased to 3,752 by October 2002 (Rawlings, 2003: 164).

Notes to Chapter 4

1   Other Structural Funds programmes operating in Wales during the 2000–6 programming period included Objective 2, Objective 3, and the Interreg IIIA, URBAN II, LEADER+, EQUAL Community Initiatives. See AGW (2002).
2   Welsh Office revenue support for the trusts to deliver agreed programmes of work for 1998/9 was £384,000 (Groundwork Wales, 2000a).
3   Interview 15, 26.07.02, voluntary/community sector, Groundwork and Objective 1 case study.
4   ISW Objective 2 Projects 1997–9 data supplied by WEFO.
5   Interview 14, 12.07.02, voluntary/community sector, Groundwork and Objective 1 case study.
6   From data supplied by WEFO.
7   The Welsh Office was accused of being too bureaucratic and seeking to control relationships between local government and the Commission. Morgan states: 'the local authority partners acidly described the Welsh Office as "Raj style of management" on account of its hierarchical and imperious attitude towards others' (2002b: 20).
8   Interview 7, 14.06.02, voluntary/community sector, Groundwork and Objective 1 case study.
9   In 1999, Groundwork Bridgend expanded to include Neath Port Talbot, and Groundwork Wrexham expanded to include Flintshire (Groundwork Wales, 2000a).

10   Interview 15, 26.07.02, voluntary/community sector, Groundwork and Objective 1 case study.
11   Interview 15, 26.07.02, voluntary/community sector, Groundwork and Objective 1 case study.
12   Interview 15, 26.07.02, voluntary/community sector, Groundwork and Objective 1 case study.
13   Objective 1 implied a £1.4 billion potential for commitment from 2000 to 2006 (excluding match funding), compared with the total of £395 million EU funding from the previous 1994–99 Structural Funds programmes (AGW, 2002: 1).
14   See E. Royles (2004) 'Civil Society and Objective 1', *Contemporary Wales*, (16) and E. Royles (2006), 'Civil society and the new democracy in post-devolution Wales: a case study of economic governance of the EU Structural Funds', *Regional and Federal Studies*, 16, 2: 137–156.
15   Chwarae Teg is an organization formed to promote and increase female economic participation and it represented the European Equality Partnership.
16   From data supplied by North Wales Economic Forum – Minutes European Task Force meeting, 16 October 1998 and Minutes European Task Force Meeting, 14 May 1999 ETF (99).
17   The chair of the Shadow Monitoring Committee was Rhodri Morgan as Economic Development Minister, and Phil Williams AM was a National Assembly for Wales public-sector representative, with Michael German AM as alternate. As the pressures on Morgan as First Secretary accumulated, Christine Chapman became chair of the PMC as the nominee of the Assembly's Minister for Economic Development in January 2001.
18   Interview 14, 12.07.02, voluntary/community sector, Groundwork and Objective 1 case study.
19   Interview 7, 14.06.02, voluntary/community sector, Groundwork and Objective 1 case study.
20   Interview 7, 14.06.02, voluntary/community sector, Groundwork and Objective 1 case study.
21   Data from WEFO (2000c).
22   Data from WEFO (2000d).
23   Interview 7, 14.06.02, voluntary/community sector, Groundwork and Objective 1 case study.
24   Data from WEFO(2001).
25   Interview 7, 14.06.02, voluntary/community sector, Groundwork and Objective 1 case study.
26   These included: through Groundwork Wales – Project Reference ERDF 52874; through RCT – Measure 3.2, 'Fernhill strategy partnership and capacity building' [ERDF 52924], 'The Greencare path to community centred sustainable development and empowerment' [ERDF 52934] and Measure 3.4 'Green social economy feasibility study and pilot for Cefn Pennar organisation' [ERDF 52936]; through Merthyr Tydfil – Measure 3.2 'The Greencare path to community centred sustainable development and empowerment (1)' [ERDF 52889].
27   Interview 7, 14.06.02, voluntary/community sector, Groundwork and Objective 1 case study.

28 Interview 14, 12.07.02, voluntary/community sector, Groundwork and Objective 1 case study.
29 Interview 7, 14.06.02, voluntary/community sector, Groundwork and Objective 1 case study.
30 Interview 7, 14.06.02, voluntary/community sector, Groundwork and Objective 1 case study.
31 Interview 7, 14.06.02, voluntary/community sector, Groundwork and Objective 1 case study.
32 Interview 15, 26.07.02, voluntary/community sector, Groundwork and Objective 1 case study.
33 Interview 15, 26.07.02, voluntary/community sector, Groundwork and Objective 1 case study.
34 Interview 15, 26.07.02, voluntary/community sector, Groundwork and Objective 1 case study.
35 Interview 15, 26.07.02, voluntary/community sector, Groundwork and Objective 1 case study.
36 Interview 15, 26.07.02, voluntary/community sector, Groundwork and Objective 1 case study.
37 Interview 15, 26.07.02, voluntary/community sector, Groundwork and Objective 1 case study.
38 Interview 15, 26.07.02, voluntary/community sector, Groundwork and Objective 1 case study.
39 Interview 12, 08.07.02, voluntary/community sector, Groundwork and Objective 1 case study.
40 Interview 15, 26.07.02, voluntary/community sector, Groundwork and Objective 1 case study.
41 Interview 15, 26.07.02, voluntary/community sector, Groundwork and Objective 1 case study.
42 Interview 15, 26.07.02, voluntary/community sector, Groundwork and Objective 1 case study.
43 Interview 10, 03.07.02, public sector, National Assembly for Wales, Groundwork and Objective 1 case study.
44 Interview 7, 14.06.02, voluntary/community sector, Groundwork and Objective 1 case study.

Notes to Chapter 5

1 Chaney & Fevre identify that the term 'movement' encompasses different aspects involved in reasserting Welsh identity. They include the main nationalist political party, Plaid Cymru, the campaign for Welsh-medium education, including Mudiad Ysgolion Meithrin, Urdd Gobaith Cymru and Cymdeithas yr Iaith (2001b: 228).
2 A number of issues contributed to generating this controversy: Anne Robinson, quiz show host's comments about Wales on the Room 101 BBC programme; Seimon Glyn's comments, discussed in Part I regarding the effects of immigrants into Gwynedd. The Higher Education and Lifelong Learning Committees' Review of Higher Education sparked controversy as did the absence of a 'Welsh' identity tick box on the 2001 census forms.

3   The year 1588 marks the first translation of the Bible into Welsh by William
     Morgan. In 1962 Saunders Lewis gave his radio lecture *Tynged yr Iaith*
     (The Fate of the Language) that led to the establishment of Cymdeithas yr
     Iaith.

4   The statistics for the decline of the Welsh language are illustrative. In 1901,
     the percentage of Welsh speakers throughout Wales was 50 per cent and by
     1981 this was under 19 per cent. There was a parallel decline in the figures
     for the traditionally Welsh-speaking counties. Carter argues that the decline
     in the numbers speaking Welsh between the 1951 and 1961 in particular
     affected Lewis (1990: 157).

5   The active cells in March 2003 were Cardiff, the Valleys, Preseli, Caerfyrddin,
     Dyffryn Teifi, North Ceredigion, Penllyn (Bala), Eifionydd, Dyffryn Conwy
     (correspondence with Cymdeithas yr Iaith, March 2003).

6   This consultation included the Confederation of British Industry, Cymdeithas
     yr Iaith Gymraeg, the Welsh Development Agency, the Welsh Counties
     Committee, the Council of Welsh Districts, Urdd Gobaith Cymru and the
     National Eisteddfod (WLB, 1991).

7   Interview 22, 07.10.02, Cymdeithas yr Iaith and Cymuned and the policy
     review case study. Original: 'oedden ni'n trio gweithredu'n uniongyrchol i
     bwysleisio rhywbeth, pwysleisio dwyster neu bwysleisio fod e'n bwysig. . . .
     A dw i'n eitha sicr nath e lwyddo . . . Os edrychi di, ar un adeg oedd na dipyn
     o weithredu mewn ymgyrch Deddf Iaith fe ddechreuwyd trafod Deddf Iaith
     dipyn mwy o ddifri.'

8   In an interview published in *Barn* (January 2001), Jenny Randerson made it
     clear that she did not think that there was a need for a Welsh Language Act
     at that time (R. Evans, 2001: 17, 19).

9   Lewis had suggested that references in the evidence presented by one academic
     to the committee were 'sexist and xenophobic' and that the committee should
     therefore 'strike from the record or not consider' the submission (Egan &
     James, 2002: 149–50). This recommendation was subsequently refused and a
     motion adopted by the Panel of Committee Chairs stated: 'any interference
     whatsoever in the process whereby papers are submitted by any contributors
     is an unacceptable and unwarranted infringement of the principles of freedom
     of thought and expression especially as defined by the Human Rights Act'
     (Rawlings, 2003: 216). Referring to this incident, Rawlings states: 'what price
     – it may be asked – inclusiveness, in the sense of the Assembly listening to
     all sides of (lawfully expressed) opinion?' (2003: 216).

10   Interview 33, 15.11.02, civil society – Cymuned, Cymdeithas yr Iaith and
     Cymuned and the policy review case study. Original: 'mi oedd y rhan yna
     o'r broses mae'n debyg y cwbl dylai ymgynghoriad cyhoeddus fod. Yr hyn
     oedd o'i le oedd nad oedd na unrhyw wir ewyllys i newid . . . yr unig sylwadau
     sy'n cael gwrandawiad go iawn yw'r rhai sy'n ffitio'r strategaeth sydd wedi
     ei phenderfynu eisioes.'

11   Interview 23, 14.10.02, civil society – Cymdeithas yr Iaith Gymraeg, Cymdeithas
     yr Iaith and Cymuned and the policy review case study. Original: 'dw i'n
     meddwl mai dim ond mater o ddiffyg adnoddau i fod yn cyflogi pobl sydd
     wedi bod yn ein rhwystro ni rhag cael rhywun fyddai yn gallu canolbwyntio

yn eitha llwyr ar y Cynulliad fel corff. Oherwydd fod na dynfa yn y bôn rhwng y math yna o waith a math o waith sydd yn ymwneud ag ymgyrchu yn gyffredinol.'

12 Interview 33, 15.11.02, civil society – Cymuned, Cymdeithas yr Iaith and Cymuned and the policy review case study. Original: 'mae mudiadau gwirfoddol dan anfantais. Dan ni'n gymharol gryf o safbwynt beth dan ni wedi llwyddo i'w drefnu ar lefel y canghennau lleol yn enwedig mewn rhai ardaloedd. Lle dan ni'n brin ydi pobl yn y canol sy'n medru gwneud y gwaith cymhleth.'

13 In December 2003, Cymuned appointed a chief executive on an unpaid and voluntary basis to ensure efficient decision-making between meetings (Brooks, 2004: 14).

14 Cymuned's Steering Group report, 'nid plaid wleidyddol mo Cymuned ac ni fydd Cymuned yn sefyll mewn etholiadau' (Cymuned, 2002a).

15 Alun Pugh AM, comment in interview on Radio Wales (Cymuned, 2002a).

16 Jenny Randerson, the minister, visited the Menter Iaith in Caerffili and outlined their work to the committee (NAW, 2002b, 2002d).

17 C. H. Williams refers to the partnership arrangement in language and governance as the 'National Assembly for Wales' conception of the triangular relationship between the Welsh Language Board, its various sponsored partners, such as the National Eisteddfod, the Urdd, the Mentrau Iaith, and the general public' (2004: 10).

18 Interview 22, 07.10.02, civil society – Cymdeithas yr Iaith Gymraeg, Cymdeithas yr Iaith and Cymuned and the policy review case study. Original: 'mae bodolaeth Bwrdd yr Iaith mewn perthynas ag ymgyrchoedd dros y Gymraeg wedi creu gwahaniaeth mawr ... Mae fe mewn ffordd wedi sbaddu lot o drafodaeth a wedi tanseilio'r cyfraniad mae lot o gyrff wedi gwneud yn y gorffennol ac wedi eu gwneud nhw'n amharod i geisio gwneud cyfraniad cyhoeddus dros y blynyddoedd diweddar. ... Y mudiadau yma yn gefnogol o ran egwyddor and yn gyhoeddus ddim yn gallu bod mor weithgar achos eu dibynniaeth nhw ar Fwrdd yr Iaith am gyllid.'

19 Interview 24, 18.10.02, public sector – National Assembly for Wales, Cymdeithas yr Iaith and Cymuned and the policy review case study. Original: 'Dw i'n meddwl mai'r ddilema fawr i'r mudiad protest nawr ydi sut mae'r mudiadau protest sy'n ymwneud yn benodol â'r Gymraeg yn ymateb i sefydliad gwleidyddol yng Nghymru sydd wedi derbyn cyfrifodeb am y Gymraeg a lle mae yna lywodraeth ... Dw i'n meddwl fod yna gwestiynau mawr yn wynebu'r mudiad protest a bod rhaid iddyn nhw weithredu i'r sefyllfa sydd wedi deillio o ddatganoli yng Nghymru.'

Notes to Chapter 6

1 Iceland's parent company, the Big Food Group (BFG), cancelled their plans to recover debt from Guyana, the compensation, and interest, that was to be paid to Booker Plc (that became BFG in 2000) due to the nationalization of its sugar industry in 1976 (Oxfam Cymru, 2003a).

2   During the minister's report to the Economic Development Committee, it
    was reported that the Welsh Assembly Government signed an agreement
    with the National Group in Homeworkers to fund an outreach worker for
    2002–3 and 2004–5. The purpose was to establish networks for homeworkers,
    firstly concentrating on the South East Wales Communities First wards and
    then broadening to target wards in north and south-west Wales. The Assembly
    Government's contribution was £44,300.
3   Interview 26, 21.10.02, civil society – Oxfam Cymru, Oxfam Cymru and Make
    Trade Fair case study.
4   Interview 31, 31.10.02, civil society – Oxfam GB, Oxfam Cymru and Make
    Trade Fair case study.
5   Interview 18, 04.10.02, civil society – Oxfam Cymru, Oxfam Cymru and Make
    Trade Fair case study.
6   Interview 18, 04.10.02, civil society – Oxfam Cymru, Oxfam Cymru and Make
    Trade Fair case study.
7   Interview 18, 04.10.02, civil society – Oxfam Cymru, Oxfam Cymru and Make
    Trade Fair case study.
8   The involvement of shops in campaigning activities was facilitated by greater
    coordination between disparate dimensions of Oxfam's work in Wales since
    2000 through an Oxfam Cymru Development Group, now the Management
    Team (Oxfam Cymru, 2000).
9   Interview 19, 04.10.02, civil society – Oxfam Cymru, Oxfam Cymru and Make
    Trade Fair case study.
10 Interview 19, 04.10.02, civil society – Oxfam Cymru, Oxfam Cymru and Make
    Trade Fair case study.
11 Interview 28, 25.10.02, civil society – Oxfam Supporter, Oxfam Cymru and
    Make Trade Fair case study.
12 Interview 18, 04.10.02, civil society – Oxfam Cymru, Oxfam Cymru and Make
    Trade Fair case study.
13 Interview 19, 04.10.02, civil society – Oxfam Cymru, Oxfam Cymru and Make
    Trade Fair case study.
14 Interview 18, 04.10.02, civil society – Oxfam Cymru, Oxfam Cymru and Make
    Trade Fair case study.
15 Interview 26, 21.10.02, civil society – Oxfam Cymru, Oxfam Cymru and Make
    Trade Fair case study.
16 Interview 26, 21.10.02, civil society – Oxfam Cymru, Oxfam Cymru and Make
    Trade Fair case study.
17 Interview 18, 04.10.02, civil society – Oxfam Cymru, Oxfam Cymru and Make
    Trade Fair case study.
18 Interview 26, 21.10.02, civil society – Oxfam Cymru, Oxfam Cymru and Make
    Trade Fair case study.
19 Interview 18, 04.10.02, civil society – Oxfam Cymru, Oxfam Cymru and Make
    Trade Fair case study.

Notes to Chapter 7

1   As discussed in Chapter 3, it is extremely difficult to identify the exact powers
    of the Assembly. This is the case in the area of equality of opportunity and
    sexual orientation. The Assembly's statutory duty to promote equality of

opportunity for all, instrumental in Stonewall Cymru's establishment, suggests that sexual orientation issues are devolved. However as Chaney and Fevre point out in relation to equality of opportunity, the situation is more complex: 'the responsibility for primary equality of opportunity legislation remains with Westminster. The equality duty applying to the Assembly relates to its functions within the complex and often opaque division of powers that characterises the current constitutional arrangements' (Chaney & Fevre, 2002b: 5).

2   As the organization is currently referred to as Stonewall Cymru, this will be the main title utilized in this chapter. However at times when referring to the early history of the organization, LGB Forum Cymru will also be utilized.

3   Interview 39, 10.06.03, civil society – Stonewall Cymru, Stonewall Cymru and Section 28 case study. Original: 'oedden ni di pretty much mynd i'r eithaf o ran bod yn agored. Ond wrth edrych nôl gyda hindsight, doedd e ddim yn gymhelliad i bobl newydd ymuno â'r mudiad.'

4   Interview 42, 20.06.03, civil society – Stonewall Cymru, Stonewall Cymru and Section 28 case study.

5   Interview 42, 20.06.03, civil society – Stonewall Cymru, Stonewall Cymru and Section 28 case study.

6   Interview 42, 20.06.03, civil society – Stonewall Cymru, Stonewall Cymru and Section 28 case study.

7   Interview 37, 10.06.03, public sector – higher education, Stonewall Cymru and Seciton 28 case study.

8   Interview 41, 12.06.03, civil society – Stonewall Cymru, Stonewall Cymru and Section 28 case study. Original: 'ar ôl i'r Blaid Lafur ddod i rym yn 1997 yn sicr oedd na dipyn o fomentwm yn y gogledd i drio ffurfio rhyw fath o strwythr rhwng y cymunedau hoyw a lesbiaidd oherwydd yr angen i weithio efo'r heddlu. A dw i'n credu mai drwy'r gwaith yna nes i ddechrau sylweddoli bod na le i gael rhyw fath o strwythr drwy Gymru er mwyn cael pobl hoyw a lesbiaidd at ei gilydd i gydweithio.'

9   Equality of Opportunity Committee minutes stated: 'taking equal opportunities forward in the Assembly, the initial focus on disability, race and gender was approved although Members noted the need to have regard to other sources of discrimination and social exclusion including age, religious beliefs and sexual orientation' (NAW, 1999a: 4.3).

10 The National Assembly funding to LGB Forum Cymru/Stonewall Cymru derived from the Assembly's Promoting Equality in Wales Project Development Fund. Funding was initially provided for three years, £25,000 for 2001–2, and then £50,000 for 2002–3. Stonewall provided £25,000 and a Heads of Partnership Agreement formalized the relationship between LGB Forum Cymru and Stonewall.

11 Observer status was granted to organizations including the Equal Opportunities Commission Wales.

12 Interview 41, 12.06.03, civil society – Stonewall Cymru, Stonewall Cymru and Section 28 case study.

13 LGB Forum Cymru's Outline Business Plan, stated under its priorities for year one (2002–3), 'during consultation exercises, education was identified to be the major priority area for Welsh lesbian, gay men and bisexual people.

Section 28 and homophobic bullying were particular issues of concern. As a result the Forum will develop an action plan of work on the theme of education' (LGB Forum Cymru, 2002c).

[14] Interview 41, 12.06.03, civil society – Stonewall Cymru, Stonewall Cymru and Section 28 case study.

[15] Jenny Randerson and Val Feld tabled a statement on 29 October 1999 and it gained eleven subscribers by 23 November 1999 (NAW, 1999c). Helen Mary Jones tabled another statement on 15 December 1999 that called 'upon all parties in the Assembly to support the repeal of Section 28' (NAW, 1999c; NAW, 1999d). By 20 March 2000, this had received twenty subscribers (NAW, 1999d). Subsequently, Conservative AM David Davies tabled a statement calling for the retention of Section 28 and four subscribers supported this (NAW, 2000j).

[16] Interview 40, 10.06.03, civil society – Stonewall Cymru, Stonewall Cymru and Section 28 case study.

[17] Interview 41, 12.06.03, civil society – Stonewall Cymru, Stonewall Cymru and Section 28 case study.

[18] Interview, 41, 12.06.03, civil society – Stonewall Cymru, Stonewall Cymru and Section 28 case study.

[19] LGB Forum Cymru conference 'Making a Difference', 13 April 2002, Cardiff County Hall.

[20] Interview 42, 20.06.03, civil society – Stonewall Cymru, Stonewall Cymru and Section 28 case study.

[21] Interview 41, 12.06.03, civil society – Stonewall Cymru, Stonewall Cymru and Section 28 case study.

[22] Interview 42, 20.06.03, civil society – Stonewall Cymru, Stonewall Cymru and Section 28 case study.

[23] Interview 40, 10.06.03, civil society – Stonewall Cymru, Stonewall Cymru and Section 28 case study.

[24] Interview 41, 12.06.03, civil society – Stonewall Cymru, Stonewall Cymru and Section 28 case study. Original: 'fysa Stonewall Cymru ddim wedi digwydd os na fasa'r Cynulliad wedi bod yno; os na fysa'r Cynulliad wedi cael ei sefydlu ar sail cydraddoldeb i bawb.'

[25] Interview 41, 12.06.03, civil society – Stonewall Cymru, Stonewall Cymru and Section 28 case study.

[26] Stonewall Cymru negotiated its work programme that set the basis for its funding with the Equality Unit. It subsequently provided quarterly and final year reports on the usage of Assembly Government funding.

[27] Interview 38, 10.06.03, public sector – National Assembly, Stonewall Cymru and Section 28 case study. Original: 'fe ddeith pwynt ac mae'n bownd o ddod, lle mae aelodaeth y fforwm isie dweud pethau nad yw llywodraeth Cymru moyn clywed. Ac mi fydd yn ddiddorol gweld mor hawdd fydd e i staff a swyddogion y fforwm gymryd yr issues na ymlaen yn gryf gyda'r llywodraeth.'

[28] Membership figures provided for 2003.

[29] There was united opposition to Section 28 by attending Assembly Members at LGB Forum Cymru's inaugural conference 'Making a Difference' in 2002 (LGB Forum Cymru, 2002b).

30 Interview 40, 10.06.03, civil society – Stonewall Cymru, Stonewall Cymru and Section 28 case study.
31 Interview 44, 05.07.03, civil society – Stonewall Cymru, Stonewall Cymru and Section 28 case study.
32 Interview 41, 12.06.03, civil society – Stonewall Cymru, Stonewall Cymru and Section 28 case study.
33 Interview 42, 20.06.03, civil society – Stonewall Cymru, Stonewall Cymru and Section 28 case study.
34 Interview 44, 05.07.03, civil society – Stonewall Cymru, Stonewall Cymru and Section 28 case study.
35 Interview 41, 12.06.03, civil society – Stonewall Cymru, Stonewall Cymru and Section 28 case study.
36 Interview 42, 20.06.03, civil society – Stonewall Cymru, Stonewall Cymru and Section 28 case study.

Notes to Chapter 8

1 At the end of August 2001, Rhodri Glyn Thomas expressed concern at the quality of submissions to the review. Betts explains: 'some submissions have been disappointing – with some of the most important Assembly-sponsored public bodies submitting evidence which said nothing about how policies needed to be changed, instead telling members what the organization had been doing during the past 12 months' (2002a). Only three organizations, Cymdeithas, Cymuned and the Mentrau Iaith, discussed alternative ideas, for example the need for a new Welsh Language Act during their review presentations (NAW, 2002e, 2001j).
2 Interview 22, 07.10.02, Cymdeithas yr Iaith and Cymuned and the policy review case study. Original: 'Mae hefyd rhyw gred mewn democratiaeth gyfranogol sy'n fwy na phleidleisio bob pum mlynedd. Swn i'n lecio meddwl fod cymdeithas sifil yn cyfrannu mewn rhyw ffordd sef rhoi cyfle i bobl i gyfrannu ti'n gwybod, mudiad ymgyrchu. . . . Swn i'n gobeithio taw rôl ein mudiad ni fel rhan o gymdeithas sifil yw i bryfocio a rhoi cyfle i bobl wneud hynny a rhoi cyfle i bobl feddwl yn wleidyddol hefyd.'
3 Interview 15, 26.07.02, voluntary/community sector – Groundwork Wales and Objective 1 case study.
4 Interview 18, 04.10.02, civil society – Oxfam Cymru, Oxfam Cymru and Make Trade Fair case study.

References

Adamson, D. L. (1991). *Class, Ideology and the Nation: A Theory of Welsh Nationalism*. Cardiff: University of Wales Press.

AGW (Auditor General for Wales) (2002). *EU Structural Funds: Maximising the Benefits for Wales*. Cardiff: National Audit Office Wales.

Alexander, J. C. (1993). 'The Return to Civil Society', *Contemporary Sociology*, 22, 6: 797–803.

Alexander, J. C. (2000). 'Contradictions: The Uncivilising Pressures of Space, Time and Function', *Soundings*, 16: 96–113.

Anderson, B. (1991). *Imagined Communities: Reflections on the Origins and Spread of Nationalism*. London: Verso.

Andrews, L. (1999). *Wales Says Yes: The Inside Story of the Yes for Wales Referendum Campaign*. Bridgend: Seren.

Arato, A. (1989). 'Civil Society, History and Socialism: Reply to John Keane', *Praxis International*, 9, 1/2 (April and July): 133–51.

Axtmann, R. (1995) 'Book Review: Civil Society and Political Theory by Jean L. Cohen and Andrew Arato', *Theory, Culture and Society*, 12, 1: 175–9.

Bachtler, J. (2002). 'Objective One in Wales: A Comparative Assessment', *Contemporary Wales*, 15: 30–41.

Baker, G. (2002). 'Introduction', in G. Baker (ed.), *Civil Society and Democracy: Alternative Voices*. London: Routledge.

Barber, B. (1984). *Strong Democracy: Participatory Politics for a New Age*. Berkeley: University of California Press.

Baynes, K. (1993). 'Cohen and Arato, Civil Society and Political Theory', *Political Theory*, 21, 3: 544–6.

Beech, M. (2000). *To what Extent does Oxfam Affect British Government Policy towards Heavily Indebted Poor Countries?* Aberystwyth: University of Wales.

Benfield, G. (2002). 'The Voluntary Sector Perspective on European Programmes 2000–2006', *Contemporary Wales*, 15: 45–51.

Benfield, G. et al. (2000). *Task and Finish Group Report on the Implementation of Objective 1 Structural Funds*. N.p.: WEFO.

Bernard, H. R. (2001). *Qualitative and Quantitative Methods*. London: Sage.

Betts, C. (2002a). 'Disagreement over Policy on Language', *Western Mail*, 25 February.

Betts, C. (2002b). 'Conference: Liberal Democrats Recognise Importance of Language Heartlands – Party Backs "Action Areas"', *Western Mail*, 22 February.

Betts, C. (2002c). 'Assembly: Dafydd Wigley Strengthens Draft Report on Preserving the Language – Curbs Likely on Holiday Homes', *Western Mail*, 30 May.

Binder, G. (1993). 'Arato & Cohen: Civil Society and Political Theory, Fukuyama: The End of History and the Last Man', *Michigan Law Review*, 91, 6: 1491–1528.

Black, M. (1992). *A Cause for Our Times: Oxfam the first Fifty Years*. Oxford: Oxford University Press.

Bobbio, N. (1988). 'Gramsci and the Concept of Civil Society', in J. Keane (ed.), *Civil Society and the State*. London: Verso.

Bogdanor, V. (1999). *Devolution in the United Kingdom*. Oxford: Oxford University Press.

Bradbury, J. and Mawson, J. (eds) (1999). *British Regionalism and Devolution: The Challenge of State Reform and European Integration*. London: Jessica Kingsley Publishers.

Brooks, S. (2002a). 'The Living Dead', *Agenda* (Spring 2000) (Cardiff: Institute of Welsh Affairs).

Brooks, S. (2002b). 'Wedi'r Arolwg', *Barn*, 470 (March 2002).

Brooks, S. (2004). 'O Gadair y Golygydd', *Gwreiddiau*, 3 (Spring).

Bryant, C. G. A. (1993). 'Social Self-Organisation, Civility and Sociology: A Comment on Kumar's "Civil Society",' *British Journal of Sociology*, 44: 396–401.

Bryant, C. G. A. (1995). 'Civic Nation, Civil Society, Civic Religion', in J. A. Hall (ed.), *Civil Society: Theory, History, Comparison*. Cambridge: Polity Press.

Calhoun, C. (1995). *Critical Social Theory*. Oxford: Blackwell Publishers.

Carter, H. (1990). 'Dirywiad yr Iaith Gymraeg yn yr Ugeinfed Ganrif', in G. H. Jenkins (ed.), *Cof Cenedl V – Ysgrifau ar Hanes Cymru*. Llandysul: Gomer.

Chaney, P. (2002a). *Social Capital and the Participation of Marginalized Groups in Government: A Study of the Statutory Partnership between the Third Sector and Devolved Government in Wales* (Paper prepared for the Fifth ISTR International Conference, Cape Town, South Africa, July 2002).

Chaney, P. (2002b). 'Social Capital and the Participation of Marginalized Groups in Government: A Study of the Statutory Partnership between the Third Sector and Devolved Government in Wales', *Public Policy and Administration*, 17, 4: 20–38.

Chaney, P. (2002c). 'An Absolute Duty: The Assembly's Statutory Equality of Opportunity Imperative', in J. B. Jones and J. Osmond (eds), *Building a Civic Culture: Institutional Change, Policy Development and Political Dynamics in the National Assembly for Wales*. Cardiff: IWA and WGC.

Chaney, P (2002d). 'New and Unexplored Possibilities – The Welsh Legislature's Statutory Duty to Promote Equality of Opportunity', *Equal Opportunities International*, 21, 2: 19–42.

Chaney, P. (2003a). *Women and Constitutional Change in Wales* (Paper presented to the Changing Constitutions, Building Institutions & (Re-)Defining Gender Relations Workshop, ECPR, Joint Sessions Workshops).

Chaney, P. (2003b). 'Increased Rights and Representation: Women and the Post-Devolution Equality Agenda in Wales', in A. Dobrowsky and V. Hart (eds), *Women, Politics and Constitutional Change*. Basingstoke: Palgrave.

Chaney, P. and Fevre, R. (2001a). 'Ron Davies and the Cultivation of "Inclusive-ness": Devolution and Participation in Wales', *Contemporary Wales*, 14: 21–50.

Chaney, P. and Fevre. R. (2001b). 'Welsh Nationalism and the Challenge of "Inclusive Politics"', *Political Opportunities, Social Movements, and Democratization*, 23: 227–54.

Chaney, P. and Fevre, R. (2001c). 'Inclusive Governance and "Minority" Groups: The Role of the Third Sector in Wales', *Voluntas: International Journal of Voluntary and Nonprofit Organizations*, 12, 2: 131–15.

Chaney, P. and Fevre, R. (2002a). 'Is there a Demand for Descriptive Representation? Evidence from the UK's Devolution Programme', *Political Studies*, 50: 897–915.

Chaney, P. and Fevre, R. (2002b). *An Absolute Duty: Equal Opportunities and the National Assembly for Wales, A Study of the Equality Policies of the Welsh Assembly Government and their implementation: July 1999 to March 2002.*
http://www.eoc.org.uk/cseng/abouteoc/absolute_duty_fr.pdf   3.6.03

Chaney, P., Hall, T. and Dicks, B. (2000). 'Inclusive Governance? The Case of "Minority" and Voluntary Sector Groups and the National Assembly for Wales' *Contemporary Wales*, 13: 203–30.

Chaney, P., Hall, T. and Pithouse, A. (eds) (2001a). *New Governance – New Democracy?* Cardiff: University of Wales Press.

Chaney, P., Hall, T. and Pithouse, A. (2001b). 'Reading the Runes', in P. Chaney, T. Hall and A. Pithouse (eds), *New Governance – New Democracy?* Cardiff: University of Wales Press.

Chaney, P., McKay, F. and McAllister, L. (2007). *Women, Politics, Constitutional Change: The First Years of the National Assembly for Wales.* Cardiff: University of Wales Press.

Chaney, P. and Williams, C. (2003). 'Getting Involved: Civic and Political Life in Wales', in C. Williams, N. Evans and P. O'Leary (eds), *A Tolerant Nation? Exploring Ethnic Diversity in Wales.* Cardiff: University of Wales Press.

Cohen, J. L. and Arato, A. (1999). *Civil Society and Political Theory.* Cambridge, MA: MIT Press.

Cohen, J. and Rogers, J. (1995). 'Secondary Associations and Democratic Governance', in E. O. Wright (ed.), *Associations and Democracy.* London: Verso.

Commons Hansard (2003a). *House of Commons Hansard Debates for March 10 2003 pt 18.*
http://www.publications.parliament.uk/pa/cm200203/cmhansrd/vo3D310/debtext/30310–18.htm

Commons Hansard (2003b). *House of Commons Hansard Debates for March 10 2003 pt 23.*
http://www.publications.parliament.uk/pa/cm200203/cmhansrd/vo3D310/debtext/30310–23.htm

Crwydren, R. (1994). 'Welsh Lesbian Feminist: A Contradiction in Terms?', in J. Aaron, T. Rees, S. Betts and M. Vincentelli (eds), *Our Sisters' Land: The Changing Identities of Women in Wales.* Cardiff: University of Wales Press.

Cymdeithas yr Iaith Gymraeg (1998). *A Working Bilingualism Working Paper 1 Welsh in Cynulliad Cenedlaethol Cymru.* Talybont: Lolfa.

Cymdeithas yr Iaith Gymraeg (1999). *Property Act Handbook, Working Paper 2 Housing and Planning in Cynulliad Cenedlaethol Cymru.* Talybont: Lolfa.

Cymdeithas yr Iaith Gymraeg (2001). *A New Welsh Language Act for a New Century.* Aberystwyth: Cymdeithas yr Iaith.

Cymdeithas yr Iaith Gymraeg (2002). *Ymateb Cychwynnol Cymdeithas yr Iaith Gymraeg i bapur safleoli Adolygiad yr Iaith Gymraeg, Pwyllgor Diwylliant Cynulliad Cenedlaethol Cymru.* N.p.

Cymuned (2001a). *What is Cymuned?*
   http://www.penllyn.com/cymuned/papurau/saesneg.html   20.1.03
Cymuned (2001b). *Answers to Questions on Culture from Assembly Members.*
   http://www.penllyn.com/cymuned/papurau/assansweseng.html   20.1.03
Cymuned (2001c). *Cymuned's evidence to the United Nations.*
   http://www.penllyn.com/cymuned/papurau/evidencetoUN.html   20.1.03
Cymuned (2001d). *The Welsh Mirror – Misleading the English-Speaking Public.*
   http://www.penllyn.com/cymuned/papurau/cwynsaes/html   20.1.03
Cymuned (2001e). *Housing, Work and Language: Recommendations by Cymuned to the National Assembly's Policy Review of the Welsh Language* Talybont: Y Lolfa.
Cymuned (2002a). *Adroddiad Pwyllgor Llywio Gorffennaf 2001 – Ebrill 2002.*
   http://www.penllyn.com/cymuned/papurau/Adroddiad%20y%20
   Pwyllgor%20Llywio.html   24.2.03
Cymuned (2002b). *Resolutions adopted in Cymuned's Annual General Meeting at Harlech, 20th April 2002.*
   http://www.penllyn.com/cymuned/papurau/resolutions.html   24.2.03
Cymuned (2002c). *Equality and Justice: Cymuned's Response to A Bilingual Future, a Welsh Assembly Government Policy Statement and Our Language: Its Future, The Policy Review of the Welsh Language by the Culture Committee and the Education and Lifelong Learning Committee of the National Assembly for Wales.*
   http://www.penllyn.com/cymuned/papurau/justice.doc   24.2.03
Cymuned (2002d). *Cyfansoddiad Cymuned.*
   http://www.penllyn.com/cymuned/papurau/cyfansoddiad%20swyddogol.
   html   24.2.03
Daily Post (2003). *Penguin's Joy as Food Firm Cancels Third World Debt*, 19 March.
Davies, C. A. (1989). *Welsh Nationalism in the Twentieth Century: The Ethnic Option to the Modern State.* New York: Praeger.
Davies, J. (1997). *Plaid Cymru since 1960.* Aberystwyth: National Library of Wales.
Davies, R. (1999). *Devolution: Process Not an Event.* Institute of Welsh Affairs, The Gregynog Papers, vol. 2 (2).
Davies, R. (2003). *Welsh Political Archive Annual Lecture 2003.* Aberystwyth: National Library of Wales.
Day, G., Dunkerley, D. and Thompson, A. (2000). 'Evaluating the "New Politics": Civil Society and the National Assembly', *Public Policy and Administration*, 15, 2: 25–37.
Deacon, R. M. (2002). *The Governance of Wales: The Welsh Office and the Policy Process 1964–99.* Cardiff: Welsh Academic Press.
Dicks, B., Hall, T. and Pithouse, A. (2001). 'The National Assembly and the Voluntary Sector: An Equal Partnership?', in P. Chaney, T. Hall, and A. Pithouse (eds), *New Governance – New Democracy?* Cardiff, University of Wales Press.
Ecotec (Ecotec Research & Consulting Ltd) (1999). *Interim Evaluation of the ISW Objective 2 Programme 1997–99 and Ex-post Evaluation of the ISW Objective 2 Programme 1996–96, Final Report on the Ex-Post Evaluation of the 1994–96 Programme.* Birmingham: Ecotec.
Edwards, M. (2004). *Civil Society.* Cambridge: Polity Press.
Egan, D. and James, R. (2002). 'Open Government and Inclusiveness: The Education and Lifelong Learning Committee', in J. B. Jones and J. Osmond (eds), *Building a Civic Culture.* Cardiff: Welsh Governance Centre & Institute of Welsh Affairs.

Ehrenberg, J. (1999). *Civil Society: The Critical History of an Idea*. London: New York University Press.

Elis-Thomas, D. (2001). *National Assembly: a Year in Power?*
http://www.contemporary-wales.com   6.7.01

Elster, J. (ed.) (1998). *Deliberative Democracy*. Cambridge: Cambridge University Press.

Equal Opportunities Commission Wales (2003). *Equality Moves on, Equal Opportunities Commission Wales Review 2002*.
http://www.eoc.org.uk/cseng/abouteoc/walesannrep.pdf   3.6.03

European Commission (2000). *Structural Actions 2000–2006: Commentary and Regulations*. Luxembourg: OOPEC.

Evans, D. T. (1995). 'Homosexual Citizenship: A Queer Kind of Justice', in A. Wilson (ed.) (1995), *A Simple Matter of Justice?* London: Cassell.

Evans, R. (2001). 'Cyfweld Jenny Randerson: Jenny, Dirprwy Delyth?', *Barn*, 455/6, (January): 14–22.

Fairclough, N. (1992). *Discourse and Social Change*. Cambridge: Polity Press.

Ferguson, A. and Forbes, D. (eds) (1966). *An Essay on the History of Civil Society 1767*. Edinburgh: Edinburgh University Press.

Fevre, R. and Thompson, A. (1999). 'Social Theory and Welsh Identities,' in R. Fevre and A. Thompson (eds), *Nation, Identity and Social Theory: Perspectives from Wales*. Cardiff: University of Wales Press.

Ffransis, F. (2002). 'Letters: Conflict of values', *Western Mail*, 12 July.

Fine, R. (1997). 'Civil Society Theory, Enlightenment and Critique', in R. Fine and S. Rai, (eds), *Civil Society: Democratic Perspectives*. London: Frank Cass.

Fine, R. (2000). 'Civil Society and Violence: A Critique of John Keane', *Soundings*, 16: 113–22.

Fine, R. and Rai, S. (eds) (1997). *Civil Society: Democratic Perspectives*. London: Frank Cass.

Foley, M. W. and Edwards, B. (1996). 'The Paradox of Civil Society', *Journal of Democracy*, 7, 3: 38–52.

Fowler, C. (2002). *The 'Cymuned Effect': Some Recent Considerations on Territory, Language and Identity in Wales* (unpublished seminar presentation, Institute of Welsh Politics, June).

Fraser, N. (1995). 'From Redistribution to Recognition? Dilemmas of Justice in a "Post-Socialist" Age', *New Left Review*, 212 (July/August): 68–93.

Fukuyama, F. (1995). *Trust: The Social Virtues and the Creation of Prosperity*. London: Hamish Hamilton.

Gargarella, R. (1998). 'Full Representation, Deliberation and Impartiality', in J. Elster (ed.), *Deliberative Democracy*. Cambridge: Cambridge University Press.

Gellner, E. (1991). 'Civil Society in Historical Context', *International Social Science Journal*, 129: 495–510.

Giddens, A. (1998). *The Third Way: The Renewal of Social Democracy*. Cambridge: Polity Press.

Giddens, A. (2000). *The Third Way and its Critics*. Cambridge: Polity Press.

Giner, S. (1995). 'Civil Society and its Future', in J. A. Hall (ed.), *Civil Society: Theory, History, Comparison*. Cambridge: Polity Press.

Gramsci, A (1998). *Selections from the Prison Notebooks of Antonio Gramsci*, ed. and trans. G. Hoare and G. N. Smith. London: Lawrence & Wishart.

Granovetter, M. (1985). 'Economic Action and Social Structure: The Problem of Embeddedness', *American Journal of Sociology*, 91, 481–510.

Griffiths, D. (1992). 'The Political Consequences of Migration into Wales', *Contemporary Wales*, 5: 65–81.

Griffiths, D. (1996). *Thatcherism and Territorial Politics: A Welsh Case Study*. Aldershot: Avebury.

Groundwork Merthyr and Rhondda Cynon Taff (2000a). *Chairman's Report*. http://www.groundworkmerthyrrct.org.uk/chairman.htm   13.5.03

Groundwork Merthyr and Rhondda Cynon Taff (2000b). *Annual Report 1999–2000*. Aberdar: Groundwork Merthyr and Rhondda Cynon Taff.

Groundwork Merthyr and Rhondda Cynon Taff (2000c). *Looking Ahead*. http://www.groundworkmerthyrrct.org.uk/looking.htm   13.5.03

Groundwork Merthyr and Rhondda Cynon Taff (2001). *Annual Report 2000–2001*. Aberdar: Groundwork Merthyr and Rhondda Cynon Taff.

Groundwork Merthyr and Rhondda Cynon Taff (2002). *Annual Report 2001–2002*. Aberdar: Groundwork Merthyr and Rhondda Cynon Taff.

Groundwork UK (2002a). *Groundwork*. http://www.groundwork.org.uk/what/index.htm   13.5.03

Groundwork UK (2002b). *Where did Groundwork Come from?* http://www.groundwork.org.uk/what/history.htm   13.5.03

Groundwork UK (2002c). *International Links*. http://www.groundwork.org.uk/int-links/index.htm   13.5.03

Groundwork Wales (2000a). *What is Groundwork?* http://www.groundworkwales.org.uk/whatisgroundwork.htm#Groundwork%20in%20Wales   13.5.03

Groundwork Wales (2000b). *Groundwork Contacts*. http://www.groundworkwales.org.uk/contacts.htm   13.5.03

Groundwork Wales (2000c). *Groundwork Wales Team*. http://www.groundworkwales.org.uk/team.htm   13.5.03

Groundwork Wales (2000d). *Welcome to Groundwork Wales*. http://www.groundworkwales.org.uk   13.8.03

Guibernau, M. (1996). *Nationalisms: The Nation-State and Nationalism in the Twentieth Century*. Cambridge: Polity Press.

Gupta, D. (2003). 'Civil Society or the State? What Happened to Citizenship?', in C. M. Eliott (ed.), *Civil Society: A Reader*. Oxford: Oxford University Press.

Gutmann, A. and Thompson, D. (1996). *Democracy and Disagreement*. Cambridge, Mass.: MIT Press.

Gwynn, J. (1993). *Introducing Oxfam*. Oxford: Oxfam.

Habermas, J. (1996). *Between Facts and Norms*. Cambridge: Polity Press.

Hain, P. (1999). *A Welsh Third Way?* (*Tribune* pamphlet). London: Tribune Publication.

Hall, J. A. (1995). 'In Search of Civil Society', in J. A. Hall (ed.), *Civil Society: Theory, History, Comparison*. Cambridge: Polity Press.

Harbeson, J. W. (1994). 'Civil Society and the Study of African Politics: A Preliminary Assessment', in J. W. Harbeson, D. Rothschild and N. Chazan (eds), *Civil Society and the State in Africa*. London: Lynne Reinner.

Hasely, R. (2005). 'Identifying Scotland and Wales: Types of Scottish and Welsh National Identities,' *Nations and Nationalism*, 11, part 2: 243–64.

Hazell, R. (ed.) (2000). *The State and the Nations: The First Year of Devolution in the United Kingdom*. London: Constitution Unit.

Healey, E. (1994). 'Getting Active: Lesbians Leave the Well of Loneliness', in A. Mason and E. Healey (eds), *Stonewall 25: The Making of the Gay and Lesbian Community in Britain*. London: Virago Press.

Hechter, M. (2000). *Containing Nationalism*. Oxford: Oxford University Press.

Hirst, P. Q. (1994). *Associative Democracy: New Forms of Economic and Social Governance*. Cambridge: Polity Press.

Hirst, P. Q. (1996). 'Democracy and Civil Society', in P. Hirst and S. Khilnani (eds), *Reinventing Democracy*. Cambridge, Mass.: Blackwell Publishers.

Hirst, P. (2002). 'Renewing Democracy through Associations', *Political Quarterly*, 73, 4: 409–21.

HMSO (1988). *Local Government Act 1988 (c.9) 1988 c.9 – continued*.
http://www.hmso.gov.uk/acts/acts1988/Ukpga_1988009_en_5.htm   3.6.03

HMSO (1998a). *Section 32 of the Government of Wales Act 1998*.
http://www.hmso.gov.uk/acts/acts1998/80038--d.htm#32   24.2.03

HMSO (1998b). *Government of Wales Act 1998*.
http://www.legislation.hmso.gov.uk/acts/acts1998/80038--d.htm#33 8.5.03

HMSO (1998c). *Government of Wales Act 1998 (c. 38) Section 48*.
http://www.hmso.gov.uk/acts/acts1998/80038--f.htm#48   5.7.03

HMSO (1998d). *Government of Wales Act 1998 (c. 38) Section 120*.
http://www.hmso.gov.uk/acts/acts1998/80038--m.htm#120   5.7.03

Hollingsworth, K. (2002). 'Reputation for Probity: The Work of the Audit Committee', in J. B. Jones and J. Osmond (eds) (2002), *Building a Civic Culture: Institutional Change, Policy Development and Political Dynamics in the National Assembly for Wales*. Cardiff: IWA and WGC.

Honneth, A. (1993). 'Conceptions of "Civil Society"', *Radical Philosophy*, 64 (Summer): 19–22.

House of Commons (2005). *Government of Wales Bill*.
http://www.publications.parliament.uk/pa/cm200506/cmbills/100/2006100.htm   10.12.05

Jeffrey-Poulter, S. (1991). *Peers, Queers and Commons: The Struggle for Gay Law Reform from 1950 to the Present*. London: Routledge.

Jones, E. H. G. (2001). 'Adfywiad', *Barn*, 457 (February).

Jones, G. (2001). *A Guide to European Funding in Wales 2000–2006*. Cardiff: Institute of Welsh Affairs.

Jones, J. B. and Osmond, J. (eds) (2001). *Inclusive Government and Party Management: The National Assembly for Wales and the Work of its Committees*. Cardiff: IWA and WGC.

Jones, J. B. and Osmond, J. (eds) (2002). *Building a Civic Culture: Institutional Change, Policy Development and Political Dynamics in the National Assembly for Wales*. Cardiff: IWA and WGC.

Keane, J. (1988a). 'Introduction', in J. Keane (ed.), *Civil Society and the State*. London: Verso.

Keane, J. (1988b). *Democracy and Civil Society*. London: Verso.

Keane, J. (1998). *Civil Society: Old Images, New Visions*. Cambridge: Polity Press.

Keane, J. (2003). *Global Civil Society?* Cambridge: Cambridge University Press.

Keating, M. (2001). *Nations against the State*. Basingstoke: Palgrave.

King, D. and Wickham-Jones, M. (1999). 'Social Capital, British Social Democracy and New Labour', *Democratization*, 6, 4: 181–213.

Kopecky, P. and Mudde, C. (2003). 'Rethinking Civil Society', *Democratization*, 10, 3: 1–14.

Kumar, K. (1993). 'Civil society: An Inquiry into the Usefulness of an Historical Term', *British Journal of Sociology*, 44: 377–95.

Kymlicka, W. and Norman, W. (2000). 'Citizenship in Culturally Diverse Societies: Issues, Contexts, Concepts', in W. Kymlicka and W. Norman (eds), *Citizenship in Diverse Societies*. Oxford: Oxford University Press.

Laffin, M. and Thomas, A. (2000). 'Designing the National Assembly for Wales', *Parliamentary Affairs*, 53: 557–76.

Laitin, D. (1995). 'The Civic Culture at 30', *American Political Science Review*, 89: 168–73.

Lambert, D. (1999). 'The Government of Wales Act: An Act for Laws to be Ministered in Wales in Like Form as it is in This Realm?', *Cambrian Law Review*, 30: 60–71.

Levi, M. (1993). 'Making Democracy Work: Civic Traditions in Modern Italy', *Comparative Political Studies*, 26, 3: 375–87.

Lewis, D. M. (2001). 'O gyhoeddi i weithredu', *Barn*, 460 (May).

LGB Forum Cymru (2002a). *Lesbian, Gay and Bisexual People Together across Wales*. N.p.

LGB Forum Cymru (2002b). *Making a Difference: Conference Report*. N.p.

LGB Forum Cymru (2002c). *LGB Forum Cymru Outline Business Plan 2002 to 2005*. N.p.

LGB Forum Cymru (2003). *LGB Forum Cymru Ballot Paper*. N.p.

Llobera, J. R. (1996). *The God of Modernity: The Development of Nationalism in Western Europe*. Oxford: Berg.

Lynch, P. (1996). 'Th Scottish Constitutional Convention 1992–5', *Scottish Affairs*, 15: 1–16.

MacCormick, N. (1996). 'Liberalism, Nationalism and the Post-sovereign State', *Political Studies*, 44: 553–67.

Mansbridge, J. (1992). 'A Deliberative Perspective on Neo-corporatism', *Politics and Society*, 20, 4: 493–505.

Mason, A. and Healey, E. (eds) (1994). *Stonewall 25: The Making of the Gay and Lesbian Community in Britain*. London: Virago Press.

Mason, J. (2001). *Qualitative Researching*. London: Sage.

Mason, T. (2001). 'Cash-Strapped Charity Plans to Pay Staff Bonuses of £617,000', *Western Mail*, 7 December.

Mason, T. (2002). 'Language Protesters Arrested', *Western Mail*, 14 February.

McAllister, I. (1980). 'The Labour Party in Wales: The Dynamics of One-Partyism', *Llafur*, 3, 1: 79–89.

McAllister, L. (2000a). 'The Road to Cardiff Bay: The Process of Establishing the National Assembly for Wales', *Parliamentary Affairs*, 53: 634–48.

McAllister, L. (2000b). 'Devolution and the New Context for Public Policy-Making: Lessons from the EU Structural Funds in Wales', *Public Policy and Administration*, 15, 2: 38–52.

McAllister, L. (2001). *Plaid Cymru: The Emergence of a Political Party*. Bridgend: Seren.

McCrone, D. (1998). *The Sociology of Nationalism*. London: Routledge.

McGuinness, P. (2003). ' "Racism" in Welsh Politics', *Planet*, 129 (June/July): 1–13.

McInness, J. (2004). *Identifying the British, or Tick Box Tyrrany* (unpublished paper).

McLaverty, P. (2002). 'Civil Society and Democracy', *Contemporary Politics*, 8, 4: 303–18.

Michael, A. (1999). *1999 Annual Lecture: The Dragon on our Doorstep*. Aberystwyth: Institute of Welsh Politics.

Midmore, P. (2002). 'West Wales and the Valleys Objective One Programme: A Personal Narrative', *Contemporary Wales*, 15: 69–78.

Mitchell, J. (1996). *Strategies for Self-Government: The Campaigns for a Scottish Parliament*. Edinburgh: Polygon.

Moore, C. and Booth, S. (1989). *Managing Competition: Meso-corporatism, Pluralism and the Negotiated Order in Scotland*. Oxford: Clarendon.

Morgan, K. (1999). 'Towards a Democratic Devolution: The Challenges of the Welsh Assembly', *Transactions of the Honourable Society of the Cymmrodorion 1998*, 5: 182–203.

Morgan, K. (2002a). 'The Two Worlds of Objective One', *Agenda: Journal of the Institute of Welsh Affairs* (Summer).

Morgan, K. (2002b). 'How Objective 1 Arrived in Wales: The Political Origins of a Coup', *Contemporary Wales*, 15: 20–30.

Morgan, K. and Mungham, G. (2000). *Redesigning Democracy: The Making of the Welsh Assembly*. Bridgend: Seren.

Morgan, K. and Price, A. (1998). *The Other Wales: the Case for Objective One Funding Post 1999*. Cardiff: Institute of Welsh Affairs.

Morgan, K. and Rees, G. (2001). 'Learning by Doing: Devolution and the Governance of Economic Development in Wales', in P. Chaney, T. Hall and A. Pithouse (eds) *New Governance – New Democracy?* Cardiff: University of Wales Press.

Morgan, R. (2000a). *Variable Geometry UK*. Cardiff: IWA Discussion Paper 13.

Morgan, R. (2000b). *2000 Annual Lecture: 'Check against Delivery'*. Aberystwyth: Institute of Welsh Politics.

Mouritsen, P. (2003). 'What's the Civil in Civil Society? Robert Putnam, Italy and the Republican Tradition', *Political Studies*, 52: 650–68.

NAW (National Assembly for Wales) (1999a). *Committee on Equality of Opportunity Minutes 22 July 1999 (EOC-01–99)*.
http://www.wales.gov.uk/assemblydata/37D520BE0006D86A00000DE80000 0000.html   3.6.03

NAW (National Assembly for Wales) (1999b). *Committee on Equality of Opportunity: Proposed Work Programme, Note from the Chair (EOC-02–99)*.
http://www.wales.gov.uk/assemblydata/37E6496B00068C64000004CA00000 000.html   3.6.03

NAW (National Assembly for Wales) (1999c). *OPIN-1999–0050 Repeal of Section 28 of the Local Government Act 1988, 29 October 1999*.
http://www.wales.gov.uk/servlet/StatementOpinion?area_code=37D6833E0 00E42E1000000F1000000000&document_code=383D6BF60005507A00003005000 00000&mmodule=dynamicpages&month_year=11 | 1999   27.6.03

NAW (National Assembly for Wales) (1999d). *OPIN-1999–0082 Repeal of Section 28, 15 December 1999.*
http://www.wales/gov.uk/servlet/StatementOpinion?area_code=37D6833E0 00E42E10000F1000000000&document_code=3858DFC20003CD91000001390000 0000&module=dynamicpages&month_year=12 | 1999   27.6.03

NAW (National Assembly for Wales) (2000a). *Voluntary Sector Scheme* (Crown Copyright).

NAW (National Assembly for Wales) (2000b). *Putting Wales First: A Partnership for the People of Wales.* N.p.

NAW (National Assembly for Wales) (2000c). *National Assembly (Official Record) Wednesday 28 June 2000, The Welsh Language.*
http://www.wales.gov.uk/assemblydata/395B7E9B000A4CBF0000198F00000 000.html#Yr%20Iaith%20Gymraeg   24.2.03

NAW (National Assembly for Wales) (2000d). *National Assembly (Official Record) 4 July 2000, The Welsh Language: Continued.*
http://www.wales.gov.uk/servlet/ChamberSession?area_code=380313AC000 46B17000028C3000000000&document_code=3964476B0005A9590001D34000000 00&module=dynamicpages&month_year=null   23.1.03

NAW (National Assembly for Wales) (2000e). *Committee on Equality of Opportunity, Minutes 13 April 2000 (EOC-03–00).*
http://www.wales.gov.uk/assemblydata/39098DB20006AC4D000008DA0000 0000.html   3.6.03

NAW (National Assembly for Wales) (2000f). *Committee on Equality of Opportunity, Minutes 29 June 2000.*
http://www.wales.gov.uk/assemblydata/39911C150002C78900000094000000 00.html   3.6.03

NAW (National Assembly for Wales) (2000g). *The National Assembly for Wales: Arrangements to promote Equality of Opportunity 1999–2000, Committee on Equality of Opportunity Report.*
http://www.wales.gov.uk/assemblydata/39A39287000C91C500002D9F00000 000.html   3.6.03

NAW (National Assembly for Wales) (2000h). *Annual Report of the Committee on Equality of Opportunity. Y Cofnod Swyddogol 12 July 2000.*
http://www.wales.gov.uk/assemblydata/396DEBE000026F8200007386000000 00.html#Adroddiad%20Blynyddol%20y%20Pwyllgor%20Cyfle%20Cyfartal
    3.6.03

NAW (National Assembly for Wales) (2000i). *Committee on Equality of Opportunity, Minutes 25 October 2000, EOC-07–00.*
http://www.wales.gov.uk/assemblydata/3A017E53000C38620000043D00000 000.html   3.6.03

NAW (National Assembly for Wales) (2000j). *OPIN-2000–026 Retention of Section 28 of the Local Government Act, 10 March 2000.*
http://www.wales.gov.uk/servlet/StatementOpinion?area_code=37D6833E0 00E42E100000F1000000000&document_code=38F1BCF20002F65500000DFA000 00000&module=dynamicpages&month_year=4 | 2000   27.6.03

NAW (National Assembly for Wales) (2001a). *Annual Report on the Voluntary Sector Scheme 2000–2001* (Crown Copyright).

NAW (National Assembly for Wales) (2001b). *Culture Committee CC-7–01(p.1): Welsh Language Review.*

http://www.wales.gov.uk/assemblydata/3AE823C3000145EF00006DA000000
00.html   25.9.02

NAW (National Assembly for Wales) (2001c). *Culture Committee CC-7–02(p.2) Paper from the Welsh Language Board.*
http://www.wales.gov.uk/assemblydata/3AE823DA0004763500006DAF0000
0000.html   25.9.02

NAW (National Assembly for Wales) (2001d). *Culture Committee, Consultation Pack.*
http://www.wales.gov.uk/keypubassemculture/content/welshlanguagere
view/consultation-e.htm   24.2.03

NAW (National Assembly for Wales) (2001e). *Culture Committee CC-7–01 (min) Minutes Committee's review of the Welsh Language, 7.05.01.*
http://www.wales.gov.uk/assemblydata/3AF7D06C0005B0AC000031F00000
0000.html   20.1.03

NAW (National Assembly for Wales) (2001f). *Culture Committee CC-13–01: Paper from Cymdeithas yr Iaith Gymraeg 17.07.01.*
http://www.wales.gov.uk/assemblydata/3B4DA93A000A14590000523600000
000.html   25.9.02

NAW (National Assembly for Wales) (2001g). *Culture Committee CC-13–01 (min): Minutes Committee's Review of the Welsh Language 17.07.01.*
http://www.wales.gov.uk/assemblydata/3B5E7DC8000124DB0000577700000
000.html   20.1.03

NAW (National Assembly for Wales) (2001h). *Press Release: 25 New Organisations to be Brought within the Scope of the Welsh Language Act 12.07.01.*
http://www.wales.gov.uk/assemblydata/3B4D76B4000C610C0000372D00000
000.html   20.1.03

NAW (National Assembly for Wales) (2001i). *Culture Committee CC-16–01 (p.2) Submission by Cymuned to the Culture Committee 7.11.01.*
http://www.wales.gov.uk/assemblydata/3BE1771C0007FA980000280A00000
000.html   25.9.02

NAW (National Assembly for Wales) (2001j). *Culture Committee CC-17–01 (min) Minutes Committee's Review of the Welsh Language 15.11.01.*
http://www.wales.gov.uk/assemblydata/3BFBBAAD000B1391000019E60000
0000.html   20.1.03

NAW (National Assembly for Wales) (2001k). *Culture Committee CC-18–01 (min) Minutes Committee's Review of the Welsh language 21.11.01.*
http://www.wales.gov.uk/assemblydata/3C04F4760003026E0000446000000
00.html   21.1.03

NAW (National Assembly for Wales) (2001l). *Committee on Equal Opportunity, Minutes 13 June 2001.*
http://www.wales.gov.uk/assemblydata/3B45872D000E1ADA00003F150000
0000.html   03.6.03

NAW (National Assembly for Wales) (2001m). *Meeting of the Voluntary Sector Partnership Council Held at the National Assembly for Wales, Cardiff Bay on Friday, 16 March 2001.*
http://www.wales.gov.uk/themesvoluntarysector/content/partnership
council/supportingpapers/160301/16mar01-e.htm#onea   18.12.05

NAW (National Assembly for Wales) (2001n). *The Voluntary Sector Partnership Council: Supporting Papers Presented to the Council 14 December 2001, VSPC (01) 31. UK Voluntary Organisations Working In Wales.*

http://www.wales.gov.uk/themesvoluntarysector/content/partnershipcouncil/supportingpapers/141201/index-e.htm 12.12.05

NAW (National Assembly for Wales) (2002a). *Culture Committee CC-2–02 (min) Minutes Review of the Welsh Language: Discussion with Members of the Local Government and Housing Committee 17.01.02.*
http://www.wales.gov.uk/assemblydata/3C4FF27600035AD9000061C900000000.html 20.1.03

NAW (National Assembly for Wales) (2002b). *Press Release: Jenny Randerson sees Menter Iaith work at first hand 30.01.02.*
http://www.wales.gov.uk/assemblydata/3C582309000514B000022FD000000000.html 20.1.03

NAW (National Assembly for Wales) (2002c). *Culture Committee CC-4–02 (min) Minutes Review of the Welsh Language Papers 6.02.02.*
http://www.wales.gov.uk/assemblydata/3C69515700074E35000043BF000000.html 20.1.03

NAW (National Assembly for Wales) (2002d). *Press Release: Jenny Randerson Outlines the Work of the Mentrau Iaith 26.02.02.*
http://www.wales.gov.uk/assemblydata/3C7BA2B90000A8030000699EB00000000.html 20.1.03

NAW (National Assembly for Wales) (2002e). *Culture Committee CC-10–02 (min) Minutes Committee's Review of the Welsh Language 15.05.02.*
http://www.wales.gov.uk/assemblydata/3CECBBE1000A5E5B0000692900000000.html 20.1.03

NAW (National Assembly for Wales) (2002f). *Press Release: 17 New Organisations to be Brought within the Scope of the Welsh Language Act 28.05.02.*
http://www.wales.gov.uk/assemblydata/3CFB3E400020D5800004D7700000000.html 20.1.03

NAW (National Assembly for Wales) (2002g). *Culture Committee CC-11–02 (min) Minutes Committee's review of the Welsh Language 29.05.02.*
http://www.wales.gov.uk/assemblydata/N000000000000000000000000000000610.html 20.1.03

NAW (National Assembly for Wales) (2002h). *Our Language: Its Future, Policy Review of the Welsh Language.* Cardiff: National Assembly for Wales.

NAW (National Assembly for Wales) (2002i). *The National Assembly for Wales: Arrangements to Promote Equality of Opportunity 2001–2002. Annex A – Annual Report of the Committee on Equality of Opportunity.* N.p.

NAW (National Assembly for Wales) (2002j). *Committee on Equal Opportunity, Minutes 26 June 2002.*
http://www.wales.gov.uk/assemblydata/N0000000000000000000000000001368.html 3.6.03

NAW (National Assembly for Wales) (2002k). *Committee on Equal Opportunity, Presentation by the Lesbian, Gay, Bisexual Forum Paper EOC 06–02.*
http://www.wales.gov.uk/assemblydata/N00000000000000000000000003426.html 3.6.03

NAW (National Assembly for Wales) (2002l). *Sex and Relationships Education in Schools, National Assembly for Wales Circular No: 11/02.*
http://www.wales.gov.uk/subieducationtraining/content/circulars/sre-e.pdf 03.6.03

NAW (National Assembly for Wales) (2002m). *Committee on Equal Opportunity, Chair's Report 24 April 2002 EOC-03–02.*
http://www.wales.gov.uk/assemblydata/3CC0169F000C9AF30000551A00000 000.html   3.6.03

NAW (National Assembly for Wales) (2002n). *Second Annual Report on the Voluntary Sector Scheme.*
http://www.wales.gov.uk/themesvoluntarysector/content/annualreport/ 2ndreport/index-e.htm   12.12.05

NAW (National Assembly for Wales) (2003a). *Iaith Pawb Provides Opportunity for Debate, Press Release 15.01.03.*
http://www.wales.gov.uk/assemblydata/N0000000000000000000000000005 789.html   24.1.03

NAW (National Assembly for Wales) (2003b). *Welsh Language Society: Written Evidence to the Richard Commission.*
http://www.richardcommission.gov.uk/content/evidence/written/cymdeithas/ index.htm   27.6.03

NAW (National Assembly for Wales) (2003c). *EDC -06–03 Minutes of the Economic Development Committee.3.04.03.*
http://www.wales.gov.uk/servlet/EconomicDevelopmentCommittee?area_ code=37D6A7190007D619000011ED00000000&document_code=N00000000000 00000000000000009026&module=dynamicpages&month_year=   8.5.03

NAW (National Assembly for Wales) (2003d). *Committee of Equality of Opportunity: Summary of Committee Activity since Last Annual Report (2002–2003)* (October 2002–March 2003). N.p.

NAW (National Assembly for Wales) (2003e). *Committee of Equality of Opportunity, Minutes 16 January 2003 EOC-01–03 (min).*
http://www.wales.gov.uk/assemblydata/N0000000000000000000000000005659. html   3.6.03

NAW (National Assembly for Wales) (2003f). *Committee of Equality of Opportunity, Minutes 20 March 2003 EOC-03–03 (min).*
http://www.wales.gov.uk/assemblydata/N0000000000000000000000000000 8987.html   3.6.03

NAW (National Assembly for Wales) (2003g). *Committee of Equality of Opportunity, 20 March 2003 Follow up to LGB Forum Presentation, EOC-03–03 (p7).*
http://www.wales.gov.uk/assemblydata/N0000000000000000000000000000 8204.html   3.6.03

NAW (National Assembly for Wales) (2003h). *OPIN-2003–0003 Sex and Relationships Education in Schools Guidance, 6 March 2003.*
http://www.wales.gov.uk/servlet/StatementOpinion?area_code=37D6833E0 00E42E100000F1000000000&document_code=N00000000000000000000000000000 7936&module=dynamicpages&month_year=3 | 2003   27.6.03

NAW (National Assembly for Wales) (2003i). *Stonewall Cymru: Written Evidence to Richard Commission.*
http://www.richardcommission.gov.uk/content/evidence/written/stonewall/ stonewall-cymru-e.htm   27.6.03

NAW (National Assembly for Wales) (2004). *Third Annual Report on the Voluntary Sector Scheme.*
http://www.wales.gov.uk/docrepos/40382/sjr/voluntary/annualreport3e? lang=en.   23.4.07

NAW (National Assembly for Wales) (2005). *Code of Practice for Funding the Voluntary Sector.*
  http://new.wales.gov.uk/docrepos/40382/sjr/voluntary/fundingcodee?lang=en.   23.4.07

NAW (National Assembly for Wales) (2007). *The Third Assembly: Changes from the Government of Wales Act 2007 and the New Standing Orders.*
  http://www.wales.gov.uk/keypubmrs/content/07-050.pdf   23.4.07

Newton, K. (2001). 'Trust, Social Capital, Civil Society and Democracy', *International Political Science Review*, 22, 2: 201–14.

North Wales Lesbian Line (2001). *Same Sex Support Services in Wales and the UK.* N.p.

Office of Public Sector Information (2006). *Government of Wales Act 2006.*
  http://www.opsi.gov.uk/acts/acts2006/ukpga_29969932_en.pdf   29.9.06

O'Leary, B. (1998). 'Ernest Gellner's Diagnoses of Nationalism: A Critical Overview, or, What is Living and What is Dead in Ernest Gellner's Philosophy of Nationalism', in J. A. Hall (ed.), *The State of the Nation: Ernest Gellner and the Theory of Nationalism.* Cambridge: Cambridge University Press.

Osmond, J. (1995). *Welsh Europeans.* Bridgend: Seren.

Osmond, J. (1998a). *New Politics in Wales.* London: Charter 88.

Osmond, J. (ed.) (1998b). *The National Assembly Agenda.* Cardiff: Institute of Welsh Affairs.

Osmond, J. (1999). *Welsh Politics in the New Millennium.* Cardiff: Institute of Welsh Affairs Discussion Paper no.11.

Osmond, J. (2000). 'A Constitutional Convention by Other Means: The First Year of the National Assembly for Wales', in R. Hazell (ed.), *The State and the Nations: The First Year of Devolution in the United Kingdom.* Throverton: Imprint Academic.

Osmond, J. (2001). 'In Search of Stability: Coalition Politics in the Second Year of the National Assembly for Wales', in A. Trench (ed.), *The State of the Nations 2001: The Second Year of Devolution in the United Kingdom.* Throverton: Imprint Academic.

Osmond, J. (ed.) (2002). *A Bilingual Wales: Monitoring the National Assembly June to August 2002.* Cardiff: Institute of Welsh Affairs.

Osmond, J. (2003). 'From Corporate Body to Virtual Parliament: The Metamorphosis of the National Assembly for Wales', in R. Hazell (ed.), *State of the Nations 2003: The Third Year of Devolution in the United Kingdom.* Exeter: Imprint Academic.

Osmond, J. (ed.) (2004). *Cull of the Quangos: Monitoring the National Assembly June–September 2004.* Cardiff: Institute of Welsh Affairs.

Osmond, J. and Jones, J. B. (eds) (2003). *Birth of Welsh Democracy: The First Term of the National Assembly for Wales.* Cardiff: IWA and WGC.

Oxfam Cymru (2000). *Annual Review May 1999–April 2000.* N.p.

Oxfam Cymru (2001a). *Oxfam Cymru Vision.* N.p.

Oxfam Cymru (2001b). *Llais: The Newsletter of Oxfam Cymru,* 4 (Spring).

Oxfam Cymru (2002a). *Llais: The Newsletter of Oxfam Cymru,* 7 (Summer).

Oxfam Cymru (2002b). *Welcome to Oxfam Cymru.*
  http://www.oxfam.org.uk/cymru/index.html   23.3.03

Oxfam Cymru (2002c). *Campaigning with Oxfam Cymru.*
  http://www.oxfam.org.uk/cymru/campaign.html   23.3.03

Oxfam Cymru (2002d). *UK Poverty Programme in Wales.*
http://www.oxfam.org.uk/cymru/ukpp.html   23.3.03

Oxfam Cymru (2002e). *Letter: Students Campaigning with Oxfam Cymru.* N.p.

Oxfam Cymru (2003a). *Welsh Food Company to Drop Huge Debt Claim* (press release, 17 March 2003).

Oxfam Cymru (2003b). *A Call for an Outward Looking Wales.* N.p.

Oxfam GB (1993). *Oxfam Campaigner: Newsletter of the Oxfam Campaigning Network,* 8 (Autumn).

Oxfam GB (1996a). *Oxfam Campaigner: Newsletter of the Oxfam Campaigning Network,* 17 (Winter 1995/6).

Oxfam GB (1996b). *Oxfam Campaigner: Newsletter of the Oxfam Campaigning Network,* 19 (Summer).

Oxfam GB (1997). *Oxfam Campaigner: Newsletter of the Oxfam Campaigning Network,* 23 (Spring).

Oxfam GB (2002a). *Welsh 'Roadshow' Launch.*
http://www.maketradefair.com/stylesheet.asp?file=17042002133346 23.3.03

Oxfam GB (2002b). *Campaigner's Diary – Thursday 12 December 2002.*
http://www.maketradefair.com/stylesheet.asp?file=12122002091741 23.3.03

Oxfam GB (2002c). *Oxfam Trade Research in Wales.* N.p.

Oxfam GB (2002d). *Oxfam Campaigner,* 44 (Summer).

Oxfam GB (2002e). *About Oxfam – Organisation of Oxfam GB.*
http://www.oxfam.org.uk/atwork/org1.htm   23.3.03

Oxfam GB (2002f). *Oxfam GB Strategic Plan Update 2002/2003–2004/5.*
http://www.oxfam.org.uk/atwork/downloads/strategicplan.doc   19.4.03

Oxfam International (2002a). *Rigged Rules and Double Standards: Trade, Globalisation, and the Fight against Poverty.* N.p., Oxfam International.

Oxfam International (2002b). *Mugged: Poverty in your Coffee Cup.* N.p.

Oxfam in Wales (1992). *Oxfam Campaigning Network: News of Wales,* (June).

Oxfam in Wales (1993). *Oxfam Campaigning Network: News of Wales,* 6 (March).

Oxfam in Wales (1994). *Oxfam Campaigning Network: News of Wales,* 6 (January).

Oxfam in Wales (1996a). *Ymgyrchwr Cymreig/The Welsh Campaigner,* 19 (Summer).

Oxfam in Wales (1996b). *Ymgyrchwr Cymreig/The Welsh Campaigner,* 20 (Autumn).

Oxfam in Wales (1997). *Ymgyrchwr Cymreig/The Welsh Campaigner,* 21 (January/ February).

Oxfam in Wales (1999). *Oxfam in Wales Campaigns Report May 1998–April 1999.* N.p.

Palmer, A. (1995). 'Lesbian and Gay Rights Campaigning: A Report from the Coalface', in A. Wilson (ed.), *A Simple Matter of Justice?* London: Cassell.

Panitch, L. (1980). 'Recent Theorizations of Corporatism: Reflections on a Growth Industry', *British Journal of Sociology,* 31, 2: 159–87.

Pateman, C. (1970). *Participation and Democratic Theory.* London: Cambridge University Press.

Paterson, L. (1996). 'Conclusion: Does Nationalism Matter?' *Scottish Affairs,* 17: 112–18.

Paterson, L. and Wyn Jones, R. (1999). 'Does Civil Society Drive Constitutional Change?' in B. Taylor and K. Thomson (eds), *Scotland and Wales: Nations Again?* Cardiff: University of Wales Press.

Pedersen, B. (1992). 'Civil Society and Political Theory, by Jean L. Cohen and Andrew Arato', *Critical Sociology,* 19, 2: 129–34.

Perez-Diaz, V. (1995). 'The Possibility of Civil Society: Traditions, Character and Challenges', in J. A. Hall (ed.), *Civil Society: Theory, History, Comparison*. Cambridge: Polity Press.

Phillips, D. (1998a). *Trwy ddulliau chwyldro . . . ? Hanes Cymdeithas yr Iaith Gymraeg 1962–1992*. Llandysul, Gomer.

Phillips, D. (1998b). *Pa Ddiben Protestio Bellach?* Talybont: Lolfa.

Pietrzyk, D. (2003). 'Democracy or Civil Society?' *Politics*, 23, 1: 38–46.

Putnam, R. D. (1993). *Making Democracy Work: Civic Traditions in Modern Italy*. Princeton: Princeton University Press.

Putnam, R. D. (2000). *Bowling Alone: The Collapse and Revival of American Community*. London: Simon & Schuster.

Putnam, R. D. and Goss., K. A. (2004). 'Introduction', in R. D. Putnam (ed.), *Democracies in Flux: The Evolution of Social Capital in Contemporary Society*. Oxford: Oxford University Press.

Rawlings, R. (1998). 'The New Model Wales', *Journal of Law and Society*, 25, 4: 461–509.

Rawlings, R. (2002). 'Towards a Parliament: Three Faces of the National Assembly for Wales', *Contemporary Wales*, 15: 1–20.

Rawlings, R. (2003). *Delineating Wales: Constitutional, Legal and Administrative Aspects of National Devolution*. Cardiff: University of Wales Press.

Rawlings, R. (2004a). *Say Not the Struggle Naught Availeth: The Richard Commission and After*. Aberystwyth: Centre for Welsh Legal Affairs.

Rawlings, R. (2005). 'Hastening Slowly: The Next Phase Of Welsh Devolution', *Public Law*, 824–852.

Rawlings, R. (2004b). *A Virtual Parliament – Mark II* (unpublished paper presented to the 'Legal Wales' Conference, November 2004).

Richard, Lord (2006). Speech to Institute of Welsh Politics Conference on 'The Future of Welsh Politics', Cardiff, 20 September 2006.

Richardson, N. (2003). 'A New Politics', in J. Osmond and J. B. Jones (eds), *Birth of Welsh Democracy: The First Term of the National Assembly for Wales*. Cardiff: IWA and WGC.

Royles, E. (2004). 'Civil Society and Objective 1', *Contemporary Wales*, 16: 101–21.

Royles, E. (2006). 'Devolution to Wales – Democratising Economic Governance? Civil Society and the Structural Funds in Wales', *Regional and Federal Studies*, 16, 2: 137–56.

Schmidt, J. (1993). 'Cohen and Arato, Civil Society and Political Theory', *Social Science Quarterly*, 74, 2: 451–2.

Schmitter, P. C. (1979). 'Still the Century of Corporatism?', in P. C. Schmitter and G. Lembruch (eds), *Trends towards Corporatist Intermediation*, London: Sage.

Scully, R. and Wyn Jones, R. (2006). 'Elections, Parties and Public Attitudes', in R. Wyn Jones and R. Scully (eds), *Wales Devolution Monitoring Report* (May) 2006. http://www.aber.ac.uk/interpol/wire/docs/cymru_wales05–06.pdf 18.7.06

Select Committee on Welsh Affairs (2000). *First Report European Structural Funds*. http://www.publications.parliament.uk/pa/cm199900/cmselect/cmwelaf/46/4603.htm   22.6.02

Select Committee on Welsh Affairs (2002a). *Second Report Objective 1 European Funding For Wales*.

http://www.publications.parliament.uk/pa/cm200102/cmselect/cmwelaf/
520/52003.htm   22.6.02

Select Committee on Welsh Affairs (2002b). *Welsh Affairs – Minutes of Evidence.*
http://www.publications.parliament.uk/pa/cm200102/cmselect/cmwelaf/
520/2012801.htm   22.6.02

Sherlock, A. (2000). 'Born Free, but Everywhere in Chains? A Legal Analysis of
the First Year of the National Assembly for Wales', *Cambrian Law Review*, 13:
61–7.

Shils, E. (1991). 'The Virtue of Civil Society', *Government and Opposition*, 26, 1
(Winter): 3–20.

Skocpol, T. (2003). *Diminished Democracy: From Membership to Management in
American Civic Life.* Norman: University of Oklahoma Press.

Smith, A. D. (1991). *National Identity.* Harmondsworth: Penguin.

Smith, A. D. (1996). 'Culture, Community and Territory: The Politics of Ethnicity
and Nationalism', *International Affairs*, 72: 445–58.

Smith, A. D. (1998). *Nationalism and Modernism.* London: Routledge.

Stacey, J. (1991). 'Promoting Normality: Section 28 and the Regulation of Sexuality',
in S. Franklin, C. Lury and J. Stacey (eds), *Off Centre: Feminism and Cultural
Studies.* London: HarperCollins Academic.

Stake, R. F. (1994). 'Case Studies', in N. K. Denzin and Y. S. Lincoln (eds), *Handbook
of Qualitative Research.* Thousand Oaks, Calif.: Sage.

Stephen, J. (2001). 'Knowledge Management in Oxfam', *Information Development*,
17, 2: 107–10.

Stonewall (2001). *Equal as Citizens: action for a new century.* N.p.

Stonewall (2003a). *Equal at School.*
http://www.stonewall.org.uk/docs/equal_at_school.PDF   3.6.03

Stonewall (2003b). *About Stonewall: Who are We?*
http://www.stonewall.org.uk/stonewall/about_stonewall/index.html
                                                                   3.6.03

Stonewall (2003c). *Stonewall Appoints New Chief Executive.*
http://www.stonewall.org.uk/stonewall/press_releases/new_ceo.html
                                                                   3.6.03

Stonewall (2003d). *Stonewall Cymru has been Invited to Give Evidence to the Richard
Commission.*
http://www.stonewall.org.uk/stonewall/news/welsh_consult.html   3.6.03

Stonewall (2003e). *Current Campaigns: Section 28.*
http://www.stonewall.org.uk/stonewall/current_campaigns/s.28.html
                                                                   3.6.03

Stonewall (2003f). *Current Campaigns: Let's Nail Section 28 Petition.*
http://www.stonewall.org.uk/stonewall/current_campaigns/s28_petition.
html   3.6.03

Stonewall (2003g). *Commons Report Stage – Local Government Bill (Day 2) New Clause
11.*
http://www.stonewall.org.uk/docs/Section_28_Commons_Report_stage_
debate_2003.doc   3.6.03

Stonewall (2003h). *News, Section 28: The Battle Gears Up 19/05/03.*
http://www.stonewall.org.uk/stonewall/news/s28_battle.html   3.6.03

Stonewall (2003i). *Current Campaigns – Sexual Offences Bill 2003.*

http://www.stonewall.org.uk/stonewall/current_campaigns/sex_offences.
html   3.6.03
Stonewall (2003j). *Current Campaigns*.
http://www.stonewall.org.uk/stonewall/current_campaigns/partnership.
html   3.6.03
Stonewall (2003k). *Lobbying*.
http://www.stonewall.org.uk/stonewall/support_us/lobbying/index.html
                                                                        3.6.03
Stonewall (2003l). *Section 28 Repeal*.
http://www.stonewall.org.uk/stonewall/current_campaigns/index.html
                                                                        11.7.03
Stonewall (2003m). *News, House of Lords Debates Section 28 Repeal*.
http://www.stonewall.org.uk.stonewall/news/hol_s28_debate.html 25.6.04
Stonewall (2003n). *House of Lords Debate 10 July 2003*.
http://www.stonewall.org.uk/docs/Lords_report_stagedebate_10July_2003.
doc   25.6.04
Stonewall Cymru (2003). *Welsh Assembly Election Manifesto 2003*. N.p.
Stonewall Scotland (n.d.). *Proud to be in Scotland* (Stonewall Lobby Group Limited).
Talfan Davies, G. and Osmond, J. (2003). 'Culture and Identity', in J. Osmond and J. B. Jones (eds), *Birth of Welsh Democracy: The First Term of the National Assembly for Wales* (Cardiff: IWA and WGC).
Tarrow, S. (1996). 'Making Science Work across Space and Time: A Critical Reflection on Robert Putnam's Making Democracy Work', *American Political Science Review*, 90, 2: 389–97.
Taylor, B., Curtice, J. and Thomson, K. (1999). 'Introduction and Conclusions', in B. Taylor and K. Thomson (eds) *Scotland and Wales: Nations Again?* Cardiff: University of Wales Press.
Thomas, A. (1997). 'Language Policy and Nationalism in Wales: A Comparative Analysis', *Nations and Nationalism*, 3, 3: 323–44.
Thomas, A. (1999). 'Politics in Wales: A New Era?' in D. Dunkerley and A. Thomson (eds), *Wales Today*, Cardiff: University of Wales Press.
Thompson, A. and Day G. (2001). 'Standing Up for Civil Society', *Radical Wales* 2001: 23–5.
Trench, A. (2006). 'The Government of Wales Act 2006: The Next Steps in Devolution for Wales', *Public Law*, 4, winter: 687–96.
Trench, A. (2007). *Old Wine in New Bottles? Relations between London and Cardiff after the Government of Wales Act 2006*. London: The Constitution Unit.
Trystan, D., Scully, R. and Wyn Jones, R. (2003). 'Explaining the "Quiet Earthquake": Voting Behaviour in the First Election to the National Assembly for Wales', *Electoral Studies*, 22: 635–50.
Turner, C. (1998). *Plaid Cymru and European Integration: An Empirical Study of Multilevel Governance*. Ph.D. thesis, University of Wales.
WAG (Welsh Assembly Government) (2002a). *Bilingual Future: A Policy Statement by the Welsh Assembly Government*. Cardiff: National Assembly for Wales.
WAG (Welsh Assembly Government) (2002b). *Iaith Pawb: A National Action Plan for a Bilingual Wales*. Cardiff: National Assembly for Wales.
WAG (Welsh Assembly Government) (2004a). *Report of the Richard Commission: Commission on the Powers and Electoral Arrangements of the National Assembly for Wales*. UK: The Stationery Office.

WAG (Welsh Assembly Government) (2004b). *Sustainable Development Action Plan 2004–2006.*
http://www.wales.gov.uk/themesustainabledev/content/action-plan-e.pdf
6.4.05

WAG (Welsh Assembly Government) (2004c). *Independent Commission to Review the Voluntary Sector Scheme Final Report*
http://new.wales.gov.uk/docrepos/40382/sjr/voluntary/reviewreport?lang=en
19.9.06

WAG (Welsh Assembly Government) (2006). *Working Within Wales: Shared Principles*
http://new.wales.gov.uk/topics/housingandcommunity/voluntarysector/
publications/workingwithinwales?lang=en
20.4.07

Waites, M. (2000). 'Homosexuality and the New Right: The Legacy of the 1980s for New Delineations of Homophobia', *Sociological Research Online*, 5, 1.
http://www.socresonline.org.uk/5/1/waites.html
1.6.03

Waites, M. (2001). 'Regulation of Sexuality: Age of Consent, Section 28 and Sex Education', *Parliamentary Affairs*, 54: 495–508.

Wales Council for Voluntary Action (2002a). *Civil Society: Civil Space.* Cardiff: WCVA.

Wales Council for Voluntary Action (2002b). *Civil Society Diamond for Wales: A Report on the CIVICUS Index on Civil Society Project in Wales.* Cardiff: WCVA.

Wales Council for Voluntary Action (2002c). *Wales Council for Voluntary Action Europe, Information Sheets.* Cardiff: WCVA.

Wales Office (2005). *Better Governance for Wales.*
http://www.wales.gov.uk/2005/better_governance_for_wales_report.pdf
15.7.05

Walzer, M. (2003). 'The Idea of Civil Society: A Path to Social Reconstruction', in C. M. Eliot (ed.), *Civil Society and Democracy: A Reader.* Oxford: Oxford University Press.

Weaver, M. R. (1993). 'Cohen, Jean L., and Andrew Arato. Civil Society and Political Theory', *The Journal of Politics*, 55, 2: 542–4.

WEFO (Welsh European Funding Office) (2000a). *West Wales and the Valleys Objective 1 Single Programming Document (SPD) 2000–2006.* Cardiff: National Assembly for Wales.

WEFO (Welsh European Funding Office) (2000b). *West Wales and the Valleys Objective 1 Programme 2000–2006 Programme Complement.* N.p.

WEFO (Welsh European Funding Office) (2000c). *Shadow Monitoring Committee Minutes of the Meeting on 7 March 2000.*
http://www.wefo.wales.gov.uk/newprogs/objective1/obj1-minutes/2000–03–07.htm
22.6.02

WEFO (Welsh European Funding Office) (2000d). *Minutes of the Shadow Monitoring Committee, 29 June 2000.*
http://www.WEFO.wales.gov.uk/newprogs/objective1/Obj1-minutes/
2000–06–29.htm
22.6.02

WEFO (Welsh European Funding Office) (2001). *Minutes of the Programme Monitoring Committee Meeting held on 22 June 2001.*
http://www.wefo.wales.gov.uk/resource/m10-(min).pdf
16.2.06

WEFO (Welsh European Funding Office) (2003). *Approved Projects.*
http://www.wefosearch.wales.gov.uk/approved-projects/newsearch/search
.asp   13.5.03

WEPE (Welsh European Programme Executive Limited). (1997). *ISW SPD 1997–99
Industrial South Wales Single Programme Document Objective 2.* N.p.

Welsh Office (1965). *Statws Gyfreithiol yr Iaith Gymraeg, Adroddiad Pwyllgor dan
Gadeiryddiaeth Syr David Parry Hughes.* London: HMO.

Welsh Office (1997). *A Voice for Wales: The Government's Proposals for a Welsh
Assembly.* HMSO. (UK: Stationery Office)

Western Mail (2002a). 'Language: Policy of Lobbying has Failed, says Pressure
Group Founder – Campaign of Civil Disobedience Urged', *Western Mail*, 20
February.

Western Mail (2002b). 'Burglary: Warning of Direct Action after Cymdeithas Pair
Given Conditional Discharge – Language Protest Pair Freed', *Western Mail*,
22 July.

Whitehead, L. (1997). 'Bowling in the Bronx: The Uncivil Interstices between
Civil and Political Society', in R. Fine and S. Rai (eds), *Civil Society: Democratic
Perspectives.* London: Frank Cass.

Williams, C. (2001). 'Can Mainstreaming Deliver? The Equal Opportunities Agenda
and the National Assembly for Wales', *Contemporary Wales*, 14: 57–79.

Williams, C. and Chaney, P. (2001). 'Devolution and Identities: The Experience
of Ethnic Minorities in Wales', *Soundings*, 18 (Summer/Autumn): 169–83.

Williams, C. H. (1977). 'Non-violence and the Development of the Welsh Language
Society, 1962–c. 1974', *Cylchgrawn Hanes Cymru*, 8, 4 (December): 426–55.

Williams, C. H. (1998). 'Operating through Two Languages', in J. Osmond (ed.),
The National Assembly Agenda. Cardiff: Institute of Welsh Affairs.

Williams, C. H. (2004). 'Iaith Pawb: The Doctrine of Plenary Inclusion,'
Contemporary Wales, 17: 1–27.

Williams, G. A. W. (1984). 'Marcsydd o Sardiniwr ac Argyfwng Cymru', *Efrydiau
Athronyddol*, 17, 1: 67–93.

Williams, G. A. W. (1985). *When Was Wales?* London: Penguin.

Williams, K. (2002). 'An Uneasy Relationship: The National Assembly and the
Press and Media', in J. B. Jones and J. Osmond (eds), *Building a Civic Culture:
Institutional Change, Policy Development and Political Dynamics in the National
Assembly for Wales.* Cardiff: IWA and WGC.

Wilson, A. (ed.) (1995). *A Simple Matter of Justice?* London: Cassell.

Wilson, F. L. (1983). 'Interest Group Politics in Western Europe: The Neo-
corporatist Approach', *Comparative Politics*, 16: 105–23.

Wilson, F. L. (1990). 'Neo-corporatism and the Rise of New Social Movements',
in R. J. Dalton and M. Kuechler (eds), *Challenging the Political Order:
New Social and Political Movements in Western Democracies.* Cambridge: Polity
Press.

Wise, S. (2000). ' "New Right" or "Backlash"? Section 28, Moral Panic and "Promoting Homosexuality" ', *Sociological Research Online*, 5, 1.
http://www.socresonline.org.uk/5/1/wise/html   1.6.03

WLB (Welsh Language Board) (1991). *Recommendations for a New Welsh Language
Act, A Report by the Welsh Language Board to the Secretary of State.* Cardiff:
Welsh Language Board.

WLB (Welsh Language Board) (1999). *The Welsh Language, Vision and Mission for 2000–05.*
http://www.bwrdd-yr-iaith.org/uploads/publications/74.pdf   24.2.03

Wood, E. M. (1990). 'The Uses and Abuses of "Civil Society"', *The Socialist Register 1990*: 60–84.

Wyn Jones, R. (1995). 'Care of the Community', *Planet: The Welsh Internationalist*, 109: 16–25.

Wyn Jones, R. (2001). 'Ysgrifennu hanes Cymdeithas yr Iaith Gymraeg', *Taliesin*, 12 (Summer) 107–24.

Wyn Jones, R. (2002). 'Dyfodol y Gymdeithas', *Barn*, 476 (September).

Wyn Jones, R. and Lewis, B. (1998). *The Wales Labour Party and Welsh Civil Society: Aspects of the Constitutional Debate in Wales.*
http://www.aber.ac.uk/~iwpwww/   25.5.99

Wyn Jones, R. and Scully, R. (2003). 'A Settling Will? Public Attitudes to Devolution in Wales', in C. Rallings, R. Scully, J. Tonge and P. Webb (eds), *British Elections and Parties Review*, 13. London: Frank Cass.

Wyn Jones, R. and Scully, R. (2004). 'Minor Tremor but Several Casualties: The 2003 Welsh Election', in J. Fisher, P. Webb and D. Broughton (eds), *British Elections and Parties Review, 14*. London: Frank Cass.

Wyn Jones, R. and Scully, R. (2007). 'The Legitimacy of Devolution', in J. Curtice (ed.), *The Variety of Devolution*. Manchester: Manchester University Press.

Wyn Jones, R. and Trystan, D. (1999). 'The 1997 Welsh Referendum Vote', in B. Taylor and K. Thomson (eds), *Scotland and Wales: Nations Again?* Cardiff: University of Wales Press.

Wyn Jones, R. and Trystan, D. (2001). 'Turnout, Participation and Legitimacy in the Politics of Post-devolution Wales', in P. Chaney, T. Hall and A. Pithouse (eds), *New Governance – New Democracy?* Cardiff, University of Wales Press.

Young, I. M. (2000). *Inclusion and Democracy.* Oxford: Oxford University Press.

Index